QUILTS *from* AMERICA'S HEARTLAND

STEP-BY-STEP DIRECTIONS FOR 35 TRADITIONAL QUILTS

Marianne Fons
and
Liz Porter

Rodale Press
Emmaus, Pennsylvania

Our Mission
We publish books that empower people's lives.

RODALE BOOKS

The authors and editors who compiled this book have tried to make all of the contents as accurate and as correct as possible. Illustrations, photographs, and text have all been carefully checked and cross-checked. However, due to the variability of materials, personal skill, and so on, neither the authors nor Rodale Press assumes any responsibility for any damages or other losses incurred that result from the material presented herein. All instructions and diagrams should be carefully studied and clearly understood before beginning any project.

Printed in the United States of America on acid-free ⊗ paper

Executive Editor: Margaret Lydic Balitas
Senior Editor: Suzanne Nelson
Senior Associate Editor: Mary V. Green
Technical Editors: Cyndi Hershey, Janet Wickell,
    Lynn Lewis Young
Copy Manager: Dolores Plikaitis
Copy Editor: Carolyn R. Mandarano
Administrative Assistant: Susan Nickol
Office Manager: Karen Earl-Braymer
Editorial Assistance: Deborah Weisel
Art Director: Michael Mandarano
Design Director: Denise M. Shade
Book Designer: Deborah Fillion
Cover Designer: Charles M. Metz
Cover Photographer: Mitch Mandel
Cover Background Photographer: Grant Heilman
    Photography, Inc., Grant Heilman
Interior Photographer: Perry Struse, except for photographs
    on pages 124, 194, and 230, which are by Mitch Mandel
Illustrator: Jack Crane

If you have any questions or comments concerning this book, please write to:
Rodale Press
Book Readers' Service
33 East Minor Street
Emmaus, PA 18098

The quilt shown on the cover is the Sawtooth Nine Patch on page 18. The cover was photographed at Harmony Barn Antiques, Harmony, New Jersey.

Library of Congress Cataloging-in-Publication Data

Fons, Marianne.
    Quilts from America's heartland : step-by-step directions for 35 traditional quilts / Marianne Fons and Liz Porter.
        p.   cm.
    ISBN 0–87596–589–X hardcover
    1. Quilting—Patterns.   2. Patchwork—Patterns.
I. Porter, Liz.   II. Title.
TT835.F665   1994
746.9'7—dc20
                                            93–6355
                                            CIP

Distributed in the book trade by St. Martin's Press

2 4 6 8 10 9 7 5 3 1   hardcover

With appreciation for their generosity,
we dedicate this book to the owners of the
antique quilts pictured within it, especially
to Marilyn Hein, for sharing so many.

Contents

Acknowledgments vii
Introduction viii
General Instructions 1

The Power of the Nine Patch 16
Sawtooth Nine Patch 18
Iowa Amish Nine Patch 25
Sweet and Simple Nine Patch 32
Reverse Double Nine Patch 37
Nine-Patch Doll Quilts 42
Snowball Nine Patch 43
Lattice Nine Patch 46
On-Point Nine Patch 48

Blue-and-White Beauties 52
Triple Irish Chain 54
Drunkard's Path 58
Burgoyne Surrounded 65
Sawtooth Medallion 72
New Burgoyne Beauty 80

Prairie Stars 86
Four Stars 88
Twinkling Stars 94
Simple Star 100
Bethlehem Star 105
Fenced Stars Crib Quilt 117

A Quilter's Garden 122
Spring Tulips 124

Hexagon Posy 130
Rose of Sharon 137
Russian Sunflower 144
Spring Tulips Wallhanging 150

Super Scrap Quilts 158
Diamond Four Patch 160
Grand Right and Left 166
Churn Dash 172
Heartland Schoolhouse Medallion 179
Katie's Grand Graduation Quilt 187

Reflections of Daily Life 192
Little Red Schoolhouses and Birds 194
Bow Tie 204
All Flags Flying 210
Grape Basket 215
Country Schools 222

Strips and Strings 230
Chinese Coins 232
Chimneys and Cornerstones 236
Bull's Eye 242
Midwest Windmill Blades 246
Roman Stripe Variations 254
Streak O' Lightning 255
Sunshine and Shadow 258
Chinese Coins Miniature Quilt 260

Acknowledgments

For sharing their quilts, we would like to thank Connie Allen, Harold and Dorothy Birkey, Lois Carty, Laura Chickering, Portia Cooper, Louise Davis, Marilyn Hein, Joan McGiverin, Sara Miller, George and Pat Montross, Katie Porter, Kathy Russi, Loretta Schnoor, Genese Sweeney, and the Warren County Historical Society.

For helping us with sewing, we would like to thank Luella Fairholm, Marty Freed, Fern Stewart, and Evalee Waltz.

For permission to shoot location photography on the grounds, we would like to thank Living History Farms in Des Moines, Iowa, and Steve Green, director. All location and studio photography, except for the cover and pages 124, 194, and 230, was by Perry Struse of Des Moines.

Introduction

Quiltmaking has an unbroken tradition in America's heartland, that part of the country also known as the Midwest. During the westward movement of the mid-1800s, women and their families brought quilts with them to establish homes deep in the rich farmlands of Ohio, Iowa, and Kansas. The fabrics of those quilts often included scraps from the clothes of parents and grandparents who weren't making the trip toward the Mississippi and might never be seen again.

The women who made a new life for themselves in the West, whether in Indiana, Nebraska, or Wisconsin, brought excellent quiltmaking skills to the frontier along with the quilts they already had. Everyday living was often hard, material goods scarce, and comforts few. It's easy to imagine that a woman's comfort might be in her quilts—her need for beauty met by joining bits of colored cloth, her satisfaction gained by creating bright, warm covers for her family.

Not only did American quilters of the past make millions of wonderful quilts, but in the late nineteenth and early-twentieth centuries, they invented and, with the help of popular magazine publishers, named most of the quilt block patterns still popular today. Inspiration came from the world around them: Log Cabin, Broken Dishes, Churn Dash, and Windmill Blades.

In addition, these early quilters created and carried on many of quiltmaking's traditions, including the sharing of patterns from one to another, holding quilting bees, expressing patriotism and political opinions through quilts, and giving quilts to others in need.

During the Depression, when few people had money, quilters could turn to their scraps for pleasure. Many women today still remember their mothers or grandmothers carefully selecting a bag of sugar or chicken feed in a brightly colored sack they could recycle as a quilt. In the Midwest, outstanding and still-renowned quilters such as Rose Kretsinger and Carrie Hall of Kansas, Grace Snyder of Nebraska, Dr. Jeannette Throckmorton of Iowa, and Bertha Stenge of Illinois created remarkable quilts prized by museums today.

With the end of the Depression and the onset

of World War II, many women went to work, and prosperity meant plenty of manufactured blankets for everyone's beds. Though the American woman's fervor for quiltmaking largely diminished, church quilting bees and sewing circles continued to exist in the Midwest.

Selecting the 28 antique quilts for inclusion in *Quilts from America's Heartland* was easy because quilts are so plentiful where we live. We loved working with our selected quilts up close—analyzing their fabrics, their construction, their beauty—and writing instructions for them. Creating our brand-new quilts inspired by the old was fun, too.

In this book, you'll find full instructions for all the quilts you see pictured, including yardage estimates, patterns for templates, step-by-step construction directions, and many full-size quilting designs. For many of the quilts, we have included modernized quick-cutting and quick-piecing techniques as well as traditional construction methods. In a few instances, we've made a subtle change or two to make the quilt simpler to sew or more appropriate for today's preference for symmetrical corners. Most of the quilts are easy to make, although some are for intermediate quilters, and three are downright challenging. We know there is a quilt you will enjoy making regardless of your skill level.

No matter where you live—East Coast, West Coast, North, South, or Middle America—we know you love making quilts as much as we do, and we hope you will enjoy *Quilts from America's Heartland*.

Happy quilting,

Liz Porter and Marianne Fons

Liz Porter and Marianne Fons

General Instructions

For each quilt in this book, the instructions include a list of all necessary fabrics and supplies, step-by-step directions for making the project, and full-size patterns. In this section, we describe the methods you'll need for many of the projects. You will be referred to these methods as needed throughout the book.

SUPPLIES TO HAVE ON HAND

You'll need some basic sewing supplies such as needles, pins, thread, and scissors. A few of the quilts require specialized supplies, which are listed with those projects. The following list includes other items to have on hand for making most of the quilts.

Rotary cutter: For greater speed and accuracy, cut all border strips and many other pieces with a rotary cutter rather than with scissors. See the section on page 21 for tips on rotary cutting. A large rotary cutter works better than a small one for cutting fabric strips.

Plastic ruler: High-quality see-through plastic rulers are available in a variety of sizes. The most useful size for rotary cutting is 6 × 24 inches, with increments marked in inches, quarter inches, and eighth inches, as well as marked guidelines for cutting 45 and 60 degree angles. Two other useful tools are a ruled plastic square, 12 × 12 inches or larger, and a 6 × 12-inch ruler handy for cutting strip sets into patchwork segments.

Cutting mat: A self-healing mat won't dull the edge of your cutter blade. A good size for a cutting mat is 18 × 24 inches.

Template plastic or cardboard: Templates are rigid master patterns used to mark patchwork and appliqué shapes on fabric. Thin, semitransparent plastic, available at quilt and craft shops, is ideal, although poster board also works well.

Plastic-coated freezer paper: Quilters have discovered many uses for freezer paper, which is sold in grocery stores. Choose a high-quality brand, such as Reynolds. We have included a method for freezer paper appliqué on page 126.

ABOUT FABRIC

The instructions for each quilt list the amount of 44/45-inch fabric you will need. When choosing fabrics, most experienced quilters insist on 100 percent cotton broadcloth or dress-weight fabric because it presses well and handles easily, whether you are sewing by hand or machine. Two of the antique quilts we have included, Midwest Windmill Blades and Chinese Coins, are made of wool and other fabrics, but these quilts can also be made in cotton.

If there is a quilt shop in your area, the sales staff there can help you choose fabrics. You'll find many reproduction fabrics available today that are ideal for achieving the period look of antique quilts. Many other fabric stores also have a section of 100 percent cotton fabrics for quilters.

Keep in mind the amount of time you will be putting into your quilt, and make it a practice to choose high-quality materials. If you have scraps left over from other sewing, use them only if they are all-cotton and of similar weight to the other fabrics you're using in your quilt.

Purchasing Fabrics

The amounts listed are based on 44/45-inch fabric, unless stated otherwise. Yardages have been double-checked for accuracy and they include a bit extra as a margin for error. Be aware, however, that occasionally fabrics are actually narrower than the width listed on the bolt, and that any quilter, no matter how experienced, can make a mistake in cutting. We recommend buying an extra half yard of *each* of the fabrics for your quilt, just to be safe.

Preparing Fabrics

For best results, prewash, dry, and press your fabrics before using them in your quilts. Use warm water and a mild detergent in your automatic washer. Dry fabric on a medium setting in the dryer or outdoors on a clothesline. Prewashing fabric takes care of shrinkage problems, removes finishes and sizing, and softens the cloth, which makes it easier to handle. It also releases excess dye, making fabrics less likely to bleed after they are combined in a quilt.

Some quilters prefer the crispness of unwashed fabric and feel that they can achieve more accurate machine patchwork by using fabric straight from the bolt. Machine quilters often prefer to use unwashed fabric and wait until the quilt is finished to wash the fabric. This creates a quilt with a crinkled and old-fashioned look, but it also raises the risk of having colors bleed in the finished quilt.

ROTARY CUTTING

We recommend rotary cutting border strips and setting pieces and have written our instructions accordingly. In addition, for some of the quilts no pattern pieces are given. Instead, the instructions will show you how to measure and rotary cut squares, triangles, rectangles, or diamonds directly from the fabric. For some quilts you will be instructed to cut strips, sew them together into strip sets, and then cut the strip sets into special units to combine with other units.

In addition to being faster than traditional cutting methods, rotary cutting is often more accurate because of the thinness of the cutting blade and the use of precisely calibrated rulers. When you are rotary cutting, here are some helpful tips to keep in mind:

- Always cover the blade when you're not using it to cut.
- Keep rotary cutters out of children's reach.
- Always cut away from yourself.
- Square off the end of your fabric before measuring and cutting any of the pieces for a quilt, as shown in **Diagram 1.** Align the ruled square exactly with the fabric fold and bring a longer cutting ruler alongside the square. Slide the square away and use your rotary cutter to slice the fabric along the edge of the cutting ruler.

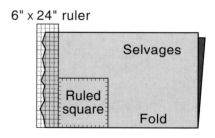

Diagram 1: Square off the uneven edges of the fabric before cutting the strips.

■ Cut strips on the crosswise grain of the fabric, as shown in **Diagram 2,** unless instructed otherwise.

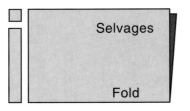

Diagram 2: Cut strips or rectangles on the crosswise grain. Cut the strips into squares.

■ Check the fabric periodically to make sure it is square and the strips remain straight.
■ To cut squares, begin by cutting one strip. Then cut that strip into squares by cutting across the width of the strip, as shown in **Diagram 2.**
■ Cut triangles from squares, as shown in **Diagram 3.** The project instructions will tell you whether to cut the square into two triangles by making one diagonal cut or into four triangles by making two diagonal cuts.

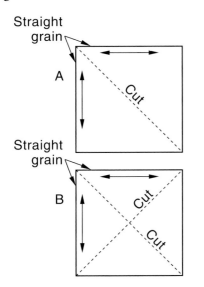

Diagram 3: Cut two triangles from a square by making one diagonal cut (A). Cut four triangles from a square by making two diagonal cuts (B).

MAKING AND USING TEMPLATES

The patterns given for patchwork and appliqué pieces are all full size. For some of the quilts you will have the option of making templates and cutting fabric pieces individually or using a rotary cutter to quick-cut them.

We favor thin, opaque plastic for templates. Carefully trace the patterns onto the plastic and cut them out with scissors. To make poster board templates, transfer each pattern to tracing paper, glue the tracing paper to the cardboard, and cut out the templates. Make sure to copy all identification letters and grain line indications onto your templates. Before using them, check your templates against the printed pattern for accuracy.

Most of the patchwork patterns in the book are printed with double lines. If you intend to sew your patchwork by hand, trace the inner line to make finished-size templates. Draw around the template on the wrong side of the fabric, leaving ½ inch between lines for seam allowances, as shown in **Diagram 4.** The lines you draw are the sewing lines. Before you cut out the pieces, add ¼-inch seam allowances around the shapes you have drawn on the fabric.

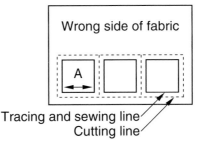

Diagram 4: If piecing by hand, mark around the template on the wrong side of the fabric. Cut it out, adding ¼-inch seam allowances on all sides.

If you plan to sew your patchwork by machine, use the outer printed line to make templates that have the ¼-inch seam allowances included. Draw around the templates on the wrong side of the fabric, as shown in **Diagram 5.** The line you draw is the cutting line. Sew with an exact ¼-inch seam for perfect patchwork.

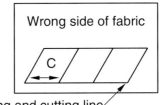

Diagram 5: If piecing by machine, use templates with seam allowances included.

Patterns for appliqué pieces are printed with a single line. Make finished-size templates for appliqué pieces. Draw around templates on the right side of the fabric, leaving ½ inch between pieces, as shown in **Diagram 6.** The lines you draw will be the fold-under lines. Then add scant ¼-inch seam allowances by eye as you cut out each piece.

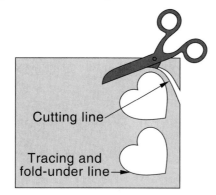

Diagram 6: Draw around the templates on the right side of the fabric for appliqué pieces. Add seam allowances as you cut out the pieces.

Freezer paper templates are another option for appliqué pieces. This method is described in "Freezer Paper Appliqué," on page 126.

MAKING MASTER PATTERNS FOR APPLIQUÉ BLOCKS

To make proper placement of appliqués on a background square easy, begin by making a full-size master pattern on a piece of tracing paper the size of your background square. You may have to tape together smaller pieces to make the paper big enough. Use your templates to position and draw outlines of the appliqué motifs on the master pattern. You can then use the master pattern either of two ways.

Method One

Lay the pattern over the background square, pinning it on at a corner or two, and then lift it to slide the appliqué pieces into position, checking the arrangement with the paper pattern.

Method Two

Darken the outlines on the paper pattern with black marker, and then lay it *under* the background square

to help you position the appliqués. If your background fabric is a light color, you can easily see the outlines through it. If your background fabric is dark, you may need to use a light box in order to see the outlines.

TIPS ON PATCHWORK

The standard seam allowance for patchwork is ¼ inch. Accurate seam allowances are a must for accurate patchwork.

When you construct patchwork blocks, keep in mind the basic principles of combining smaller pieces to make larger units, combining larger units into rows or sections, and joining sections into complete blocks. We have included piecing diagrams and step-by-step instructions to help you construct patchwork blocks easily and efficiently.

Whether you sew by hand or machine, lay out the pieces for a block right side up, as shown in the piecing diagrams, before you sew. For quilts with multiple blocks, you may want to cut out the pieces for a sample block first. Piecing this block will allow you to make sure that your fabrics work well together and that you are cutting accurately before you go on to cut out the pieces for the rest of the blocks.

Hand Piecing

For hand patchwork, use finished-size templates to cut your fabric pieces. Join pieces by pin matching marked sewing lines and sewing with a running stitch from seam line to seam line, as shown in **Diagram 7,** rather than from raw edge to raw edge. As you sew, check to see that your stitching is staying on the lines. Make a backstitch every four or five stitches

Diagram 7: Join the pieces with a running stitch, backstitching every four or five stitches.

to reinforce and strengthen the seam. Secure corners with an extra backstitch.

When you cross seam allowances of previously joined smaller units, make a backstitch just before and just after you cross. Leave the seam allowances free, as shown in **Diagram 8,** rather than stitching them down. When your block is finished, press the seam allowances either toward darker fabrics or so they will be out of the way of your planned quilting.

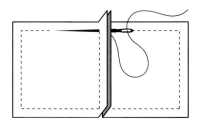

Diagram 8: When hand piecing, leave the seam allowances free by slipping through without stitching them down.

Machine Piecing

For machine patchwork, cut fabric pieces using either templates with ¼-inch seam allowances included or a rotary cutter to quick-cut them as instructed. Before sewing a block, sew a test seam to make sure you are sewing accurate ¼-inch seams. Cut two 3-inch squares and sew them together along one side. Then press the seam, open up the squares, and press the seam again. Measure across the joined squares. If they do not measure exactly 5½ inches, adjust your seam width accordingly.

On many sewing machines, you can use the edge of the presser foot as an accurate seam guide. Another option is to place a piece of masking tape on the throat plate ¼ inch to the right of the needle and use it as a guide.

Adjust the stitch length on your machine to 10 to 12 stitches per inch. Select a neutral-color thread that blends well with the fabrics you are using.

When you join pieces by machine, sew from raw edge to raw edge. Press all seams before crossing them with other seams. When you cross seams, you will be sewing seam allowances down, so before you press, think about the direction in which you want them to lie. When possible, press seam allowances toward

darker fabrics to prevent them from showing through lighter ones in the finished quilt. See page 7 for more information on pressing.

When you join rows, press the seams in opposite directions from row to row, as shown in **Diagram 9.** That way, you can abut the seam allowances when you join the rows and produce precisely matched seams.

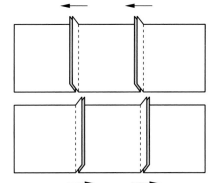

Diagram 9: Press seams in opposite directions from row to row.

When you make multiple blocks, sew pieces together assembly-line fashion whenever possible, as shown in **Diagram 10.** Chain piece pairs of pieces or units one after another without cutting the thread between them. Snip units apart, press the seams, and add the next element to growing sections of blocks.

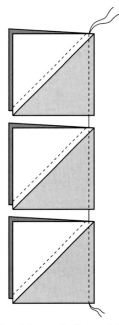

Diagram 10: Feed the units through the machine without cutting the thread.

SETTING-IN PIECES

Not all patchwork patterns can be assembled with continuous straight seams. Examples of quilts with set-in pieces are the Four Stars quilt on page 88, the medium stars of the Bethlehem Star quilt on page 105, and the Bow Tie quilt on page 204.

Setting-in pieces by hand is simple. Because you have a marked sewing line, you can easily stop your stitching exactly at the corner, pivot the fabric, adjust and pin the other side of the piece, and complete the seam.

Set-in pieces can be accurately stitched on the sewing machine by adapting hand sewing methods to machine sewing. Follow the instructions below to learn some marking and sewing tricks that can make precision machine stitching easier.

Making Templates

To make the templates, trace both the cutting (outer solid) line and sewing (inner dashed) line onto the template plastic. Carefully cut out the templates along the outer line. Check for accuracy by matching your template to the original pattern.

Use a sewing machine needle or other large needle to make holes in the templates at the corners of the sewing (inner dashed) lines, as shown in **Diagram 11.** The holes need to be large enough to allow the point of a pencil or other fabric marker to poke through.

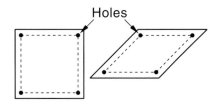

Holes

Diagram 11: For setting-in pieces by machine, make templates with holes at the setting-in points.

Marking the Fabric

On the wrong side of the fabric, draw around the template. Then, using a pencil, mark dots on the fabric through the holes in the template to create matching points on the fabric piece. Since the templates include seam allowances, you can position pieces next to each other so they share cutting lines. Cut out the fabric pieces along the drawn lines. Check to be sure all the pieces have matching points marked on them.

If you have forgotten to mark some, reposition the template atop the cutout fabric piece and add the matching points.

Preparing to Sew

Place two fabric pieces right sides together. Put a pin through the matching point on the top piece. Using the same pin, pierce the corresponding matching point on the underneath piece and pin the pieces together. In the same manner, pin the pieces together at the matching point at the end of the seam. **Diagram 12** shows two diamonds pinned at the matching points. Align the raw edges of the pieces between the points, and add additional pins along the seam line as needed.

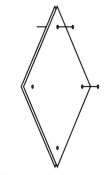

Diagram 12: Place pieces right sides together and pin match at the marked points.

Stitching a Seam

Taking an exact ¼-inch-wide seam, machine stitch from the first matching point to the matching point at the end of the seam, as shown in **Diagram 13.** Stitch only between the points; do not stitch into the seam allowance at the beginning or end of the seam. Secure the beginning and end of your stitching with a few backstitches.

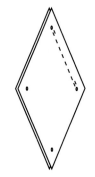

Diagram 13: Stitch from point to point, backstitching at each end of the seam.

To set in a piece, begin by pin matching the piece you want to set in to one side of the opening. Sew the seam from matching point to matching point, as shown in **Diagram 14.** Remove the work from the sewing machine.

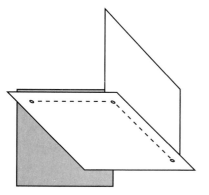

Diagram 14: Pin the piece to one side of the opening, matching dots. Stitch from the edge into the corner.

Align the adjacent edge of the piece you are setting in with the corresponding side of the opening. Pin match and stitch the adjacent seam, sewing from matching point to matching point, as shown in **Diagram 15.** The seam should be smooth, and the corner will lie flat without puckers if you have marked, pinned, and stitched accurately.

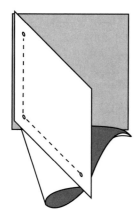

Diagram 15: Pin match the adjacent side of the piece and stitch.

Pressing

Because seam allowances at the ends of seams are left unsewn with this method, you are free to wait to make final pressing decisions until the block is assembled. Press the seams in the direction that will make the block lie the flattest, pressing toward the darker fabric whenever possible.

PRESSING BASICS

Proper pressing can make a big difference in the appearance of a finished block or quilt top. Quilters are divided on the issue of whether steam or dry pressing is superior. Experiment to see which works best for you. We have included pressing instructions with each of the quilts, but here are some general guidelines you can apply to all your projects:

■ Press a seam before crossing it with another seam.

■ Press seam allowances to one side rather than open.

■ Whenever possible, press seams toward darker fabrics.

■ Press seams of adjacent rows of patchwork, or rows within blocks, in opposite directions so they will abut as the rows are joined.

■ Press, don't iron. Bring the iron down gently and firmly on the fabric from above—don't slide it across the surface of the patchwork and risk distortion.

■ Avoid pressing appliqués after they are stitched to the background fabric. They are prettiest when slightly puffed rather than flat.

TIPS ON APPLIQUÉ

The goal for successful appliqué is smoothly turned, crisp edges without unsightly bumps or gaps. Stitches should be almost invisible.

Three popular appliqué methods are:

1. Basting back the seam allowances on appliqué pieces before stitching them to the background fabric;

2. Needle turning the edges of appliqué pieces and stitching them in place on the background fabric as you go;

3. Using freezer paper pressed to the right side of appliqué pieces as a guide to fold under seam allowances (explained in "Freezer Paper Appliqué" on page 126).

For all of these methods, use thread that matches the appliqué pieces, and stitch the appliqués to the background fabric with a blind hem or appliqué stitch, as shown in **Diagram 16.** Use long, thin size 11 or size 12 needles marked "sharps." Make stitches at ⅛-inch intervals and keep them snug.

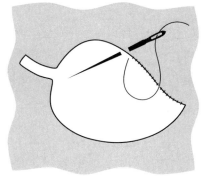

Diagram 16: Stitch the appliqués to the background with a blind hem stitch. The stitches should be nearly invisible.

When constructing appliqué blocks, always work from background to foreground. When one appliqué piece will be covered or overlapped by another, stitch the underneath piece to the background fabric first.

Basting Back Method

Mark around finished-size templates on the right side of the fabric to draw the turning lines. Cut out pieces, adding a scant ¼-inch seam allowance to the outside of the marked line.

For each appliqué piece, turn the seam allowance under, folding along the marked line, and thread baste close to the fold with white or natural thread. Clip concave curves and clefts, as shown in **Diagram 17.**

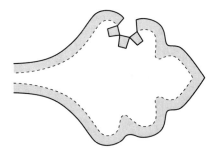

Diagram 17: Clip any concave curves, then baste back the seam allowances.

Do not baste back edges that will be covered by another appliqué piece. Pin each appliqué in place and stitch it to the background fabric, layering pieces where necessary. Remove all basting threads after the pieces are stitched down. Cut away the background fabric from behind pieces when appropriate, as described below.

Needle-Turning Method

For this method, cut appliqué pieces a generous ⅛ inch larger than the finished size. Turn under the seam allowances with your needle as you stitch the pieces to the background. Clip concave curves as needed.

Cutting Away Background Fabric behind Appliqués

When appliqué pieces are layered on top of one another, such as the petals of the Rose of Sharon quilt on page 137, or when quilting is planned on an appliqué piece, then the background fabric should be trimmed away to reduce thickness and make quilting easier. It's also a good idea to trim away the background fabric or underneath layer if they are a darker fabric than the appliqués.

Working from the back, pinch the background or underlying fabric and gently separate it from the appliqué piece. Make a small cut in the background fabric. Insert scissors in the hole and cut a scant ¼ inch to the inside of the line of appliqué stitches.

ASSEMBLING QUILT TOPS

Most of the quilts we have included have simple settings in which the blocks are sewn together in straight or diagonal rows. On many of our quilt diagrams, we've used heavier lines to indicate rows. For more complicated settings, such as medallions like the Bethlehem Star or the Sawtooth Medallion, or unusual ones, like the Hexagon Posy or Country Schools, pay close attention to the quilt diagram and the detailed assembly instructions.

After all the blocks for a quilt are complete, lay them out right side up, along with any plain blocks and setting pieces, positioned as they will be in the finished quilt. If there are quilting designs for plain setting blocks, it may be helpful to mark them before you sew the top together.

Pin and sew the blocks together in vertical or horizontal rows for straight-set quilts, as shown in **Diagram 18,** and in diagonal rows for diagonal sets, as shown in **Diagram 19.**

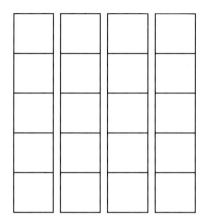

Diagram 18: Join straight-set quilts in vertical rows.

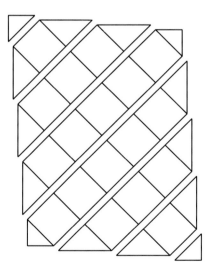

Diagram 19: Join diagonally set quilts in diagonal rows.

Press the seams in opposite directions from row to row. Once all the rows are constructed, join the rows, abutting the pressed seam allowances for accuracy in matching seams. To make the task of assembling a large quilt top manageable, first join rows into pairs and then join those pairs, rather than adding each row to an increasingly unwieldy top.

For medallion-style tops, follow the individual project instructions for constructing the quilt, generally pressing seams toward areas with less patchwork.

When you press a completed quilt top, press the wrong side first, carefully clipping and removing excess threads. Then press the right side, making sure that all of the seams lie flat.

Adding Borders

Directions for adding the appropriate borders are included with the instructions for each quilt. Here are some general tips for successful borders:

■ Cut borders the desired finished width plus ½ inch for seam allowances. Always cut border strips several inches longer than needed just to be safe. (Our cutting instructions for borders already include seam allowance and extra length.)

■ Before you add borders, measure your completed inner quilt top. Measure through the center of the quilt rather than along the edges, which may have stretched from handling. Use this measurement to determine the exact length to mark and cut borders.

■ Measure and mark the sewing dimensions on the borders before sewing them onto the quilt; wait to trim off excess fabric until after the borders are joined to the quilt.

■ Fold the border strips in half and press lightly to indicate the halfway mark on each. Align this mark with the center side of your quilt when you pin the border to the quilt.

■ When a quilt has multiple mitered borders, such as the Spring Tulips quilt on page 124, join the border strips first, then sew them to the quilt as one unit, mitering the corners as described below. Press the border seam allowances away from the center of the quilt.

Mitering Borders

Measure your finished quilt top as described above and prepare and sew each border as follows:

1. With a ruler and pencil, mark a ¼-inch sewing line on the wrong side along one long edge of the border strip. Fold the strip in half crosswise and press it lightly to mark the halfway point.

2. Measure out from the halfway point along the drawn line, and mark one-half the desired finished border length at each end of the border.

3. Using a ruler with a 45 degree angle line, mark the sewing line for the miter as shown in **Diagram 20,** measuring from the end mark made in Step 2 to the outer edge of the border strip. Mark a cutting line ¼ inch to the outside of the sewing line, but do not trim the excess fabric away until after the border is sewn to the quilt top.

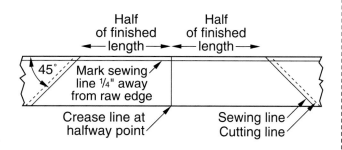

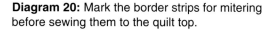

Diagram 20: Mark the border strips for mitering before sewing them to the quilt top.

4. Pin the marked border strip to the quilt top, matching the crease at the halfway point to the midpoint on the side of the quilt. Match the end marks of the sewing lines on the border strips to a point ¼ inch in from the raw edges of the quilt top.

5. Stitch the borders to the quilt top, starting and stopping at the end marks, exactly ¼ inch in from the corner of the quilt top. Backstitch to secure the beginning and end of each seam, without stitching into the seam allowances. Press the seams away from the quilt top.

6. Fold the quilt diagonally right sides together and align the marked miter lines on adjacent borders. Sew on the angled stitching line from the inner corner mark all the way to the outer raw edge. Backstitch at the beginning and the end of the seam, without stitching into the seam allowance at the inside corner.

7. Check the accuracy of each mitered corner and then trim away any excess fabric, creating a ¼-inch seam allowance at each corner.

QUILTING DESIGNS

Along with our quilt instructions, we've included many full-size quilting designs and suggestions for quilting.

Outline quilting is quilting that follows the seams of patchwork, either in the ditch, i.e., right next to the seam, or ¼ inch away from the seams. In-the-ditch quilting does not need to be marked. For ¼-inch outline quilting, you can work by eye or use ¼-inch masking tape as a stitching guide. You can also mark these and other straight lines lightly with a pencil and ruler.

Motifs such as the feather designs for the Sawtooth Medallion on page 72, the Bethlehem Star on page 105, the Rose of Sharon on page 137, and the Russian Sunflower on page 144 should be marked before the quilt top is layered with batting and backing. The method to use for marking quilting designs depends on whether your fabric is light or dark.

Marking Light Fabrics

If your fabric is a light one that you can see through easily, such as muslin, place the pattern under the quilt top and trace the quilting design onto the fabric. First, trace the design from the book onto good-quality tracing paper or photocopy it. Darken the lines with black permanent marker if necessary. If the pattern will be used many times, glue it to cardboard to make it sturdy. Carefully mark the designs on the fabric, marking a thin, continuous line that will be covered by the quilting thread. We recommend marking tools such as a silver artist's or quilter's pencil, a mechanical pencil with thin (0.5 mm), medium (B) lead, or a washable graphite pencil sold at quilt shops.

Marking Dark Fabrics

Using a light box, you can trace quilting designs directly onto dark fabrics with the pattern positioned underneath the quilt, as described above. You can also mark quilting designs from the top with a hard-edged template. To make a simple quilting design template, trace the design onto template plastic and cut it out. Draw around the outer edge of the template onto fabric and add any inner lines by eye.

QUILT BACKINGS

The materials list that accompanies each quilt includes yardage for the quilt backing. For the small quilts that are narrower than 44 inches wide, simply use a full width of fabric cut several inches longer than the quilt top. For the majority of the quilts, the quilt backing must be pieced, but another option is to purchase 90-inch-wide or 108-inch-wide fabric sold especially for quilt backings.

Whenever possible, piece quilt backings in vertical panels. Backings for quilts that are 80 inches wide or less can easily be pieced this way from two widths of fabric. You should avoid piecing a back with a seam down the center. The routine folding of a finished quilt can cause creases to form, and a center back seam can lead to a more noticeable fold line. For best results, divide one of the fabric backing pieces in half lengthwise, and sew a narrow panel to each side of a full-width central one, as shown in **Diagram 21.** Press all the seams away from the center of the quilt.

Diagram 21: Divide the yardage in half crosswise; divide one of the pieces in half lengthwise. Sew one of those halves to each side of the full-width piece, as shown.

For quilts that are wider than 80 inches, piecing the back with horizontal seams may make more economical use of your fabric. If this is the case, use three horizontal panels, as shown in **Diagram 22.** Join the full-width panels, layer the backing with the batting and the quilt top, and trim the excess from one of the panels.

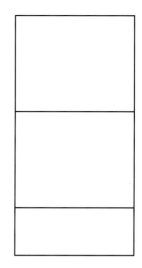

Diagram 22: Divide the yardage crosswise into three equal panels. Sew the three full-width panels together side by side. Layer the backing, batting, and quilt top with the seams running parallel to the short side of the quilt top, as shown. Trim the excess from one panel as needed.

TYPES OF QUILT BATTING

Quilters generally spend a lot of time selecting the fabrics for their quilts, but often not enough time choosing the batting they will use. When purchasing a batt, take the time to read the manufacturer's literature and think about the intended use of your quilt. It's also a good idea to talk to experienced quilters about their batting preferences.

One hundred percent polyester battings are very durable and warm. They launder without shrinking and needle easily for hand quilting. All-cotton battings are popular with quilters who like a very flat, old-fashioned appearance, though some cotton battings are more difficult to hand quilt. Another option is cotton/polyester blend batting, which combines the low-loft, sculpted look of cotton with the stability of polyester. Cotton flannel may be substituted for batting for miniature quilts or to give a very thin, flat look.

Before layering the batting with the quilt backing and top, open the package, unroll the batt, and let it relax for several hours to soften the folds, or tumble it in a clothes dryer set on low heat for five to ten minutes.

LAYERING AND BASTING

Once your quilt top is complete and marked for quilting, the batting relaxed, and the backing prepared, you are ready to assemble and baste the layers of the quilt together. Whether you plan to hand or machine quilt, the layers must first be basted evenly, so that the finished quilt will lie flat and smooth. Baste with thread for hand quilting and with safety pins for machine quilting. Follow these steps:

1. Fold the backing in half lengthwise and press to form a centerline. Place the backing, wrong side up, on a large flat surface, such as two tables pushed together or the floor. To keep the backing taut, secure it with masking tape or clamp it to the table with large binder clips.

2. Fold the batting in half lengthwise and lay it on top of the quilt backing, aligning the fold with the center crease line of the backing. Open out the batting, and smooth out and pat down any wrinkles.

3. Fold the quilt top in half lengthwise, right sides together, and lay it on top of the batting, aligning the fold with the center of the batting. Open out the top and remove any loose threads. Check to make sure that the backing and batting are 2 to 3 inches larger than the quilt top on all four sides.

4. To prepare for hand quilting, use a long darning needle and white sewing thread to baste the layers together, basting lines of stitches approximately 4 inches apart. Baste from the center outward in a radiating pattern, or make horizontal and vertical lines of basting in a grid-work fashion, using seams as guidelines. To prepare for machine quilting, use 1-inch rust-proof brass safety pins to secure the layers together, pinning from the center out approximately every 3 inches.

QUILTING

All of the antique quilts in this book are hand quilted, but most of our new projects are machine quilted. Follow these tips for successful hand or machine quilting:

Hand Quilting

- Use a hoop or frame to hold the quilt layers taut and smooth while you quilt.
- Use short quilting needles called "betweens" in size 9, 10, or 12.
- Use quilting thread rather than regular sewing thread.
- Pop the knot through the fabric into the batting layer at the beginning and ending of each length of thread so that no knots show on the front or back of the quilt.
- Quilt through all three layers of the quilt with running stitches about ⅛ inch long.

Machine Quilting

- Use a walking or even-feed presser foot for quilting straight lines.
- Use a darning or machine embroidery presser foot for free-motion quilting of curved lines.
- For the top thread, use a color that matches the fabric or clear monofilament nylon thread. Use regular sewing thread in the bobbin.
- To secure the thread at the beginning and end of a design, take extra-short stitches.
- For free-motion quilting, disengage the feed dogs of the sewing machine so you can manipulate the quilt freely. Choose continuous-line quilting designs to reduce the number of times you will need to begin and end a stitching line. Guide the marked design under the needle with both hands, working at an even pace to form even stitches.

FINISHING

The most common edge finish for quilts is binding, cut either on the bias or straight of grain. A few of the quilts in this book are finished without binding. Directions for those finishes are included with the quilt instructions.

We recommend French-fold (double-fold) binding for most quilts. Double-fold binding is easier to apply than single fold binding, and the double thickness adds durability to your quilt. Cut double-fold binding 2 inches wide for quilts with thin batting, such as cotton, and 2¼ inches wide for quilts with thicker batting.

The amount of binding needed for each quilt is included with the finishing instructions. Generally, you will need enough binding to go around the perimeter of the quilt, plus 8 to 10 inches for mitering corners and ending the binding. Three-quarters to 1 yard of fabric will usually make enough binding to finish a full-size quilt.

Making Continuous Bias Binding

1. Measure and cut a square of fabric. A 27-inch square of fabric will yield approximately 350 inches of 2-inch cut binding, which is enough to bind most of the quilts in this book. If you need more than that amount, it's easy to make more binding by cutting another square of fabric in a smaller size. Here's a handy formula for estimating the number of inches of binding you can get from a particular size fabric square: Multiply one side of the square by another side of the square. Divide the result by whatever cut width you desire for the binding strips.

2. After you've cut the size square of fabric you need for making continuous binding, fold the square in half diagonally and press it lightly. Cut the square into two triangles, cutting on the pressed line.

3. Place the two triangles right sides together as shown in **Diagram 23.** Stitch them together with a ¼-inch seam and press the seam open.

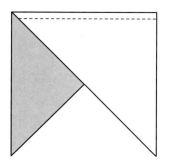

Diagram 23: Place the triangles right sides together as shown and stitch.

4. As shown in **Diagram 24,** mark the cutting lines on the wrong side of the fabric at intervals of the desired strip width, parallel to the bias edges.

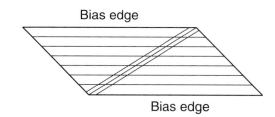

Bias edge

Bias edge

Diagram 24: Open out the two pieces and press the seam open. On the wrong side, mark cutting lines parallel to the bias edges.

5. Place the marked fabric right side up and fold as shown in **Diagram 25,** bringing the two nonbias edges together and offsetting the edges by one strip width.

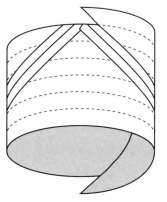

Diagram 25: Bring the nonbias edges together, offsetting them by one strip width. Sew the edges together to create a tube.

6. Pin the edges together and sew the fabric into a tube, sewing a ¼-inch seam. Press the seam open.

7. Cut on the marked lines, turning the tube as you cut, to make one long bias strip.

8. To make double-fold binding, fold the long strip in half lengthwise, wrong sides together, and press.

Joining Straight Strips for Continuous Binding

1. Refer to the individual project instructions for the amount of binding the quilt requires. Estimate the needed number of strips and cut them across the fabric width.

2. Join the strips, placing right sides together and sewing diagonal seams as shown in **Diagram 26.**

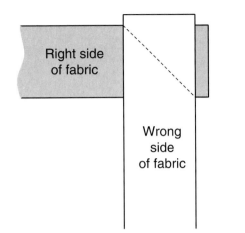

Diagram 26: Place the strips right sides together, positioning each strip $\frac{1}{4}$ inch in from the end of the other strip. Join with a diagonal seam.

3. For double-fold binding, fold and press the long strip in half lengthwise, wrong sides together.

Preparing a Quilt for Binding

Wait to trim excess batting and backing until after you sew the binding strips to the quilt. If the edges of the quilt are uneven after you're finished quilting, use a ruler and pencil to mark a straight line as close as possible to the raw edges of the quilt top. This will help in placing the binding accurately. For best results, use a ruled square to mark placement lines at 90 degree angles at the corners.

Binding a Quilt with Continuous Binding and Mitered Corners

1. If you have a "walking foot" or even-feed presser foot for your sewing machine, use it to sew on the binding. If you do not have a walking foot, thread baste around the perimeter of the quilt to help avoid puckers.

2. When you begin to sew on the binding, start at a point that's away from a corner. Place the raw edges of the binding strip even with the raw edge of the quilt top or the placement line.

3. Turn under the short raw edge approximately 2 inches at the beginning of the binding strip, creating a folded edge. Begin sewing 1 inch away from this fold. With a $\frac{1}{4}$-inch seam allowance, sew the binding to the quilt, stitching through all three layers.

4. When you approach a corner, stop stitching exactly $\frac{1}{4}$ inch away from the corner. Backstitch and remove the quilt from the sewing machine.

5. Fold the binding up and away from the corner, as shown in **Diagram 27A,** forming a fold at a 45 degree angle.

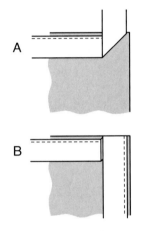

Diagram 27: Stop stitching $\frac{1}{4}$ inch from the corner and fold the binding up at a 45 degree angle (A). Fold the binding strip back down, align the raw edges with the side of the quilt top, and stitch the binding in place (B).

6. Fold the binding strip back down, creating a fold along the top edge of the quilt. Align the raw edges with the adjacent side of the corner.

7. Begin stitching the next side at the top fold of the binding, as shown in **Diagram 27B.** Miter all four corners in this manner.

8. To complete the binding, lay the end of the binding strip over the beginning of the binding. Trim the end of the binding strip so that it extends 1 inch beyond the folded edge at the beginning of the binding and complete the binding seam. The beginning and ending sections overlap approximately 1 inch.

9. Trim away any excess batting and backing from the edges of the quilt top using scissors or a rotary cutter and ruler. Testing a small section, turn the binding to the back of the quilt to determine the right amount of excess to trim from the quilt. The binding will look fuller and be more durable if it is filled rather than hollow.

10. Turn the binding to the back of the quilt and blindstitch the folded edge in place, covering the machine stitches with the folded edge of the binding. Finish the miters at the corners by folding in the adjacent sides on the back of the quilt and placing several blind stitches in the miter, both front and back.

11. If you plan to add a hanging sleeve to your quilt, follow the instructions below to make and attach the sleeve before turning and finishing the binding.

Making a Hanging Sleeve for a Quilt

Many quilters put hanging sleeves on bed quilts as well as on wallhangings so that their work can be exhibited at quilt shows. Use the following procedure to add a 4-inch-wide hanging sleeve.

1. Cut a strip of muslin or other fabric that is 8½ inches wide and 1 inch shorter than the width of the finished quilt.

2. Machine hem the short ends by turning under ½ inch on each end of the strip and pressing the fold. Turn under another ½ inch and stitch next to the fold.

3. Fold the strip in half lengthwise, wrong sides together, align the two long raw edges, and press.

4. After stitching the binding to your quilt and trimming the excess backing and batting, align the raw edges of the sleeve with the top raw edges of the quilt back, centering the sleeve on the quilt. Pin the sleeve in place.

5. Machine stitch the sleeve to the back of the quilt, stitching from the front by sewing over the stitches used to sew on the binding.

6. Turn the binding to the back of the quilt and hand stitch in place as described previously. When you turn over the binding along the edge of the quilt with the hanging sleeve, you may need to trim away extra batting and backing in order to turn the binding more easily.

7. Hand stitch the bottom loose edge of the sleeve in place on the back of the quilt, being careful not to sew through to the front of the quilt.

Labeling Your Quilt

The makers of most of the antique quilts in this book are anonymous, since quilters of the nineteenth and early twentieth centuries rarely signed their work. Once you have completed your quilt, however, be sure to sign and date it. If the backing is muslin, or other light-color fabric, you can embroider on it, or use a permanent pen and write the information directly on the fabric. Another option is to make a muslin label and blindstitch it to the back.

The Power of the Nine Patch

Throughout American quilt history, women have empowered the simplest of all patchwork blocks, the humble Nine Patch, through wonderful settings and inspired fabric use. Since the Nine Patch was often the first block little girls learned to sew, we designed three charming doll quilts for the new projects in this chapter. Each of the antique quilts we've included is powerful in its own way, from the strong simplicity of the zigzag Amish blocks to the stunning array of scrap fabrics in the Sawtooth Nine-Patch quilt.

Sawtooth Nine Patch

We named this delightful pattern ourselves after looking in vain through all the quilt block identification books we could find. The Nine-Patch structure of the larger blocks and the important Nine-Patch sashing blocks make this quilt a perfect complement to the other, simpler quilts in this chapter. This quilt's special feature is the vibrant red-and-black paisley sashing fabric, which is as bright today as the day the quilt was made, around 1890.

SKILL LEVEL: *Intermediate*

SIZE:

Finished quilt is approximately 70½ × 84 inches
Finished Sawtooth Nine-Patch block is 10½ inches square
Finished Nine-Patch setting block is 3 inches square

NUMBER OF PIECED BLOCKS:

30 Sawtooth Nine-Patch blocks
42 Nine-Patch sashing blocks

FABRICS AND SUPPLIES

To create the Sawtooth Nine-Patch blocks and the sashing blocks, you can use many different fabrics, as in the quilt shown, or a single print fabric in each value (dark, medium, and light). If you want to match the colors closely to the antique quilt shown, the list below provides a key to the predominant fabrics used. Refer to the **Block Diagram** to determine the placement of the various colors.

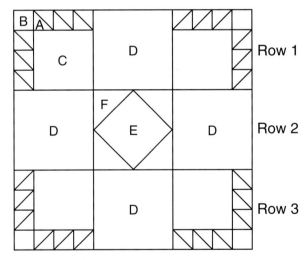

Block Diagram

Fabric Name	Colors Used in the Antique
Dark print fabric I	Navy, red, dark green, black, brown
Medium print fabric I	Light blue, medium gray
Light print fabric I	White, light gray, beige
Dark print fabric II	Dark blue, black, gray, dark brown
Medium print fabric II	Red, brown
Light print fabric II	White with red dot
Dark print fabric III	Black, gray, navy

- 2½ yards of red paisley fabric for sashing strips
- 1½ yards, or the equivalent in scraps, of medium print fabric I for D squares
- 1¼ yards, or the equivalent in scraps, of dark print fabric I for A triangles and B squares
- 1 yard, or the equivalent in scraps, of light print fabric I for A triangles
- 1 yard, or the equivalent in scraps, of black print fabric for C squares
- ½ yard, or the equivalent in scraps, of medium print fabric II for F triangles
- ⅓ yard, or the equivalent in scraps, of dark print fabric II for E squares
- ⅓ yard, or the equivalent in scraps, of light print fabric II for the Nine-Patch sashing blocks
- ⅓ yard, or the equivalent in scraps, of dark print fabric III for the Nine-Patch sashing blocks
- ¼ yard, or the equivalent in scraps, of red print fabric for the Nine-Patch sashing blocks
- 5¼ yards of fabric for the quilt back
- ¾ yard of fabric for binding
- Batting, larger than 70½ × 84 inches
- Template plastic (optional)
- Rotary cutter, ruler, and mat

CUTTING

Make templates for patterns A, B, C, D, E, and F on page 24, and mark and cut the fabric pieces. If you prefer, follow the quick-cutting instructions below. All measurements include seam allowances. Cut all strips across the fabric width.

From the red paisley fabric, cut:

- Seventy-one 3½ × 11-inch sashing strips
  Quick-cut twenty-four 3½-inch-wide strips. Cut the strips into 3½ × 11-inch rectangles.

From the various print fabrics for the blocks, cut:

- 120 medium print I D squares
  Quick-cut twelve 4-inch-wide strips. Cut the strips into 4-inch squares.
- 720 dark print I A triangles
  Quick-cut fifteen 1¾-inch-wide strips. Cut the strips into 1¾-inch squares; you will need 360

squares. Divide each square in half diagonally to produce two triangles.
- 120 dark print I B squares
  Quick-cut four 1⅜-inch-wide strips. Cut the strips into 1⅜-inch squares.
- 720 light print I A triangles
  Quick-cut as described above.
- 120 black print C squares
  Quick-cut ten 3⅛-inch-wide strips. Cut the strips into 3⅛-inch squares.
- 120 medium print II F triangles
  Quick-cut four 2⅝-inch-wide strips. Cut the strips into 2⅝-inch squares; you will need 60 squares. Divide each square diagonally into two triangles.
- 30 dark print II E squares
  Quick-cut three 3-inch-wide strips. Cut the strips into 3-inch squares.

From the fabric for the Nine-Patch sashing blocks, cut the following number of 1½-inch-wide strips. You will combine these strips into strip sets for quick piecing.
- 7 strips from light print II
- 6 strips from dark print III
- 2 strips from red print

MAKING THE SAWTOOTH NINE-PATCH BLOCKS

1. Referring to the **Fabric Key** for correct placement, join 24 dark and 24 light A triangles, as shown in **Diagram 1**. You will have 24 triangle-square units.

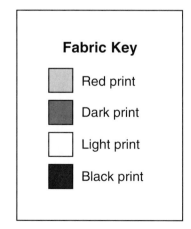

Fabric Key

Red print

Dark print

Light print

Black print

Diagram 1

2. Join the triangle-squares into strips of three. Referring to **Diagram 2** for correct positioning, make four strips as shown in **2A** and four strips as shown in **2B.**

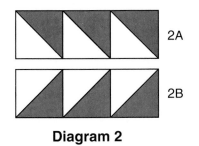

Diagram 2

3. Referring to **Diagram 3**, add a dark print B square to the end of each of the four **Diagram 2A** strips. Press the seams toward the B squares.

Diagram 3

4. Referring to **Diagram 4**, add a black print C square to the side of each of the four **Diagram 2B** strips. Press the seams toward the C squares.

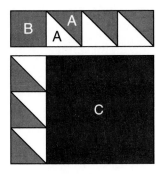

Diagram 4

5. Sew a Step 3 strip to the adjacent side of each C square as shown in **Diagram 4.** Press the seams toward the C squares. Make four of these Corner Units.

6. Referring to the **Block Piecing Diagram,** combine Corner Units and D squares to make Rows 1 and 3 of the block. Press the seams toward the D squares.

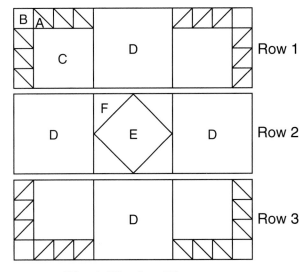

Block Piecing Diagram

7. Referring to **Diagram 5,** sew matching F triangles to two opposite sides of an E square. Press the seams away from the square. Sew two more matching F triangles to the remaining two sides of the square. Press the seams away from the square.

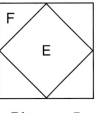

Diagram 5

8. Referring to the **Block Piecing Diagram,** sew D squares to two opposite sides of the Step 7 unit to form Row 2 of the block. Press the seams toward the D squares.

9. Join the three rows to complete the block. Repeat to make 30 blocks.

MAKING THE NINE-PATCH SASHING BLOCKS

1. Join 1½-inch-wide strips as shown in **Diagram 6** to make strip sets. Make three sets as shown in **6A** and two sets as shown in **6B.** Press seams toward the darker fabric strips.

2. Cut the strip sets into 1½-inch-wide segments. You will need 84 **Diagram 6A** segments and 42 **Diagram 6B** segments.

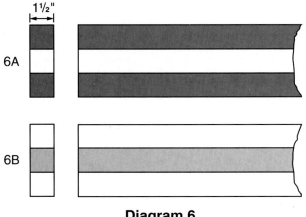

Diagram 6

3. Combine the segments to make Nine-Patch blocks, as shown in **Diagram 7.** Make 42 Nine-Patch sashing blocks. The blocks should measure 3½ inches square including seam allowances.

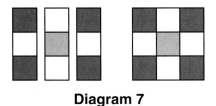

Diagram 7

ASSEMBLING THE QUILT TOP

1. Referring to the **Quilt Diagram,** make five vertical rows of blocks by joining seven red paisley sashing strips and six Sawtooth Nine-Patch blocks per row. The heavy vertical lines on the diagram help to define the rows. Press the seams toward the sashing strips.

2. Make six vertical sashing strip rows by joining seven Nine-Patch sashing blocks and six red paisley sashing strips per row, as shown in the **Quilt Diagram.** Press the seams toward the sashing strips.

3. Join the rows as shown in the diagram.

QUILTING AND FINISHING

1. Mark quilting designs as desired. On the quilt shown, the blocks have straight-line quilting as in **Diagram 8.** A diamond pattern is quilted in the sashing strips, as shown in **Diagram 9.** The full-size diamond design is provided on page 24.

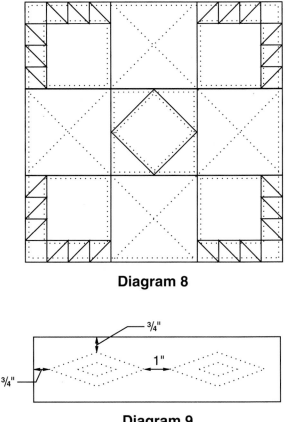

Diagram 8

Diagram 9

2. Piece the quilt back. Begin by dividing the backing fabric crosswise into two equal pieces. Cut one of the pieces in half lengthwise. Trim the selvages, and sew a narrow panel to each side of the full-width panel.

3. Layer the backing, batting, and quilt top; baste. Quilt as desired.

4. Make approximately 9 yards (324 inches) of bias or straight-grain binding for the quilt. See page 13 in the "General Instructions" for details on making and attaching binding.

70½"

84"

Quilt Diagram

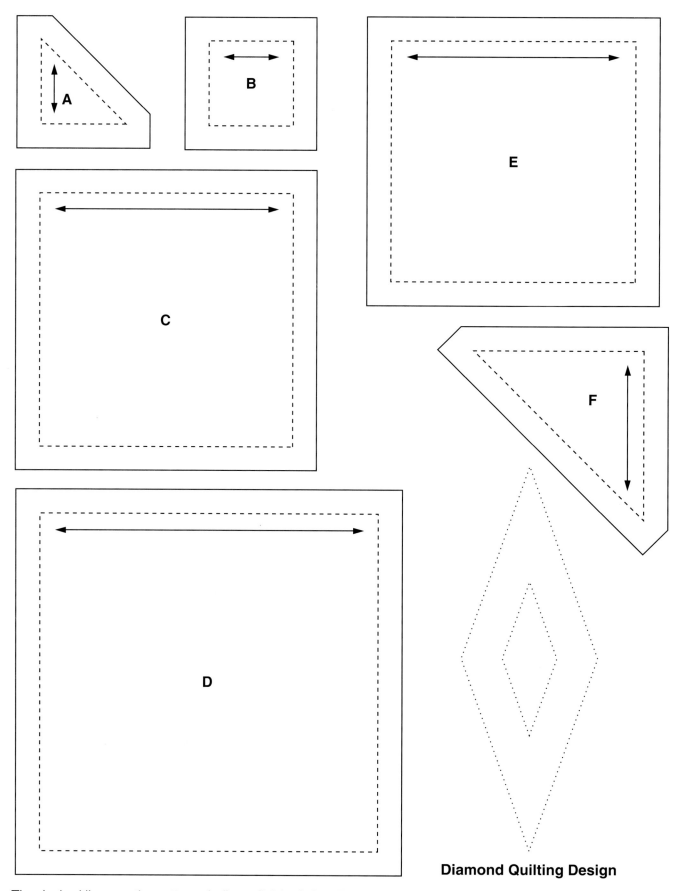

Diamond Quilting Design

The dashed lines on the patterns indicate finished size. The solid lines include seam allowances.

Iowa Amish Nine Patch

This prime example of a midwestern Amish-style quilt was made in 1926 near Kalona, Iowa. It features a simple Nine-Patch block made interesting by its zigzag set. Typical of midwestern Amish work, solid, rather than printed, fabrics were used in the top, and the backing is a tiny print fabric. Our instructions call for quick-and-easy rotary cutting of the many fabric squares for the Nine-Patch blocks.

SKILL LEVEL: *Easy*

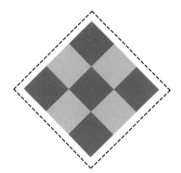

SIZE:

Finished quilt is approximately 63½ × 73 inches
Finished block is 6¾ inches square (approximately 9½ inches on the diagonal)

NUMBER OF PIECED BLOCKS: 32

FABRICS AND SUPPLIES

- 3½ yards of tan fabric for outer borders and setting pieces
- 1½ yards of black fabric for blocks, inner borders, and binding
- ½ yard of forest green fabric for blocks
- ⅜ yard of maroon fabric for blocks
- ¼ yard *each* of the following four fabrics for blocks: taupe, red-brown, brown, and light green
- 4 yards of fabric for the quilt back
- Batting, larger than 63½ × 73 inches
- Rotary cutter, ruler, and mat

CUTTING

The instructions for this quilt are for quick-cutting. If you prefer to use a template for marking and cutting the squares for the Nine-Patch blocks, draw a pattern for a 2¾-inch square on graph paper. This pattern includes seam allowances. Trace the square to make a cardboard or plastic template.

All measurements include ¼-inch seam allowances. Measurements for the border strips include extra length. Trim them to size when you add them to the quilt top. Unless otherwise directed, cut all strips across the fabric width.

From the tan fabric, first cut off a 68-inch-long piece. From this piece, cut:
- Four 6½ × 68-inch outer border strips
- One 10¾ × 68-inch strip. From this strip, cut six 10¾-inch squares. Cut each square diagonally both ways to make four **X** setting triangles. You will get a total of 24 **X** setting triangles from the six squares.

From the remaining tan fabric, cut:
- Three 10¾-inch-wide strips. From the strips, cut eight more 10¾-inch squares. Cut each square

diagonally both ways into four triangles to produce 32 more **X** setting triangles. You will need a total of 54 **X** triangles; you will have 2 extra.

■ One 5⅝-inch-wide strip. From the strip, cut six 5⅝-inch squares. Cut each square in half diagonally one way only, to produce two **Y** setting triangles per square. You will need all 12 of the triangles for the quilt.

From the black fabric, cut:
■ Six 2½-inch-wide border strips
■ 50 squares for patchwork
  Quick-cut four 2¾-inch-wide strips. Cut the strips into 2¾-inch squares.
■ Reserve the remaining fabric for binding

From the six remaining fabrics: Cut 2¾-inch squares for the blocks. First cut the fabrics into 2¾-inch-wide strips; then cut squares from the strips. You can cut 15 to 16 squares per strip, depending on the width of your yardage. The following list indicates the number of squares of each color used in the quilt shown:

■ Forest green: 85 squares (6 strips)
■ Maroon: 52 squares (4 strips)
■ Taupe: 36 squares (3 strips)
■ Red-brown: 25 squares (2 strips)
■ Brown: 20 squares (2 strips)
■ Light green: 20 squares (2 strips)

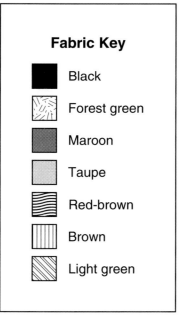

Fabric Key

■ Black
▨ Forest green
▨ Maroon
▨ Taupe
▨ Red-brown
▨ Brown
▨ Light green

MAKING THE BLOCKS

1. Referring to the **Fabric Key** and **Diagram 1,** combine the cut squares to make 32 Nine-Patch blocks in the color combinations and quantities shown in the diagram.

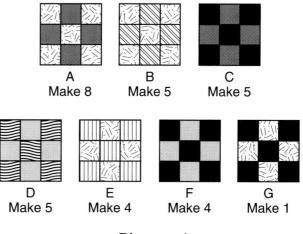

A
Make 8

B
Make 5

C
Make 5

D
Make 5

E
Make 4

F
Make 4

G
Make 1

Diagram 1

2. Sew the squares together into three rows of three squares per row, as shown in **Diagram 2,** pressing seams in opposite directions from row to row. Join the rows. Your blocks should measure 7¼ inches square from raw edge to raw edge.

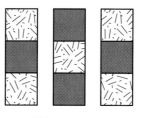

Diagram 2

ASSEMBLING THE QUILT TOP

1. Referring to the **Quilt Diagram** on page 29 for color placement, lay out the completed Nine-Patch blocks, the **X** setting triangles, and the **Y** setting triangles. Position the pieces in five vertical rows. The heavy lines on the diagram define the rows.

2. The first, third, and fifth rows have six blocks each. Referring to **Diagram 3,** join the blocks and the setting triangles for the first row into sections. Join the sections to complete one row. Press the seams away from the blocks. Repeat for the third and fifth rows.

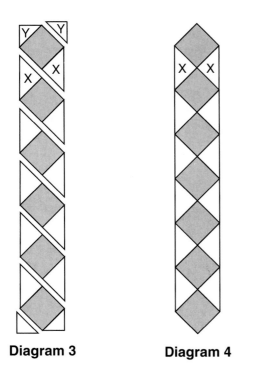

Diagram 3   **Diagram 4**

3. The second and fourth rows have seven blocks each. The block at each end will be trimmed in half after the borders are added. Referring to **Diagram 4,** join the blocks and the setting triangles for one row into sections. Join the sections to complete the row. Repeat for the other seven-block row.

4. Join the five rows to form the inner quilt top.

5. Cut two of the 2½-inch-wide black border strips in half. Sew a half strip to each full strip. Make a total of four long borders.

6. Measure the length of the quilt top (approximately 57½ inches including seam allowances). Trim two of the black borders to this length, and sew them to the sides of the quilt top.

7. Measure the width of the quilt top, including the side borders (approximately 52 inches including seam allowances). Trim the two remaining black borders to this length, and sew them to the top and bottom of the quilt. After sewing, trim off the excess half blocks at the top and bottom of the second and fourth rows. Trim even with the raw edge of the border strip.

8. Add the tan borders to the sides and then the ends of the quilt top, measuring and trimming as described previously.

QUILTING AND FINISHING

1. Mark quilting designs as desired. The quilt shown has horizontal double-line quilting through the Nine-Patch blocks, as shown in **Diagram 5.** The tan background fabric is quilted in a grid of 1-inch squares. The black borders have diagonal double-line quilting, and the wide tan borders have a Baptist fan motif. The fan motif is given full size on page 31. Adjust as needed to fit the borders of your quilt.

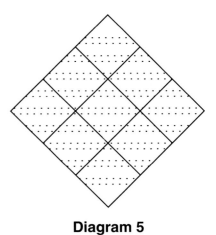

Diagram 5

2. To piece the quilt back, begin by dividing the 4 yards of backing fabric into two equal lengths. Trim the selvages and sew the two pieces together. Press the seam to one side.

3. Layer the quilt back, batting, and quilt top; position the quilt back so that the seam will be parallel to the short ends of the quilt. Baste the layers together.

4. Quilt as desired.

5. From the remaining black fabric, make approximately 8 yards (288 inches) of straight-grain binding. Sew the binding to the quilt, using squared rather than mitered corners. See "Binding with Overlapped Corners" on page 30 for details.

Quilt Diagram

Quilter's Schoolhouse

BINDING WITH OVERLAPPED CORNERS

Binding with overlapped, rather than mitered, corners is typical of Amish quilts, not only in the Midwest but also in most Amish quiltmaking communities. When you make an Amish-style quilt, you may wish to finish the edges in keeping with the quilt's character.

Follow these instructions for overlapping corners. Although we generally recommend double-fold binding, single-fold binding is less bulky and slightly easier to work with at the corners. Wait to trim off excess batting and backing until after you have sewn the binding to the quilt.

1. Make enough straight-grain binding so that you have four long pieces, each 2 to 3 inches longer than the side of the quilt it is intended for. The thickness of the batting you used will determine how wide you should cut the binding strips. For flatter cotton batts, $1\frac{1}{4}$-inch strips are wide enough. Puffier polyester batts call for wider binding, for example, $1\frac{1}{2}$ inches.

2. Sew the binding to two opposite sides of your quilt. Machine stitch the binding to the quilt top, aligning the raw edge of the binding with the raw edge of the quilt top.

3. Trim excess batting and backing. Fold over the binding on the sides and finish it by hand on the back of the quilt. Trim the ends of the binding even with the adjacent, unbound sides of the quilt.

4. Stitch binding to the two remaining sides of the quilt, allowing 1 to $1\frac{1}{2}$ inches of excess at each end.

5. Trim the ends of the unfinished binding so they are only $\frac{1}{2}$ inch longer than the adjacent bound edge.

6. To finish one corner, work with the back of the quilt facing you. Fold the raw end of the binding toward you over the edge of the quilt. Fold in the long raw edge of the binding so it is even and covers the machine stitching and the raw edges of the previously bound corner. Hand stitch the end of the binding at the corner; then continue to hand finish along the length of the binding. Finish the other corners in the same manner.

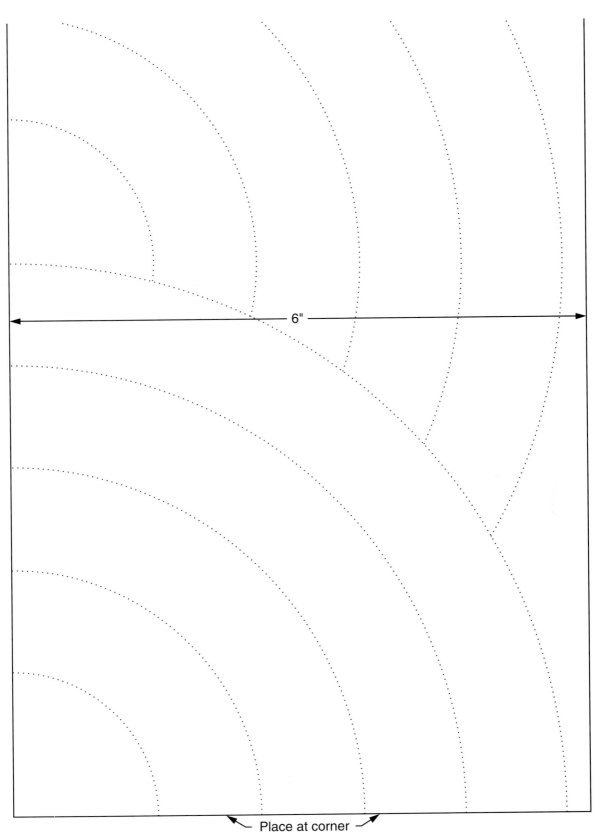

6"

Place at corner

Border Quilting Design

Sweet and Simple Nine Patch

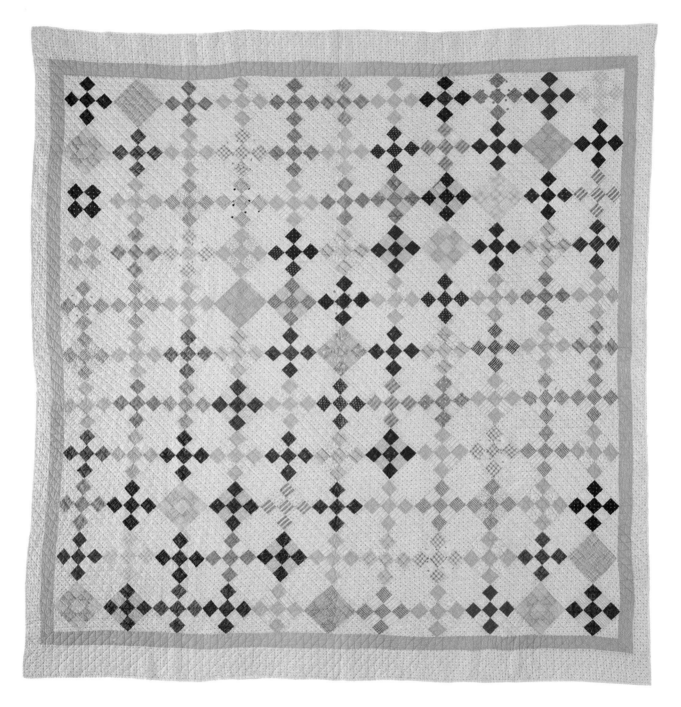

Over the years, innovative quilters have found variations galore to jazz up their quilts. An often-successful energizer is turning a block on point, as the maker of this simple Nine Patch did. Its summery combination of crisp white shirting prints, indigo blues, plaids, and bright solid pink inspires images of country farmhouses and freshly cleaned laundry snapping in the breeze.

SKILL LEVEL: *Easy*

SIZE:

Finished quilt is approximately 77¼ × 81¾ inches
Finished block is 4½ inches square (approximately 6⅜ inches on the diagonal)

NUMBER OF PIECED BLOCKS: 121

FABRICS AND SUPPLIES

- 3¾ yards of white-and-blue background print fabric for setting pieces and outer border
- Approximately 2½ yards total of assorted medium and dark print fabrics for blocks. (You can use a variety of fabrics, as in the quilt shown, or all one fabric. If you wish to use several fabrics, buy ¼ yard each of ten different fabrics. The fabrics used in the quilt shown include indigo blue prints; blue, brown, and pink checks and plaids; and a small amount of solid gold.)
- Approximately 2 yards total of assorted light print fabrics for blocks. (As described above, this yardage can be a variety of fabrics or all one fabric. If using several fabrics, buy ¼ to ½ yard each of eight fabrics. The fabrics used in the quilt shown include white with black stripes; white with black, red, or blue dots; and several white fabrics with small black motifs.)

- 1 yard of pink solid fabric for inner border and patchwork
- 5 yards of fabric for the quilt back
- ¾ yard of fabric for binding
- Batting, larger than 77¼ × 81¾ inches
- Rotary cutter, ruler, and mat

CUTTING

The instructions for this quilt call for quick-cutting and quick-piecing. If you prefer to use a template for marking and cutting the pieces for the Nine-Patch blocks, draw a pattern for a 2-inch square on graph paper. This pattern includes seam allowances. Use the pattern to make a cardboard or plastic template.

All measurements include ¼-inch seam allowances. Measurements for the border strips include extra length. They will be trimmed to size when you add them to the quilt top. Unless directed otherwise, cut all strips across the fabric width.

From the white-and-blue background print, first cut off an 86-inch-long piece. From this piece, cut:
- Two 2¼ × 86-inch borders
- Two 4½ × 78-inch borders

■ 85 setting squares
Quick-cut five 5 × 86-inch strips. Cut the strips into 5-inch squares.

From the other piece of white-and-blue fabric, cut:
■ 15 additional setting squares
Quick-cut two 5-inch-wide strips. Cut the strips into 5-inch squares. You will need a total of 100 setting squares.
■ 40 side setting triangles
Quick-cut two 7⅝-inch-wide strips. Cut the strips into 7⅝-inch squares; you will need ten squares. Cut each square in half diagonally both ways to produce four triangles.
■ 4 corner setting triangles
Quick-cut two 4¼-inch squares. Divide each square in half diagonally one way to produce two triangles per square.

From the medium and dark print fabrics, cut:
■ Ten sets of three matching 2-inch-wide strips for blocks (30 strips total)

From the light print fabrics, cut:
■ Ten sets of three matching 2-inch-wide strips for blocks (30 strips total)
■ One set of six matching 2-inch-wide strips for the pink blocks

From the pink solid fabric, cut:
■ Eight 2¼-inch-wide border strips. (Label strips and set them aside so you won't mix them up with the strips for patchwork.)
■ Seven 2-inch-wide strips for blocks

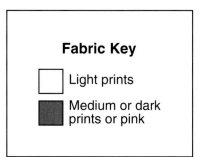

Fabric Key

☐ Light prints

■ Medium or dark prints or pink

MAKING THE PINK BLOCKS

1. Using the seven 2-inch-wide pink strips and the six 2-inch-wide light print strips, make strip sets, as shown in **Diagram 1**. Referring to the **Fabric Key**, make two strip sets as shown in **1A** and one strip set as shown in **1B**. Use the remaining two pink and matching light print strips to make a half strip set of each type. Press the seams toward the pink strips.

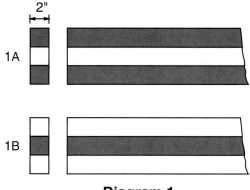

Diagram 1

2. Cut the strip sets into 2-inch-wide segments. You should get approximately 21 segments per *full* strip set and 10 from the *half* strip sets.

3. Referring to **Diagram 2**, sew the segments together into blocks. Make approximately 25 pink-and-white Nine-Patch blocks.

Diagram 2

MAKING THE OTHER BLOCKS

1. In the same manner as for the pink blocks, make strip sets using dark, medium, and light print strips. Make ten **Diagram 1A** strip sets and ten **Diagram 1B** strip sets. Press the seams toward the darker strips.

2. Cut 2-inch-wide segments from the strip sets, keeping matching fabrics together. You should get approximately 21 segments per set.

3. Keeping matching fabrics together, make sets of matching blocks like the one shown in **Diagram 2**. Make a total of 121 blocks, including the pink-and-white blocks. You will have some leftover segments.

Quilter's Schoolhouse

MAKING EXTRA NINE-PATCH BLOCKS

This quilt requires a total of 121 Nine-Patch blocks, most of which are of the five dark/four light configuration of squares shown in **Diagram 1.** Depending on the width of your yardage, you may have sewn and cut all the strip sets as instructed and still need a few more blocks. If necessary, combine the leftover segments you have to make blocks of

Diagram 1   **Diagram 2**

the five light/four dark configuration of squares shown in **Diagram 2.** The quilt shown has two blocks of this type.

ASSEMBLING THE QUILT TOP

1. Referring to the **Quilt Diagram** on page 36 and the photo on page 32, lay out the completed Nine-Patch blocks, setting squares, side setting triangles, and corner triangles.

2. Join the pieced blocks and setting pieces in diagonal rows. The heavy lines on the diagram define the rows. Press the seams toward the setting squares.

3. Join the rows. If necessary, trim the outside edges of the setting triangles so that the outer edge of the quilt top is even.

4. To make the four pink borders, sew pairs of 2¼-inch-wide pink border strips end to end. See page 9 in the "General Instructions" for details on piecing border strips.

5. Measure the width of the completed quilt top, measuring through the center of the quilt rather than along the edges, which may have stretched. Trim two of the pink borders to length (approximately 70½ inches). Sew the borders to two opposite ends of the quilt. Press the seams toward the borders.

6. In the same manner, measure the length of the quilt top, including the pink borders, from raw edge to raw edge. Trim two pink borders to this length (approximately 74 inches) and add them to the sides of the quilt top. Press the seams toward the borders.

7. In the same manner, measure, trim, and sew the two 4½-inch-wide white-and-blue outer border strips to the top and bottom of the quilt top. Trim and sew the 2¼-inch white-and-blue borders to the two sides of the quilt. Press the seams toward the borders.

QUILTING AND FINISHING

1. Mark quilting designs as desired. The original quilt has straight-line quilting in both the patchwork blocks and the setting squares.

2. Piece the quilt back. Begin by dividing the backing fabric crosswise into two equal pieces. Cut one of the pieces in half lengthwise. Trim the selvages, and sew a narrow panel to each side of the full-width panel. Press the seams toward the narrow panels.

3. Layer the backing, batting, and quilt top; baste.

4. Quilt as desired.

5. Make approximately 9 yards (324 inches) of straight-grain or bias binding. See page 13 in the "General Instructions" for details on making and attaching binding.

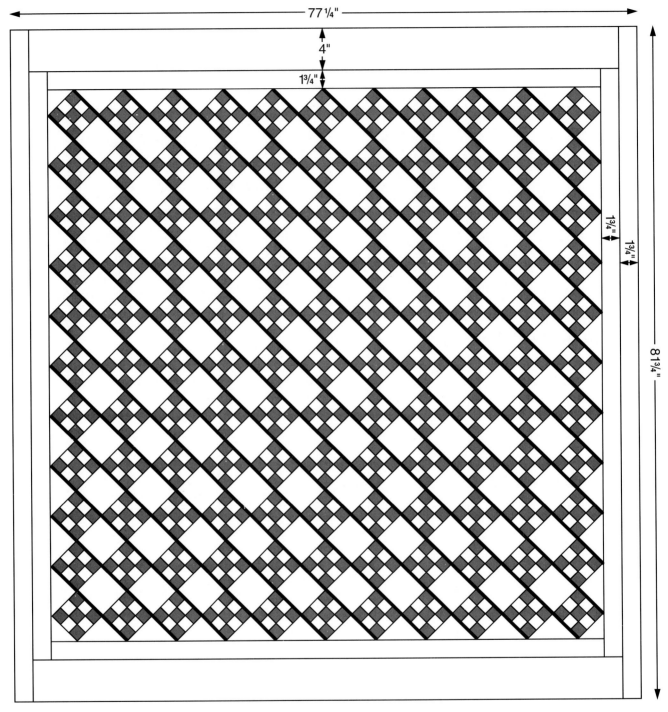

Quilt Diagram

Reverse Double Nine Patch

Traditionally, Double Nine-Patch blocks are made from five small Nine-Patch blocks and four plain squares. The turn of the century maverick quiltmaker who made this quilt broke with tradition, either by intent or by accident, and instead used four Nine Patches and five plain squares to create her own unique design.

SKILL LEVEL: *Easy*

SIZE:

Finished quilt is approximately 66½ × 76 inches
Finished Double Nine-Patch block is 6¾ inches
   square (approximately 9½ inches on the diagonal)
Finished Nine-Patch unit is 2¼ inches square

NUMBER OF PIECED BLOCKS: 56

FABRICS AND SUPPLIES

- 3½ yards of medium blue fabric for setting squares and triangles
- 3¼ yards of muslin for blocks
- Approximately 2¼ yards total of assorted medium and dark print fabrics (red, brown, green, gold, pink, purple, and beige) for blocks. (One 31 × 1¼-inch strip is enough to make the Nine-Patch units for one Double Nine-Patch block.)
- 4½ yards of fabric for the quilt back
- ¾ yard of pink print fabric for binding
- Batting, larger than 66½ × 76 inches
- Rotary cutter, ruler, and mat

CUTTING

The instructions for this quilt call for quick-cutting and quick-piecing. If you prefer to use templates for marking and cutting the pieces for the blocks, draw patterns for the two sizes of squares on graph paper and make templates. The A square is 1¼ inches, including seam allowances, and the larger B square is 2¾ inches.

All measurements include ¼-inch seam allowances. Cut all strips across the width of the fabric unless directed otherwise.

From the medium blue fabric, cut:
- 42 setting squares
  Quick-cut nine 7¼-inch-wide strips. Cut the strips into 7¼-inch squares.
- 26 side setting triangles
  Quick-cut three 10¾-inch-wide strips. Cut seven 10¾-inch squares from the strips. Cut each square diagonally in both directions into four triangles. You will have two extra triangles.
- 4 corner setting triangles
  Quick-cut two 5½-inch squares. Cut each square in half diagonally into two triangles.

From the muslin, cut:
- Forty-three 1¼-inch-wide strips for Nine-Patch units
- 280 B squares
  Quick-cut nineteen 2¾-inch-wide strips. Cut the strips into 2¾-inch squares.

From the assorted medium and dark print fabrics, cut:

■ Fifty-six 1¼-inch-wide strips for Nine-Patch units. Cut each strip into two 12-inch-long pieces and one 7-inch-long piece to make a set of four small Nine-Patch units.

MAKING THE NINE-PATCH UNITS

This quilt calls for 56 blocks, with four Nine-Patch units in each block. Use the assembly-line method described here to speed up construction of the small Nine-Patch units.

1. Referring to **Diagram 1,** sew one 12-inch-long strip each of three different medium or dark print fabrics to one side of a 44-inch-long muslin strip, allowing approximately 1 inch of space between each print strip.

Diagram 1

2. Sew 12-inch-long strips of the same three fabrics to the opposite side of the muslin strip, so that matching strips are opposite each other. Press the seam allowances away from the muslin. Cut the strip set into three sections, one for each fabric.

3. Repeat Steps 1 and 2 to make a total of 56 fabric sections.

4. Referring to **Diagram 2,** cut each fabric section into eight 1¼-inch-wide segments. From each fabric section you will get enough segments for four small Nine-Patch units.

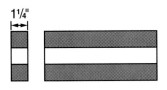

Diagram 2

5. Referring to **Diagram 3,** sew five different 7-inch-long medium or dark print fabric strips to one side of a muslin strip, leaving approximately 1 inch of space between each print strip. Sew a second muslin strip to the opposite side of the dark strips. Press the seam allowances away from the muslin strips. Cut the strip set into five fabric sections, one for each fabric.

Diagram 3

6. Repeat Step 5 to make a total of 56 fabric sections.

7. Cut each fabric section into four 1¼-inch-wide segments. From each fabric section, you will have enough segments for four small Nine-Patch units.

8. Refer to **Diagram 4** to make the Nine-Patch units. Choose segments that contain matching fabric, and join the three rows to make a unit. Press the seam allowances away from the center row. Make 56 sets of four matching Nine-Patch units, for a total of 224 Nine-Patch units.

Diagram 4

MAKING THE REVERSE DOUBLE NINE-PATCH BLOCKS

1. For each block, lay out four matching small Nine-Patch units and five muslin B squares, as shown in **Diagram 5.**

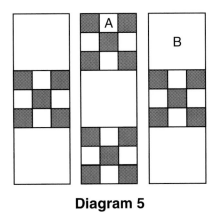

Diagram 5

2. Join the Nine-Patch units and muslin squares into three vertical rows. Press the seam allowances toward the muslin squares.

3. Join the rows; press the seam allowances away from the center row.

4. Repeat to make a total of 56 blocks.

ASSEMBLING THE QUILT TOP

1. Lay out the blocks on point in eight horizontal rows with seven blocks in each row, as shown in the **Quilt Diagram.**

2. Fill in between the blocks with blue setting squares. Add setting triangles around the outer edge and a corner triangle at each corner.

3. Sew the quilt together in diagonal rows. The heavy lines on the diagram help define the rows. Press the seams toward the blue setting pieces.

4. Join the rows.

QUILTING AND FINISHING

1. Mark quilting designs as desired. The quilt shown has double-line quilting running vertically through some blocks and horizontally through others. Although there is no set pattern in the original, you might choose to quilt all the pieced blocks one way and all the plain blocks the other way.

2. Divide the quilt back fabric crosswise into two equal pieces. Cut one piece in half lengthwise into two long panels. Trim the selvages, and stitch a narrow panel to each long side of the full-width panel. Press the seams away from the center panel.

3. Layer the quilt back, batting, and quilt top; baste. Quilt as desired.

4. From the binding fabric, make approximately 8½ yards (306 inches) of bias or straight-grain binding. See page 13 in "General Instructions" for details on making and attaching binding.

Row 7   Row 6   Row 5   Row 4   Row 3   Row 2   Row 1

Row 8

Row 9

Row 10

Row 11

Row 12

Row 13

Row 14

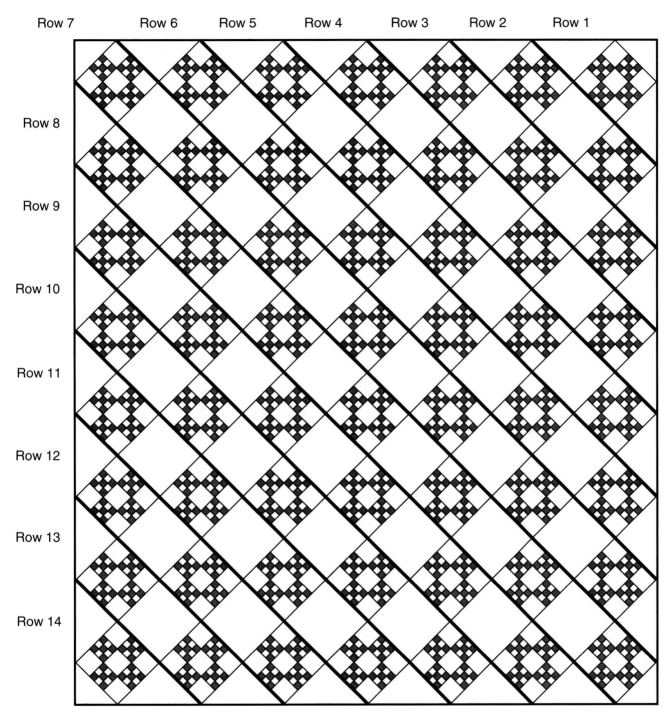

Quilt Diagram

Nine-Patch Doll Quilts

The simple Nine Patch was the pattern used by nineteenth-century mothers and grandmothers to teach the little girls in the family how to piece patchwork. In a way, the Nine Patch represents the ABCs of quiltmaking—the basics of choosing colors, cutting, piecing, and quilting are all covered by the time the quilt is completed. Continue the tradition of teaching with a Nine Patch as you work with your own budding quilter to create one or all of our charming Nine-Patch doll quilts. Of course, you should feel free to make these even if there aren't any children around!

The Snowball Nine Patch (lower right in photo) is a traditional two-block pattern. For the Lattice Nine Patch (left), the blocks are separated by sashing strips and squares. In the On-Point Nine Patch (upper right), the blocks are set diagonally and then "squared off" with pastel scrap triangles.

Snowball Nine Patch

SKILL LEVEL: *Easy*

SIZE:

Finished quilt is approximately 14¼ × 18¾ inches
Finished block is 2¼ inches square

NUMBER OF PIECED BLOCKS:

18 Nine-Patch blocks
17 Snowball blocks

FABRICS AND SUPPLIES

■ 1 yard of medium blue print fabric for borders, blocks, and quilt back
■ ½ yard of dark blue print fabric for borders, blocks, and binding
■ ¼ yard of light blue print fabric for blocks
■ Batting, larger than 14½ × 18¾ inches
■ Rotary cutter, ruler, and mat
■ Template plastic (optional)

CUTTING

The instructions for this quilt call for quick-cutting and quick-piecing the Nine-Patch blocks, and include a special method for making the Snowball blocks. If you prefer to use templates for marking and cutting patchwork pieces, make templates for A, B, and C using the patterns on page 51.

Measurements below for quick-cutting include ¼-inch seam allowances. Measurements for borders include extra length. Trim the borders to size when you add them to the quilt top. Cut all strips across the fabric width.

From the medium blue print fabric, cut:

■ Two 1¼-inch-wide border strips
■ One 1¼-inch-wide strip for strip sets. (If using templates, cut 18 A squares.)

- Two 2¾-inch-wide strips for Snowball blocks. (If using templates, cut 17 B pieces.)
- Reserve an 18 × 22-inch rectangle for the quilt back

From the dark blue print fabric, cut:
- Two 1¼-inch-wide border strips
- Six 1¼-inch-wide strips for strip sets and Snowball blocks. (If using templates, cut 72 A squares and 68 C triangles.)
- Two 1¼-inch-wide strips for binding

From the light blue print fabric, cut:
- Three 1¼-inch-wide strips for strip sets. (If using templates, cut 72 A squares.)

MAKING THE NINE-PATCH BLOCKS

If you are using traditional piecing to make the blocks, combine four dark A squares, four light A squares, and one medium A square, as shown in **Diagram 3**. Make a total of 18 blocks.

If quick-piecing, follow the instructions below to make strip sets to produce the 18 blocks for the quilt.

1. Referring to the **Fabric Key** and **Diagram 1**, combine two 1¼-inch-wide light blue strips and one 1¼-inch-wide dark blue strip to make a strip set as shown. Press the seams toward the dark strip. From additional strips, cut two 10-inch-long light blue strips and one 10-inch-long dark blue strip. Combine them in the same manner to make a short strip set. Cut the two strip sets into 1¼-inch-wide segments. You will need 36 segments.

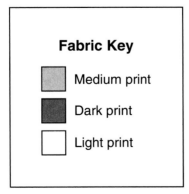

Fabric Key

■ Medium print

■ Dark print

□ Light print

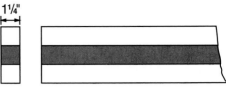

Diagram 1

2. Trim two dark blue strips and one medium blue strip to 25 inches long. Combine them to form one **Diagram 2** strip set. Press the seams toward the dark strips. Cut the strip set into 1¼-inch-wide segments. You will need 18 segments.

Diagram 2

3. Combine two Step 1 segments and one Step 2 segment to form each Nine-Patch block, as shown in **Diagram 3**. Repeat to make 18 blocks. The blocks should measure 2¾ inches square including seam allowances.

Diagram 3

MAKING THE SNOWBALL BLOCKS

If you are using traditional piecing to make the blocks, combine one B piece and four C triangles, as shown in **Diagram 4.** Make a total of 17 blocks.

Diagram 4

If quick-piecing, follow the instructions below to make 17 blocks.

1. Using two full-length 1¼-inch-wide dark blue strips and one leftover short dark blue strip, cut sixty-eight 1¼-inch squares. On the wrong side of the fabric, draw a diagonal pencil line across each square as shown in **Diagram 5.**

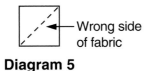

Diagram 5

2. From the two 2¾-inch-wide medium blue fabric strips, cut seventeen 2¾-inch squares.

3. Place a 1¼-inch square at each corner of a 2¾-inch square, right sides together, as shown in **Diagram 6.** Pin in place if you desire. Stitch on the drawn lines as shown. Repeat for all 17 squares.

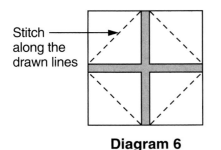

Diagram 6

4. Trim the corners as shown in **Diagram 7,** cutting ¼ inch to the outside of the stitching. Open out the dark triangles and press seams toward the corners. The blocks should measure 2¾ inches including seam allowances. Use a ruled square and rotary cutter to square up the blocks if necessary.

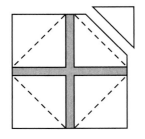

Diagram 7

ASSEMBLING THE QUILT TOP

1. Referring to the **Quilt Diagram,** lay out the 18 Nine-Patch blocks and 17 Snowball blocks in five vertical rows.

2. Join the blocks to form the rows, pressing the seams toward the Snowball blocks. Join the rows to form the inner quilt.

3. Make four small four-patch blocks for the corners of the quilt. To do so, cut eight 1¼-inch dark blue squares and eight 1¼-inch light blue squares from remaining strips. Combine the squares as shown in **Diagram 8.**

Diagram 8

4. Combine the two medium blue border strips and the two dark blue border strips into two strip sets with one medium and one dark strip in each set.

5. Measure the length and width of the quilt top, measuring through the middle rather than along the edges. From the above Step 4 strip sets, cut two border sections the length of the quilt (approximately 16¼ inches including seam allowances) and two border sections the width of the quilt (approximately 11¾ inches including seam allowances).

6. Sew the two side borders to the quilt top with the medium blue strip on the outside. Press the seams toward the borders.

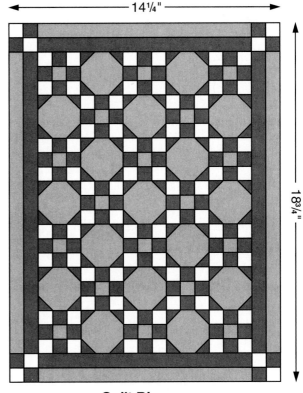

Quilt Diagram

7. Sew a Four-Patch block to each end of the remaining borders, referring to the **Quilt Diagram** for correct fabric placement. Press the seams toward the border strips. Sew the borders to the top and bottom of the quilt with the medium blue strip on the outside.

QUILTING AND FINISHING

1. Mark quilting designs as desired. We used a pumpkin seed design in the center of the Snowball blocks, and simple straight-line quilting in the patch-work areas. The pumpkin seed design is printed on the B pattern piece on page 51.

2. Layer the backing, batting, and quilt top; baste. Quilt as desired.

3. To make binding, join the remaining two 1¼-inch-wide dark print strips with a diagonal seam, making one long strip. Sew the binding to the quilt and hand finish. See page 13 in the "General Instructions" for details on making and attaching binding.

Lattice Nine Patch

SKILL LEVEL: *Easy*

SIZE:
Finished quilt is approximately 14¼ × 17¼ inches
Finished block is 2¼ inches square

NUMBER OF PIECED BLOCKS: 16

FABRICS AND SUPPLIES
- ⅝ yard of white-and-blue print fabric for borders, sashing, and quilt back
- ⅛ yard or a "quilter's eighth" (9 × 22 inches) *each* of three yellow and three blue print fabrics for patchwork
- ⅛ yard of tiny gold check fabric for sashing squares and binding
- Batting, larger than 14¼ × 17¼ inches
- Rotary cutter, ruler, and mat
- Template plastic (optional)

CUTTING
The instructions for this quilt are for quick-cutting and quick-piecing the Nine-Patch blocks. If you prefer to use a template for marking and cutting the squares for the blocks, make a template using pattern A on page 51.

If you are using a template, cut five yellow and four blue squares per block for each of the 16 blocks.

All measurements for quick-cutting include ¼-inch seam allowances. Measurements for the border strips include extra length. Trim the borders to size when you add them to the quilt top. Cut all strips across the fabric width.

From the white-and-blue print fabric, cut:
- One 18 × 22-inch rectangle for the quilt back
- Four 2¾ × 22-inch border strips

- Thirty-one 1¼ × 2¾-inch sashing strips
  Quick-cut two 2¾ × 22-inch strips. Cut the strips into 1¼-inch rectangles.

From *one* of the yellow print fabrics, cut:
- One 1¼ × 22-inch strip for Strip Set A

From *each* of the other two yellow print fabrics, cut:
- Two 1¼ × 22-inch strips for Strip Set B

From *one* of the blue print fabrics, cut:
- Two 1¼ × 22-inch strips for Strip Set A

From *each* of the other two blue print fabrics, cut:
- One 1¼ × 22-inch strip for Strip Set B

From the gold check fabric, cut:
- Twenty 1¼-inch sashing squares
  Quick-cut one 1¼-inch-wide strip. Cut the strip into squares.
- Two 1¼-inch-wide binding strips. (Label and set aside.)

MAKING THE BLOCKS

If you used a template to cut individual squares for the Nine-Patch blocks, combine the squares into rows of three squares per row, as shown in **Diagram 11**. Make a total of 16 blocks.

To quick-piece the Nine-Patch blocks, follow the steps below to make strip sets and combine segments into blocks.

1. Referring to the **Fabric Key** and **Diagram 9**, combine the one yellow and the two blue strips to make Strip Set A. Press the seams toward the blue strips. Cut the strip set into 1¼-inch-wide segments; you will need 16 segments.

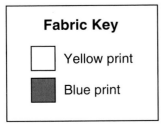

Fabric Key

☐ Yellow print

■ Blue print

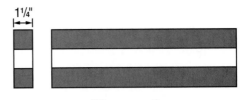

Diagram 9
Strip Set A

2. Combine two matching yellow strips and one blue strip as shown in **Diagram 10** to make Strip Set B. Press the seams toward the blue strip. Repeat with the second set of two matching yellow strips and the one remaining blue strip to form a second Strip Set B. Cut the strip sets into 1¼-inch segments; you will need a total of 32 segments.

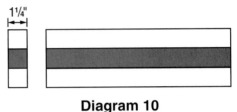

Diagram 10
Strip Set B

3. To complete one block, join one Strip Set A and two Strip Set B segments as shown in **Diagram 11**. The block should measure 2¾ inches square including seam allowances.

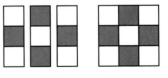

Diagram 11

ASSEMBLING THE QUILT TOP

1. Lay out the blocks, sashing strips, and sashing squares as shown in the **Quilt Diagram** on page 48.

2. Make four vertical rows with five sashing squares and four sashing strips per row. Press the seams toward the strips.

3. Make three vertical rows with five sashing strips and four Nine-Patch blocks per row. Press the seams toward the strips.

4. Join the rows.

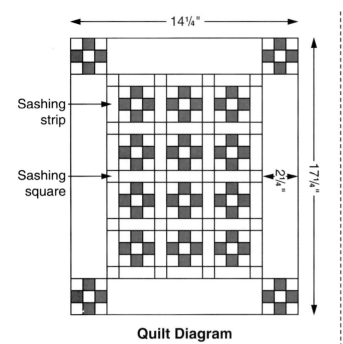

Quilt Diagram

5. Measure the length of the quilt top through the center from raw edge to raw edge (approximately 13¼ inches). Trim two 2¾-inch-wide border strips to this length. Measure the width of the quilt top (approximately 10¼ inches) through the center from raw edge to raw edge. From the remaining border strips, trim two strips to this length.

6. Sew the longer borders to the sides of quilt. Press the seams toward the borders.

7. Sew a Nine-Patch block to each end of the two shorter borders. Press the seams toward the borders. Sew the borders to the top and bottom of the quilt.

QUILTING AND FINISHING

1. Mark quilting designs as desired. We used simple straight-line quilting for the project shown.

2. Layer the backing, batting, and quilt top; baste. Quilt as desired.

3. Join the two gold binding strips together with a diagonal seam to make one long strip. Sew the binding to the quilt and hand finish. See page 13 in the "General Instructions" for details on making and attaching binding.

On-Point Nine Patch

SKILL LEVEL: *Easy*

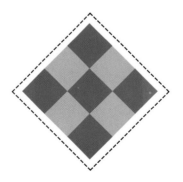

SIZE:

Finished quilt is approximately 12¾ × 16 inches
Finished block is 2¼ inches square (approximately 3¼ inches on the diagonal)

NUMBER OF PIECED BLOCKS: 12

FABRICS AND SUPPLIES

- ⅝ yard of lavender print fabric for borders and quilt back
- ¼ yard or a "quilter's quarter" (18 × 22 inches) of white-and-pink print for blocks and pieced border
- Scraps or "quilter's eighths" (9 × 22 inches) of 18 different pastel print fabrics (pink, peach, yellow,

blue, and green) for the blocks, setting pieces, pieced border, and binding
- Batting, larger than 12¾ × 16 inches
- Rotary cutter, ruler, and mat
- Template plastic (optional)

CUTTING

The instructions for this quilt call for quick-cutting and quick-piecing the Nine-Patch blocks and quick-cutting the setting pieces. If you prefer to use a template for marking and cutting the squares for the blocks, make a template for pattern A on page 51.

All measurements include ¼-inch seam allowances. Measurements for the border strips include extra length. Trim the borders to size when you add them to the quilt top. Cut all strips across the fabric width.

If you are using a template to mark and cut squares for the blocks, cut five pastel print squares and four light background print squares per block for each of the 12 blocks.

From the lavender print fabric, cut:
- One 18 × 22-inch rectangle for the quilt back
- Four 1¼ × 22-inch border strips
- One 1¼ × 22-inch strip; cut the strip into 7-inch segments for strip sets

From the white-and-pink print fabric, cut:
- Five 1¼ × 22-inch strips for strip sets

From the pastel print fabrics, cut:
- Twenty-four 1¼ × 7-inch strips
- 48 setting triangles
  Quick-cut two 2½-inch squares from *each* of 12 fabrics. Cut each square in half diagonally into two triangles. You will have 12 sets of triangles with four matching triangles in each set.

MAKING THE BLOCKS

If you used a template to cut individual squares for the Nine-Patch blocks, combine the squares into rows of three squares per row, as shown in **Diagram 14.** Make a total of 12 blocks.

To quick-piece the Nine-Patch blocks, review the following steps to make strip sets and combine segments into blocks.

1. Referring to the **Fabric Key** and **Diagram 12,** combine two 1¼ × 22-inch white-and-pink background strips and three 1¼ × 7-inch pastel print strips as shown. Press the seams toward the pastel strips. Cut the three sections apart, then cut the sections into 1¼-inch-wide segments. You will need 12 segments.

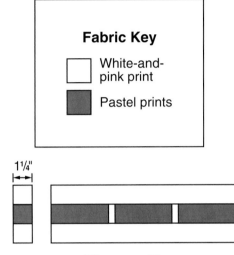

Diagram 12

2. Make three **Diagram 13** strip sets. For each set, combine one 22-inch-long white-and-pink print strip and six 7-inch-long pastel print strips. The pastel strips do not need to match. Press the seams toward the pastel strips. Cut the strip sets into a total of 24 segments, each 1¼ inches wide.

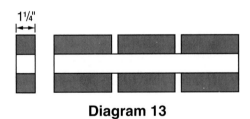

Diagram 13

3. To form a block, combine one Step 1 and two Step 2 segments as shown in **Diagram 14.** The block should measure 2¾ inches square including seam allowances.

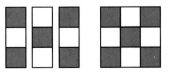

Diagram 14

ASSEMBLING THE QUILT TOP

1. "Square off" each diagonal block as shown in **Diagram 15** by adding four matching setting triangles. Sew triangles to two opposite sides of a block, centering the long side of the triangle on the side of the block. Press seams toward the triangles. Sew the remaining two triangles to the remaining sides of the block and press. If necessary, use a ruled square to trim the squared-off block.

Diagram 15

2. Lay out the 12 squared-off blocks as shown in the **Quilt Diagram.**

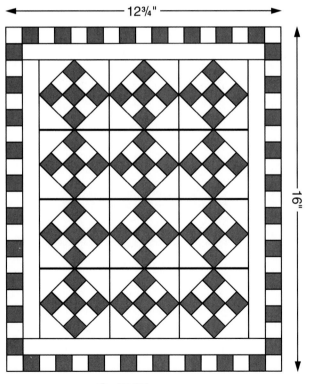

Quilt Diagram

3. Join the squared-off blocks into four horizontal rows with three blocks per row. The heavy lines on the diagram define the rows. Join the rows.

4. Measure the length of the quilt top (approximately 13½ inches). Trim two 1¼-inch-wide lavender border strips to this length. Sew the borders to the sides of the quilt top. Press the seams toward the borders.

5. Measure the width of the quilt top from raw edge to raw edge (approximately 11¾ inches). Trim two lavender border strips to this length. Sew the borders to the top and bottom of the quilt. Press the seams toward the borders.

6. To make the pieced border, use leftover strip set segments or cut individual 1¼-inch squares and alternate white-and-pink print squares with pastel print squares. Make two side borders, using 19 squares in each border and having pastel squares at each end. Sew the side borders to the quilt top. It may be necessary to take slightly narrower seams between squares to make the pieced strip fit.

In the same manner, make top and bottom borders using 17 squares each, with a background print square at each end. Sew the borders to the top and bottom of the quilt, adjusting seams as needed.

QUILTING AND FINISHING

1. Mark quilting designs as desired. We used simple straight-line quilting for the project shown.

2. Layer the backing, batting, and quilt top; baste. Quilt as desired.

3. From one of the pastel print fabrics, cut 1¼-inch-wide strips and join with diagonal seams to make a piece of binding approximately 60 inches long. Sew binding to the quilt and hand finish. See page 13 in the "General Instructions" for details on making and attaching binding.

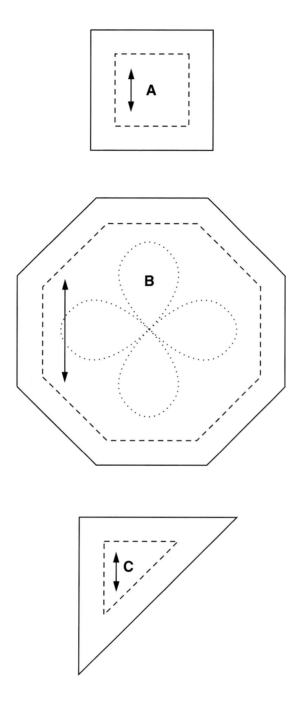

The dashed lines on the patterns indicate finished size.
The solid lines include seam allowances.

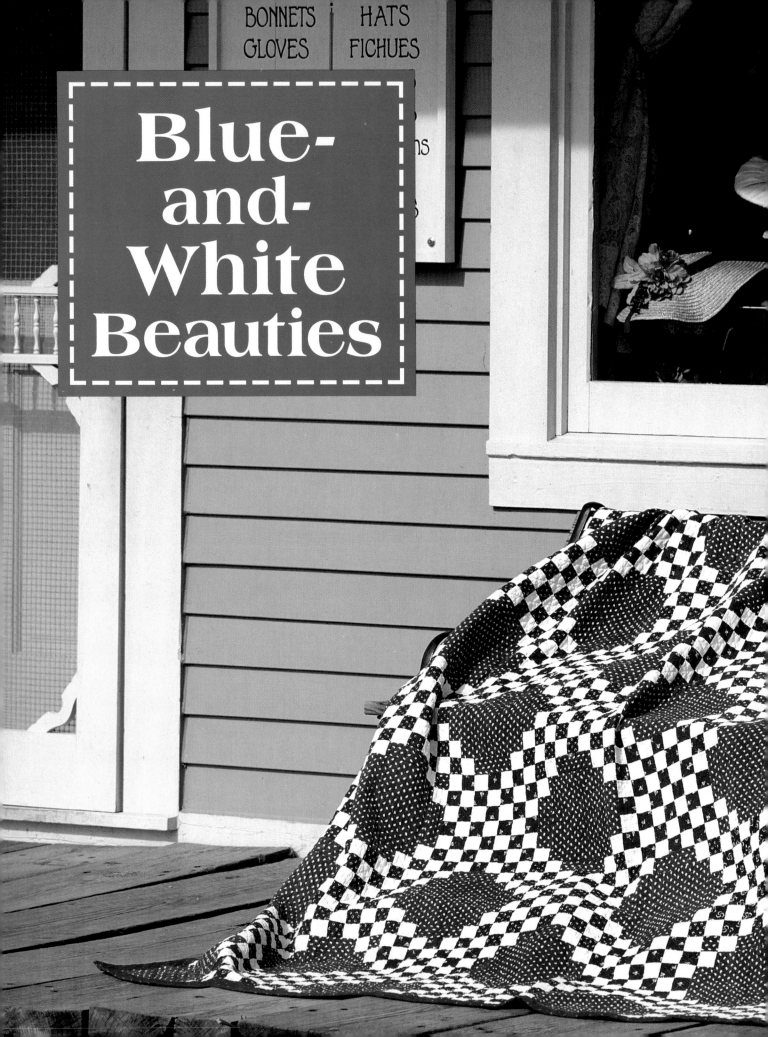

Blue-
and-
White
Beauties

A strictly blue-and-white color scheme for quilts has enjoyed unbroken popularity since around 1840. Between 1875 and 1925, dark indigo blue was often combined with shirting prints—white fabric with small isolated figures—rather than with the plain muslin of earlier examples. Pastel blue-and-white quilts are most likely from the twentieth century.

The Triple Irish Chain, Burgoyne Surrounded, and our New Burgoyne Beauty are excellent projects for modern strip-piecing techniques, and we have written instructions accordingly. For the classic Sawtooth Medallion, you have the option of traditional patchwork or a timesaving grid method to create the many triangle-squares needed for the quilt. Piece the curved patchwork for the Drunkard's Path either by hand or machine.

Triple
Irish Chain

This simple quilt from the early 1900s is constructed from two types of blocks that alternate to create the chain design. In writing the instructions, we altered the layout slightly, adding enough blocks so that the quilt has checkerboard blocks at all four corners and is large enough to fit a full-size bed. Our directions call for quick-cutting with a rotary cutter and speedy machine piecing.

SKILL LEVEL: *Easy*

SIZE:

Finished quilt is approximately 78¾ × 96¼ inches
Finished blocks are 8¾ inches square

NUMBER OF PIECED BLOCKS:

50 A blocks
49 B blocks

FABRICS AND SUPPLIES

- 6½ yards of navy blue print fabric
- 4 yards of unbleached muslin
- 6 yards of fabric for the quilt back
- ¾ yard of fabric for binding
- Batting, larger than 78¾ × 96¼ inches
- Rotary cutter, ruler, and cutting mat

CUTTING

All measurements include ¼-inch seam allowances. Cut all strips across the fabric width, using a rotary cutter and ruler.

From the navy print fabric, cut:

- Sixty-three 1¾-inch-wide strips
- Eight 4¼-inch-wide strips
- Forty-nine 6¾-inch squares
  Quick-cut nine 6¾-inch-wide strips. Cut the strips into squares.

From the muslin, cut:

- Seventy-three 1¾-inch-wide strips

MAKING THE A BLOCKS

Both types of blocks are constructed in the same basic manner. You will combine cut strips into strip sets, cut the strip sets into segments, then join the segments to form the blocks.

1. Using four 1¾-inch muslin strips and three 1¾-inch navy print strips per strip set, make a total of nine strip sets, as shown in **Diagram 1**. Press the seams toward the dark fabric.

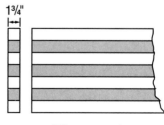

Diagram 1

2. Cut the strip sets into 1¾-inch segments. You will need a total of 200 segments.

3. Using four 1¾-inch navy print strips and three 1¾-inch muslin strips per strip set, make a total of seven strip sets as shown in **Diagram 2.** Press the seams toward the dark fabric.

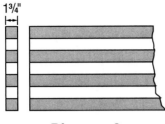

Diagram 2

4. Cut the **Diagram 2** strip sets into 1¾-inch segments. You will need 150 segments.

5. For each Block A, combine four Step 2 segments and three Step 4 segments to make a checkerboard as shown in **Diagram 3.** The finished block should measure 9¾ inches square including seam allowances. Make 50 Block A checkerboard blocks.

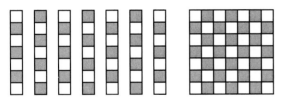

Diagram 3

Block A Diagram

MAKING THE B BLOCKS

Depending on the width of your fabric, the instructions that follow may not produce quite enough segments to make the 49 blocks. The instructions assume the fabric is a full 44 inches wide; if your fabric is narrower than that, cut and combine additional strips as necessary.

1. Using two 1¾-inch navy print strips, one 4¼-inch navy print strip, and two 1¾-inch muslin strips per strip set, make four strip sets like the one shown in **Diagram 4.** Press the seams toward the dark fabric.

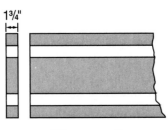

Diagram 4

2. Cut the strip sets into 1¾-inch segments. You will need a total of 98 segments.

3. Using two 1¾-inch muslin strips and one 4¼-inch navy print strip per strip set, make four **Diagram 5** strip sets. Press the seams toward the dark fabric.

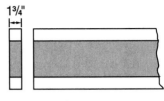

Diagram 5

4. Cut the Step 3 strip set into 1¾-inch segments. You need a total of 98 segments.

5. Combine two Step 2 segments, two Step 4 segments, and one 6¾-inch navy print square, as shown in **Diagram 6,** to make one Block B. Add the Step 4 segments to the navy print square first, then the Step 2 segments. Press the seams away from the center square as you piece the block. The blocks should measure 9¼ inches square including seam allowances. Make 49 of these blocks.

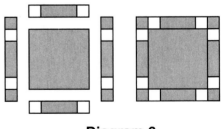

Diagram 6

Block B Diagram

ASSEMBLING THE QUILT

1. Referring to the **Quilt Diagram,** join the A and B blocks in nine vertical rows, alternating the blocks in the rows as shown. The heavy lines on the diagram help define the rows. Press the joining seams toward the B blocks each time.

2. Join the rows.

QUILTING AND FINISHING

1. Mark quilting designs as desired. The quilt shown has diagonal-square grid quilting over the entire quilt. The lines of the grid bisect the patchwork as shown by the lines in **Diagram 7.** See page 10 in the "General Instructions" for tips on marking quilting designs.

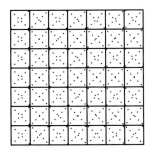 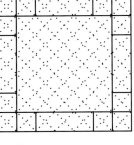

Diagram 7

2. Piece the quilt back. Begin by dividing the backing fabric crosswise into two equal pieces. Cut one of the pieces in half lengthwise. Trim the selvages, and sew a narrow panel to each side of the full-width piece. Press the seams toward the narrow panels.

3. Layer the backing, batting, and quilt top; baste. Quilt as desired.

4. Make approximately 10½ yards (378 inches) of bias or straight-grain binding to bind the edges of the finished quilt. See page 13 in the "General Instructions" for details on making and attaching binding.

78¾"

96¼"

		A	B	A	B	A	B	A
B	A	B	A	B	A	B	A	B
A	B	A	B	A	B	A	B	A
B	A	B	A	B	A	B	A	B
A	B	A	B	A	B	A	B	A
B	A	B	A	B	A	B	A	B
A	B	A	B	A	B	A	B	A
B	A	B	A	B	A	B	A	B
A	B	A	B	A	B	A	B	A
B	A	B	A	B	A	B	A	B
A	B	A	B	A	B	A	B	A

Quilt Diagram

Drunkard's Path

Aflowing vine and leaf appliqué border frames the patchwork center of this stunning late-nineteenth-century Drunkard's Path quilt. The popular pattern and its variations have gathered many names over the years, including Solomon's Puzzle, Robbing Peter to Pay Paul, Wonder of the World, Love Ring, and Falling Timbers. For patterns with curved pieces such as this one, we recommend piecing the units by hand, then using the machine to join the units into blocks and then to join the blocks.

SKILL LEVEL: *Intermediate*

SIZE:

Finished quilt is approximately 77 × 89 inches
Finished block is 6 inches square

NUMBER OF PIECED BLOCKS:

120 blocks
22 half blocks
1 quarter block

FABRICS AND SUPPLIES

Note: For best results, use a ½-inch-wide flat metal or heat-resistant plastic "bias bar" to prepare the long bias strip for the border vine. Sets of bars in several widths used for preparing strips for Celtic and other appliqué are sold in quilt shops.

- 6¼ yards of white fabric for blocks, borders, and binding
- 4½ yards of navy print fabric for blocks, vine, and leaves
- 6 yards of fabric for the quilt back
- Batting, larger than 77 × 89 inches
- Template plastic
- ½-inch-wide bias bar for pressing the bias vines (optional)

CUTTING

Make templates for patterns A, B, C, D, and the leaf on pages 63–64. If you will be piecing by hand, trace the inner dashed line on the patterns to make finished-size templates. Then add seam allowances as you cut out the fabric pieces. If you will be machine piecing, trace the outer solid lines on the patterns to make templates that include seam allowances. Transfer the register marks on the patterns to your templates. These marks indicate the centers of the curves. As you mark the fabric pieces, transfer these register marks to the fabric to help you align the curved edges when pinning and sewing.

The leaf pattern is finished size; add seam allowances when cutting the pieces from fabric. All other pattern pieces include a ¼-inch seam allowance.

The border measurements include seam allowances and extra length. Trim the borders to the exact length needed before you add them to the quilt top.

To make the bias vine, refer to the instructions for making bias binding in the "General Instructions" on page 13.

From the white fabric, cut:
- Four 7½ × 80-inch borders
- 262 A pieces

- 1 B piece
- 60 C pieces
- 11 D pieces
- Reserve the remaining fabric for binding

From the navy print fabric, cut:
- 263 A pieces
- 262 B pieces
- 48 leaves
- Approximately 350 inches of 1½-inch-wide bias. (Cut bias strips and piece them together to achieve the needed length.)

MAKING THE BLOCKS

1. Begin by making units like the one shown in **Diagram 1.** Pin the curved edge of a white A piece to the curved edge of a navy print B piece, matching the center curve marks and outer edges. To make pinning along the curved edges easier, start by pinning at the corners and the center of the curve, and take up only a few threads with each pin. Stitch the curved seam, clipping as needed. Press the seam away from the A piece. Repeat to make a total of 262 units.

Diagram 1

2. Join four Step 1 units into a square, as shown in **Diagram 2.** Make a total of 60 of these units.

Diagram 2

3. Sew pairs of Step 1 units together into rectangles, as shown in **Diagram 3.** You will have a total of 11 of these units.

Diagram 3

4. Sew the white B piece to a navy print A piece, as shown in **Diagram 4.** Press the seam away from the A piece. There is only one unit of this type.

Diagram 4

5. Referring to **Diagram 5,** pin and sew the curved edge of a navy print A piece to each curved edge of a C piece. Press the seams away from the A pieces. Make 60 of these units.

Diagram 5

6. Sew the curved edge of a navy print A piece to each curved edge of a D piece, as shown in **Diagram 6.** Make 11 of these units.

Diagram 6

ASSEMBLING THE QUILT TOP

1. Referring to the **Quilt Diagram** and the photograph on page 58, lay out the various patchwork units. The numbers on this diagram correspond to the diagram numbers for the various types of units.

2. Sew the units together into rows, pressing the seam allowances in alternate directions from row to row. Join the rows.

3. Measure the length of the quilt top. Trim two borders to this length (approximately 75½ inches) and sew them to the sides of the quilt top. Press the seams toward the borders.

4. Measure the width of the quilt top, including the side borders. Trim the remaining two borders to this length (approximately 77½ inches) and sew them to the top and bottom of the quilt top. Press the seams toward the borders.

77"

89"

Quilt Diagram

5. Prepare a bias strip for a vine that finishes approximately ½ inch wide. Use your favorite method for making appliqué vines, or use the bias bar method described here.

To prepare the bias with a bias bar, begin by folding the long bias strip in half with wrong sides facing. Stitch the long raw edges together with a ⅛-inch seam. Insert a ½-inch-wide bias bar in the fabric tube. Adjust the fabric so the seam is centered along one flat side of the bar; press on both sides. Work the bar through the tube until the entire strip is pressed flat.

6. Using your favorite technique, prepare the leaves for appliqué. The technique described in "Freezer Paper Appliqué" on page 126 works well for shapes such as these leaves.

7. Referring to the **Quilt Diagram,** curve the vine along the borders and baste or pin in place. Position the leaves along the vine as shown. Appliqué the vine and leaves to the borders.

QUILTING AND FINISHING

1. Mark quilting designs as desired. The quilting design used for the C pieces on the antique quilt is printed on the C pattern piece on page 64. The quilt shown has outline quilting around the vine and leaves, with additional quilting through the center of the vine and echo quilting within the leaves. A grid of ½-inch squares fills all other areas. If you do not wish to quilt this closely, you can outline quilt ¼ inch from the patchwork pieces, and then fill in the open areas in the borders with a ½-inch or larger grid of squares.

2. Divide the quilt back fabric crosswise into two equal lengths. Cut one piece in half lengthwise. Trim the selvages, and stitch a half panel to each long side of the full-width panel. Press the seams away from the full panel.

3. Layer the quilt back, batting, and quilt top; baste. Quilt as desired.

4. Make approximately 10 yards (360 inches) of bias or straight-grain binding to finish the edges of the quilt. See page 13 in the "General Instructions" for details on making and attaching binding.

Quilter's Schoolhouse

DRUNKARD'S PATH VARIATIONS

A single Drunkard's Path unit, shown at right, is a versatile building block for many different patchwork designs that are variations of the basic Drunkard's Path pattern. Design variations are created by altering the light and dark placement in the units, turning the units, and combining different numbers of units. The drawings here show some of the popular variations of this classic quilt design.

One unit

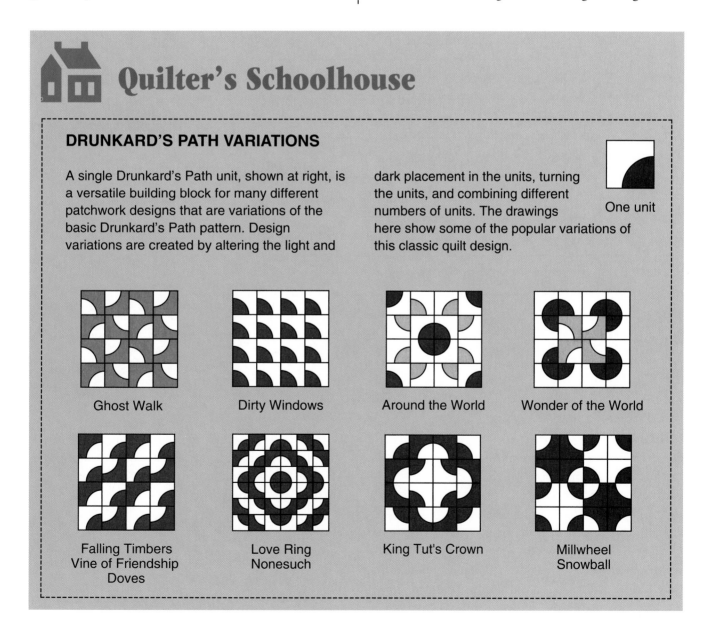

Ghost Walk

Dirty Windows

Around the World

Wonder of the World

Falling Timbers
Vine of Friendship
Doves

Love Ring
Nonesuch

King Tut's Crown

Millwheel
Snowball

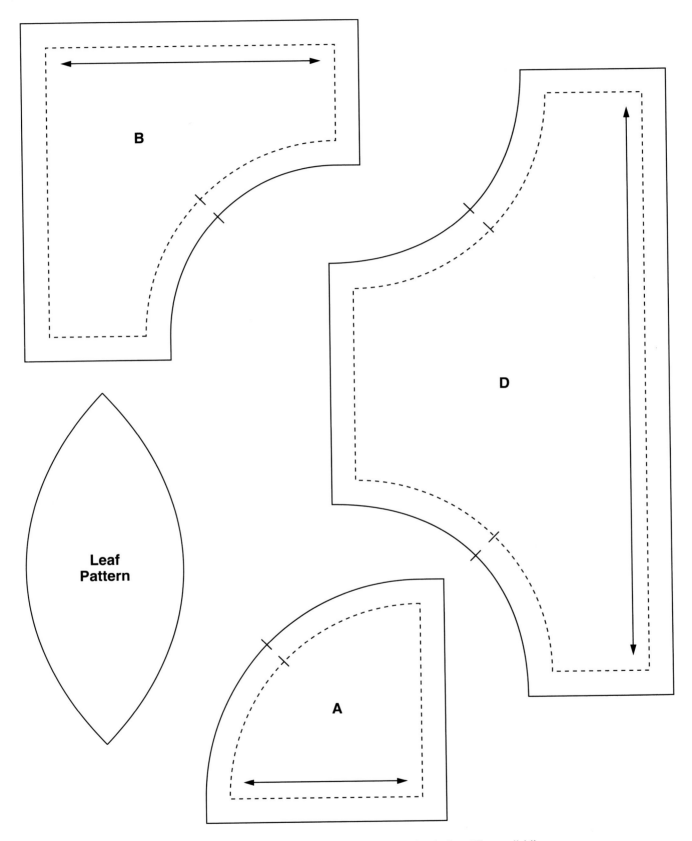

The dashed lines on the patterns indicate finished size. The solid lines include seam allowances. For the appliqué pattern, add seam allowances when cutting the piece from fabric.

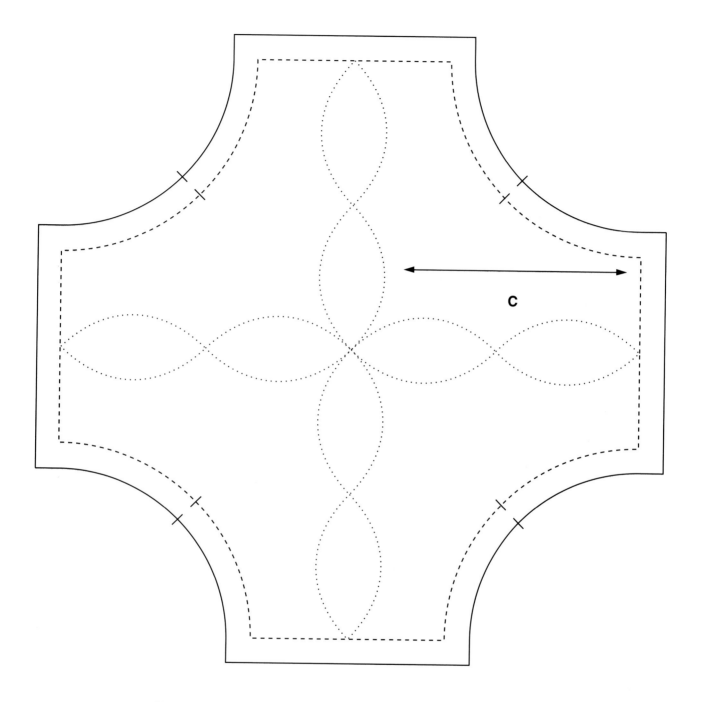

The dashed lines on the pattern indicate finished size.
The solid lines include seam allowances.

Burgoyne Surrounded

British general John Burgoyne surrendered, with his entire army, to Revolutionary forces at Saratoga, New York, in 1777. The lost battle was a turning point of the war. American women, who would not be able to vote for almost 150 years, expressed their patriotism by commemorating Burgoyne's defeat in a quilt. Our instructions, written for quick-cutting and quick-piecing the 97-piece Burgoyne Surrounded blocks, express appreciation for modernized quiltmaking techniques.

SKILL LEVEL: *Easy*

SIZE:

Finished quilt is approximately 77½ × 93⅜ inches
Finished block is 11¼ inches square (approximately 15⅞ inches on the diagonal)

NUMBER OF PIECED BLOCKS: 20

FABRICS AND SUPPLIES

- 8 yards of blue fabric for patchwork, setting squares, setting triangles, and borders
- 2 yards of white fabric or muslin for patchwork
- 5¾ yards of fabric for the quilt back
- ¾ yard of fabric for binding
- Batting, larger than 77½ × 93⅜ inches
- Rotary cutter, ruler, and mat

CUTTING

The instructions for this quilt are for quick-cutting and quick-piecing. All the cutting dimensions that follow include seam allowances. Measurements for the border strips include extra length. They will be trimmed to size when you add them to the quilt top. Unless otherwise directed, cut strips across the fabric width.

From the blue fabric, first cut off two 85-inch-long pieces. From the first piece, cut:
- Two 7½ × 85-inch borders
- 12 setting squares
  Quick-cut two lengthwise strips, each 11¾ inches wide. Cut 11¾-inch squares from the strips.

From the second 85-inch-long piece, cut:
- Two 7½ × 85-inch borders
- 14 side setting triangles
  Quick-cut four 17⅛-inch squares. Divide each square in half diagonally both ways to produce four triangles. You will have two extra triangles.
- 4 corner setting triangles
  Quick-cut two 8⅞-inch squares. Divide each square in half diagonally one way to produce two triangles.

From the remaining blue fabric, cut:
- Twenty-one 1¼-inch-wide strips
- Eight 2-inch-wide strips
- 160 A rectangles
  Quick-cut eight 2¾-inch-wide strips. Cut the strips into 2 × 2¾-inch rectangles.
- 80 B rectangles
  Quick-cut six 4¼-inch-wide strips. Cut the strips into 2¾ × 4¼-inch rectangles.

From the white fabric or muslin, cut:
- Twenty-two 1¼-inch-wide strips
- Ten 2-inch-wide strips

MAKING THE BLOCKS

The Burgoyne Surrounded blocks are made of four types of pieced units, plus two sizes of blue rectangles. To create the pieced units, you will combine strips to make strip sets, cut the strip sets into segments, and reposition the segments to form the units. As you piece the strip sets, press the seams toward the blue strips.

1. Make a strip set, as shown in **Diagram 1A,** sewing a 1¼-inch-wide white strip to a 1¼-inch-wide blue strip. Make five strip sets of this type. Cut the strip sets into 1¼-inch-wide segments. You will need 160 segments.

2. Combine pairs of segments into Four-Patch units as shown in **Diagram 1B.** You should have 80 units.

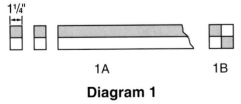

Diagram 1

3. Make a strip set, as shown in **Diagram 2A,** sewing together two 2-inch-wide blue strips and one 1¼-inch-wide white strip. Make three strip sets of this type. Cut the strip sets into 1¼-inch-wide segments. You will need a total of 80 segments.

4. In the same manner, sew together two 2-inch-wide white strips and one 1¼-inch-wide blue strip into a strip set, as shown in **Diagram 2B.** Make three

strip sets of this type. Cut the strip sets into 1¼-inch-wide segments. You will need 80 segments.

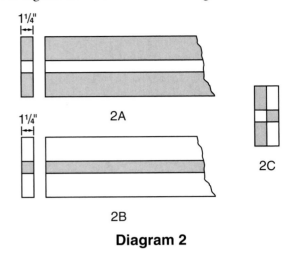

Diagram 2

5. Combine the two types of segments into units like the one shown in **Diagram 2C.** You should have a total of 80 units.

6. To make a strip set, as shown in **Diagram 3A,** combine two 1¼-inch-wide white strips and one 1¼-inch-wide blue strip. Make five strip sets of this type. Cut the strip sets into 1¼-inch-wide segments. You will need a total of 160 segments.

7. Make a similar strip set using two blue strips and one white strip, as shown in **Diagram 3B.** Make three strip sets of this type. Cut 1¼-inch-wide segments from the strip sets. You will need 80 segments. Use the segments to make 80 Nine-Patch units as shown in **3C.**

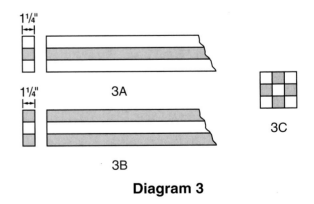

Diagram 3

8. Use two 2-inch-wide white strips and one 1¼-inch-wide blue strip to make two strip sets, as shown in **Diagram 4A** on page 68. Cut 2-inch-wide segments from the strip sets. You will need 40 segments.

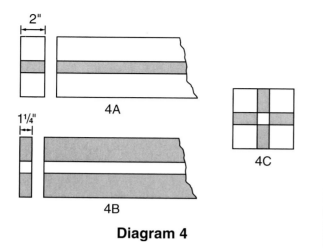

Diagram 4

9. Make a similar strip set using two blue strips and one white strip, as shown in **Diagram 4B.** Cut 20 segments, each 1¼ inches wide, from the strip set.

10. Combine the two types of segments to make the square unit shown in **Diagram 4C.** Make 20 of these units.

11. Combine the four types of pieced units and the blue A and B rectangles into rows, as shown in **Diagram 5.** Press the seams toward the unpieced blue rectangles.

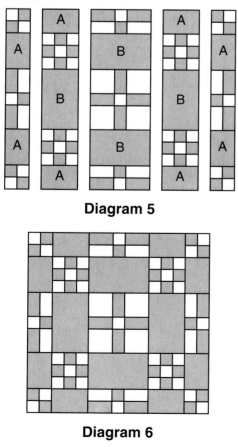

Diagram 5

Diagram 6

12. Join the rows to form the block. It should measure 11¾ inches square from raw edge to raw edge. See **Diagram 6.** Make a total of 20 blocks.

ASSEMBLING THE QUILT TOP

1. Referring to the **Quilt Diagram,** join pieced blocks, setting squares, side setting triangles, and corner setting triangles in diagonal rows to form the inner quilt top. The heavy lines on the diagram define the rows.

2. Measure the length of the quilt through the center. Trim two borders to this measurement (approximately 79⅞ inches). Sew the borders to the sides of the quilt top, pressing the seams toward the borders.

3. Measure the width of the quilt through the center, including the side borders. Trim two borders to this length (approximately 78 inches) and sew them to the top and bottom of the quilt.

QUILTING AND FINISHING

1. Mark quilting designs. The quilt shown has straight-line quilting in the block areas, as shown by the dashed lines in **Diagram 7.**

The fan-style quilting design used in the setting

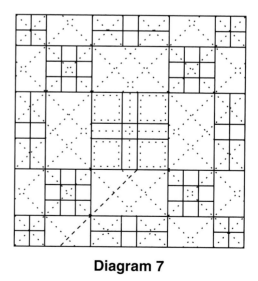

Diagram 7

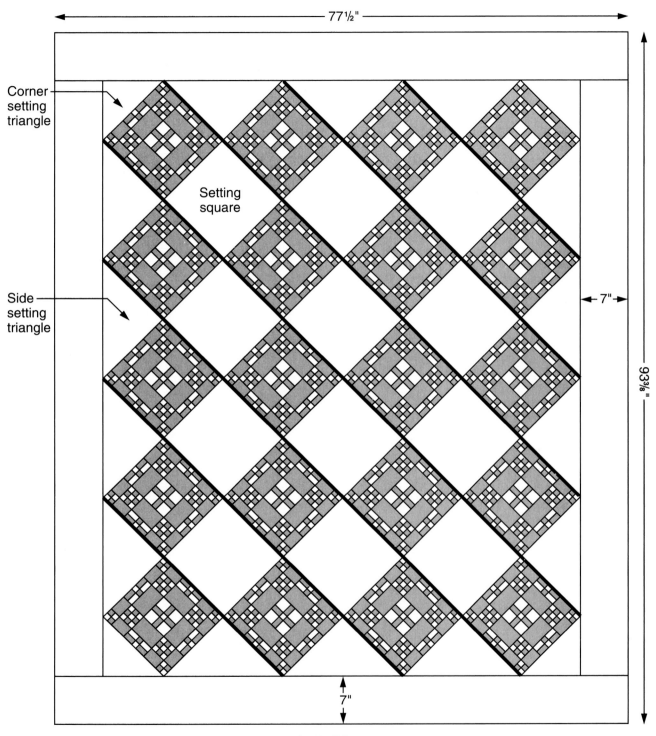

77½"

Corner setting triangle

Setting square

Side setting triangle

7"

7"

93⅜"

Quilt Diagram

squares is provided on the opposite page. **Diagram 8** shows the placement of the fan design on the blue squares. The overlapping cable design for the borders

is shown below. Adjust the cable as needed to fit in the borders.

2. Piece the quilt back. Begin by dividing the quilt back fabric crosswise into two equal pieces. Cut one piece in half lengthwise. Trim the selvages, and sew a narrow panel to each side of the full-width panel. Press the seams toward the narrow panels.

3. Layer the backing, batting, and quilt top; baste. Quilt as desired.

4. Make approximately 10 yards (360 inches) of bias or straight-grain binding to bind the edges of the finished quilt. See page 13 in the "General Instructions" for details on making and attaching binding.

Diagram 8

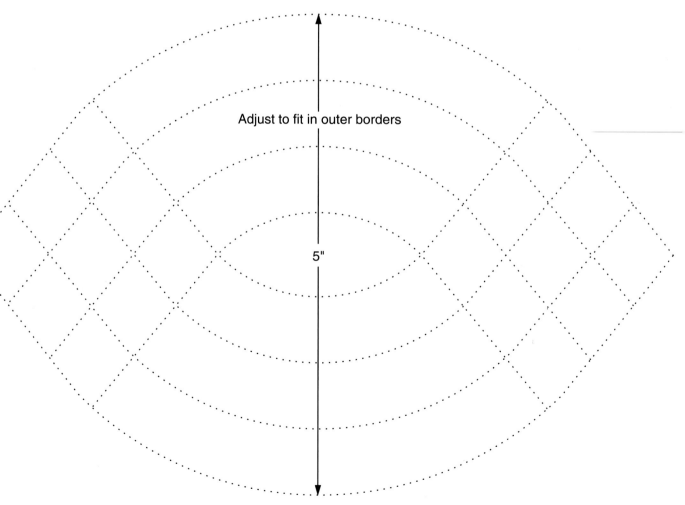

Adjust to fit in outer borders

5"

Border Quilting Design

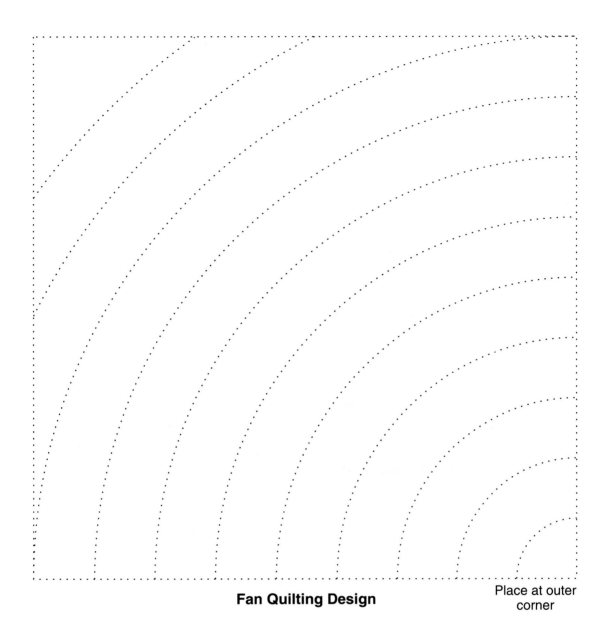

Fan Quilting Design

Place at outer
corner

Sawtooth Medallion

The crisp beauty of this classic Sawtooth quilt is enhanced by lovely quilted feathers, cables, grids, and clamshells. The full-size patterns for the feathered quilting motifs for the blue center square and the large blue triangles are given on pages 78–79. If you love this pattern but prefer to make a smaller project, stop the design before adding the wide, innermost white borders (borders D and E) and you'll have a 25½-inch-square wallhanging. If you stop the design before adding the four blue inner borders (borders F and G), you will have a 40½-inch-square quilt that would make a lovely baby quilt or larger wallhanging.

SKILL LEVEL: *Intermediate*

SIZE:
Finished quilt is approximately 67½ × 76½ inches

FABRICS AND SUPPLIES
- 4¾ yards of blue fabric for patchwork and binding
- 4 yards of white fabric for patchwork
- 4¾ yards of fabric for the quilt back
- Quilt batting, larger than 67½ × 76½ inches
- Rotary cutter, ruler, and mat

CUTTING
Over 300 triangle-square units are needed for this quilt. We've included two methods for making the triangle-squares. The traditional method calls for cutting individual triangles and then joining them in pairs. Our quick-piecing technique uses the timesaving grid method.

The instructions are written to cut all the pieces for this quilt with a rotary cutter and ruler. If you plan to piece the triangle-squares traditionally, cut individual triangles from both the white and blue fabrics. If you plan to quick-piece the triangle-square units, cut rectangles to use for the piecing grids.

All measurements include ¼-inch seam allowances. Since the size of the quilt at each stage is critical for the pieced borders to fit, cut the long fabric borders to the exact lengths given in the cutting instructions. The letters for the borders correspond to the border labels on the **Quilt Diagram** on page 77. Pin identifying labels onto the borders as you cut them. Cut all other pieces across the width of the fabric.

From the blue fabric, first cut off one 77-inch-long piece. From this piece, cut:
- Two 3½ × 77-inch strips for the L borders
- Two 5 × 53-inch I borders
- Two 5 × 50-inch G borders
- Two 5 × 41-inch F borders
- 4 C triangles
  Quick-cut two 12⅛-inch squares. Cut each square in half diagonally to make two triangles.
- One 6½-inch A square
- Four 2-inch squares for border corners

From the remaining blue fabric, cut either individual small triangles or large rectangles for quick-piecing.

- For traditional piecing, cut 350 small triangles. **Quick-cut** eleven 2⅜-inch-wide strips. Cut the strips into 2⅜-inch squares. You will need 175 squares. Cut each square in half diagonally into two triangles.
- For quick-piecing, cut four 20 × 22-inch rectangles to use for making grids for triangle-squares.
- Reserve the remaining fabric for the binding

From the white fabric, first cut off one 77-inch-long piece. From this piece, cut:
- Two 5 × 77-inch K borders
- Two 6½ × 77-inch strips. From each strip, cut one 38-inch-long E border and one 26-inch-long D border.
- Two 5 × 53-inch H borders
- Two 3½ × 53-inch J borders
- Six 2-inch squares for border corners

From the remaining white fabric, cut either individual small triangles or large rectangles for quick-piecing.
- For traditional piecing, cut 350 small triangles. **Quick-cut** eleven 2⅜-inch-wide strips. Cut the strips into 2⅜-inch squares. You will need 175 squares. Cut each square in half diagonally into two triangles.
- For quick-piecing, cut four 20 × 22-inch rectangles to use for making grids for triangle-squares.
- Two 8½ × 26-inch D borders
- 4 B triangles
  Quick-cut two 7¼-inch squares. Cut each square in half diagonally to make two triangles.

MAKING THE TRIANGLE-SQUARE UNITS
Make 350 triangle-square units using either of the following two methods.

Traditional Method
1. Sew a small blue triangle to a small white triangle along the long sides to form a square. Press the seam allowance toward the blue fabric. The triangle-square unit should measure 2 inches square, including seam allowances.

2. Repeat to make a total of 350 triangle-square units for the Sawtooth borders.

Grid Method
Note: Before beginning, read through all the instructions in this section to be sure you understand the procedure. This method is a great time-saver, but accurate marking and sewing are crucial for good results.

Work with one pair of rectangles, a blue one and a white one, at a time. Repeat to make additional triangle-squares from the remaining sets of rectangles.

1. Referring to **Diagram 1,** draw a seven-square by eight-square grid of 2⅜-inch squares on the wrong side of a white rectangle. Position the grid of squares so there is at least a ½-inch fabric margin around the outside of the grid. Draw the squares carefully, making sure that they are the correct size.

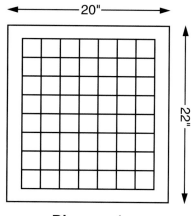

Diagram 1

2. Draw a diagonal line through each square exactly, as shown in **Diagram 2.** Only one diagonal line should go through each square.

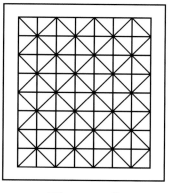

Diagram 2

3. With right sides facing and raw edges aligned, pin the marked white rectangle to the blue rectangle. You will stitch on both sides of the marked diagonal lines, ¼ inch away from the lines. To ensure an accurate seam width, you may want to mark stitching guides ¼-inch away on both sides of the lines.

4. Referring to **Diagram 3,** begin at the starting point and follow the arrows to stitch continuously around the grid. Stitch along one side of the lines until you've completed the grid. Some of your stitching will fall in the margin outside the grid. When you've completed the grid along one side of the diagonal line, switch to the other side and follow the pattern again to stitch on the other side of the lines.

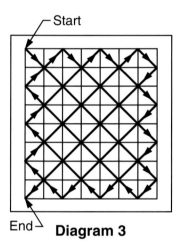

Diagram 3

5. Check to make sure you have stitched on both sides of all diagonal lines, as shown in the detail drawing in **Diagram 4.**

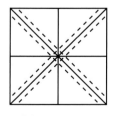

Diagram 4

6. Cut the grid apart on all the vertical and horizontal lines, cutting the grid into squares like the one shown in **Diagram 5.** You will have 56 squares.

Diagram 5

7. Cut each square into two triangles by cutting on the diagonal line between the rows of stitching, as shown in **Diagram 6.**

Diagram 6

8. Open out the pieces and press the seam allowances toward the blue fabric. Trim excess seam allowances (triangle tips) that extend beyond the edge of the square. From each square in the original grid, you will get two triangle-squares like those shown in **Diagram 7.** Since you began with 56 squares in the grid, you should have 112 triangle-squares. Each triangle-square should measure 2 inches square including seam allowances; the finished size will be 1½ inches square. Discard any units that are too small, and trim to size any that are too large. Repeat with all pairs of blue and white rectangles until you have the 350 triangle-square units required.

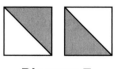

Diagram 7

ASSEMBLING THE QUILT TOP

As you piece the Sawtooth borders from the triangle-square units, refer to the diagrams for the correct angle for the triangle seams in the borders. Check also for the correct placement of the solid and pieced corner squares. Press seam allowances toward the blue fabric whenever possible.

Strips of joined triangle-square units are stretchy. When adding pieced borders to the precut borders and other pieces, you may need to adjust the seams that join the triangle-squares by making them slightly wider or narrower.

1. Referring to **Diagram 8** on page 76, sew sets of four triangle-square units together into four Sawtooth border strips, paying careful attention to the angle of the diagonal seams in each border.

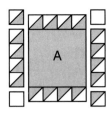

Diagram 8

2. Sew a pieced border to two opposite sides of the blue A center square. Press the seams toward the A square.

3. Using two white 2-inch squares and two additional triangle-square units, add corners to the other two pieced borders as shown. Sew the borders to the remaining two sides of the A square. Press the seams toward the A square.

4. Referring to **Diagram 9,** sew a B triangle to two opposite sides of the center unit. Press seams toward the B triangles. Sew a B triangle to the remaining two sides. Press seams toward the B triangles.

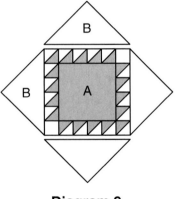

Diagram 9

5. Referring to **Diagram 10,** sew sets of eight triangle-square units together into four pieced borders, paying attention to the angle of the diagonal seams. Take narrower seams (closer to ⅛ inch than to ¼ inch) as you join the triangle-squares so the pieced strips are the same length as the sides of the quilt center.

6. Sew pieced borders to two opposite sides of the center unit. Press the seams toward the center. Using two blue 2-inch squares and two additional triangle-square units, add corners to the remaining two pieced borders. Refer to **Diagram 10** for correct placement of the corner squares. Sew the borders to the center unit and press.

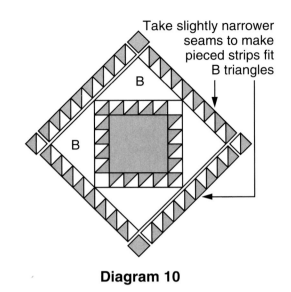

Diagram 10

7. Sew a C triangle to two opposite sides of the center unit. Press seams toward the C triangles. Sew C triangles to the remaining two sides. Press seams toward the triangles.

8. Sew sets of 15 triangle-square units together to make four pieced borders. Referring to the **Quilt Diagram,** sew two borders to the center unit. Using two white 2-inch squares and two triangle-square units, add border corners to the other two borders, then sew them to the center unit.

9. Referring to the **Quilt Diagram,** sew D borders to two opposite sides of the center unit, stretching or easing the pieces as needed to fit. Press seams toward the D borders. In a similar manner, sew E borders to the remaining two sides.

10. Sew sets of 25 triangle-square units together to make four pieced borders. Sew two pieced borders to opposite sides of the center unit. Add border corners to the two remaining borders, using two blue 2-inch squares and two triangle-square units; sew the borders to the quilt.

11. Sew F borders and G borders to the quilt as shown in the diagram.

12. Sew sets of 33 triangle-square units together to make four pieced borders. Sew two pieced borders to opposite sides of the center unit. Add border corners to the two remaining borders, using two white 2-inch squares and two triangle-square units. Add the borders to the quilt.

13. Make a border set by sewing together the H, I, and J borders; repeat to make a second set. Referring to the **Quilt Diagram,** sew the border sets to two opposite sides of the quilt top, with the H border toward the center unit and the J border toward the outside edge.

14. In the same manner, sew the K and L borders together into two border sets. Sew the borders to the sides of the quilt with the L borders on the outside edge.

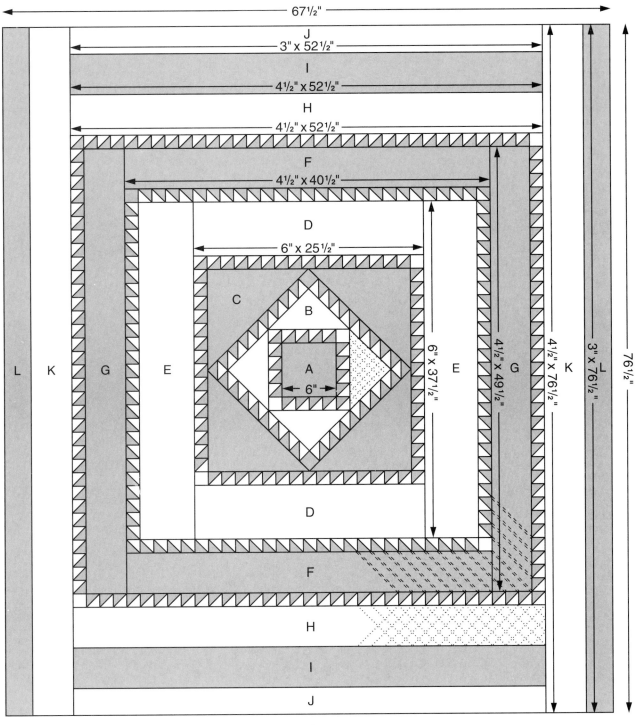

Quilt Diagram

QUILTING AND FINISHING

1. Mark quilting designs as desired. The full-size quilting motif for the center A square is shown below, and the motif for the C triangles is on the opposite page. Dashed lines on the **Quilt Diagram** show suggested straight-line quilting for the B triangles, F and G borders, and H and K borders. The quilt shown has a cable design in the D and E borders and a curving feather design running through the K and L borders and the I and J borders. A clamshell motif was used at the outer edges.

2. Divide the quilt back fabric crosswise into two equal lengths. Cut one piece in half lengthwise into two long panels. Sew a half panel to each side of the full-width panel; press the seam allowances away from the center panel.

3. Layer the quilt back, batting, and quilt top; baste. Quilt as desired.

4. Make approximately 8½ yards (306 inches) of bias or straight-grain binding from the reserved blue fabric. Sew the binding to the quilt, mitering the corners. See page 13 in the "General Instructions" for details on making and attaching binding.

Quilting Design for A Square

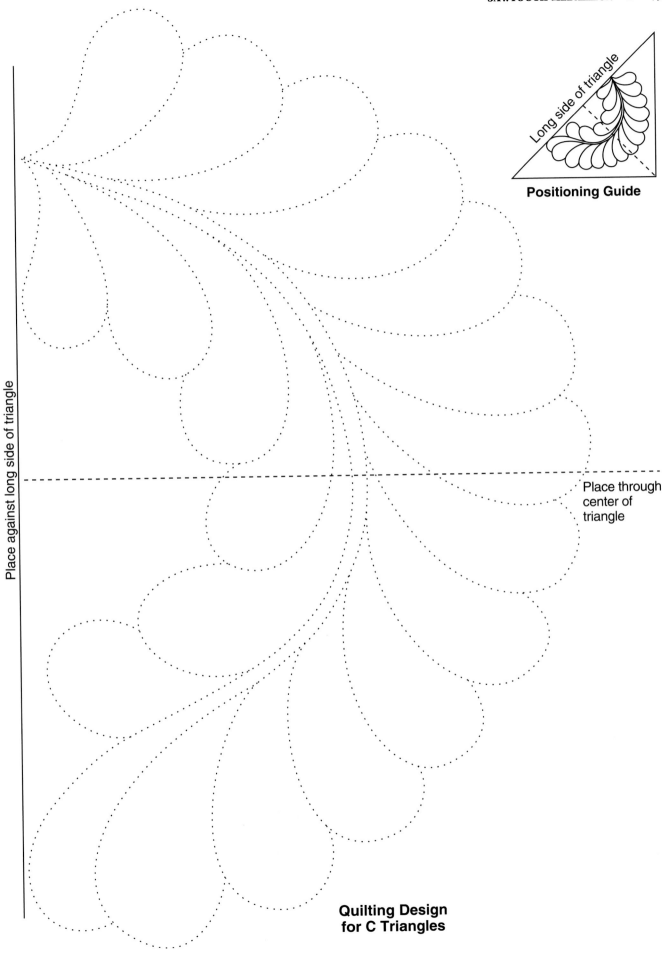

Positioning Guide

Long side of triangle

Place against long side of triangle

Place through center of triangle

Quilting Design for C Triangles

New · Burgoyne · Beauty

This classically beautiful quilt was inspired by the antique Burgoyne Surrounded on page 65. Here, we used a straight set and eliminated the alternating setting squares. A checkerboard border adds a snappy finishing touch. To avoid working with the 5,000-plus pieces individually, we used strip-piecing methods for the blocks and the pieced border. Though our method streamlines and modernizes this quilt, you'll still want to install a brand new blade in your cutter and eat a good breakfast the day you plan on cutting all your strips! Before sewing, wind extra bobbins so you won't have to stop for long once you're on a roll.

SKILL LEVEL: *Intermediate*

SIZE:
Finished quilt is approximately 78 × 100½ inches
Finished block is 11¼ inches

NUMBER OF PIECED BLOCKS: 48

FABRICS AND SUPPLIES
■ 6½ yards of white-and-blue print fabric for patchwork
■ 6 yards of blue print fabric for patchwork, borders, and binding
■ 6 yards of fabric for the quilt back
■ Batting, larger than 78 × 100½ inches
■ Rotary cutter, ruler, and mat

CUTTING
The instructions for this quilt call for quick-cutting and quick-piecing. All measurements include ¼-inch seam allowances. Measurements for the plain border strips include extra length; trim them to the exact size when adding them to the quilt top. Cut all strips across the fabric width. Label and set aside the groups of strips as you cut them so you won't get confused later.

From the white-and-blue print fabric, cut:
■ Forty-seven 1¼-inch-wide strips for the blocks
■ Sixteen 2-inch-wide strips for the blocks
■ 384 A rectangles
  Quick-cut twenty-six 2-inch-wide strips. Cut the strips into 2 × 2¾-inch rectangles.
■ 192 B rectangles
  Quick-cut thirteen 4¼-inch-wide strips. Cut the strips into 4¼ × 2¾-inch rectangles.
■ Twenty-one 1¼-inch-wide strips for the pieced border

From the blue print fabric, cut:
■ Seventeen 2-inch-wide strips for the plain borders
■ Twenty-one 1¼-inch-wide strips for the pieced border
■ Fifty 1¼-inch-wide strips for the blocks
■ Twenty-two 2-inch-wide strips for the blocks
■ Reserve the remaining fabric for binding

MAKING THE BLOCKS

The Burgoyne Surrounded blocks are made up of four types of pieced units, plus two sizes of white print rectangles. To create the pieced units, combine strips to make strip sets, cut the strip sets into segments, and reposition the segments as described to form the units. Combine the units with the plain rectangles to make the blocks. As you piece the strip sets, press the seams toward the darker fabric.

1. Make a strip set, as shown in **Diagram 1A,** sewing a 1¼-inch-wide blue strip to a 1¼-inch-wide white print strip. Make 12 strip sets of this type. Cut the strip sets into 1¼-inch-wide segments. You will need 384 segments. Combine pairs of segments into 192 Four-Patch units as shown in **Diagram 1B.**

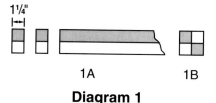

Diagram 1

2. Make a strip set, as shown in **Diagram 2A,** sewing together two 2-inch-wide blue strips and one 1¼-inch-wide white print strip. Make six strip sets of this type. Cut the strip sets into 1¼-inch-wide segments. You will need 192 segments.

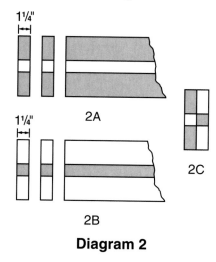

Diagram 2

3. In the same manner, combine two 2-inch-wide white strips and one 1¼-inch-wide blue strip into a strip set, as shown in **Diagram 2B.** Make six strip sets of this type. Cut the strip sets into a total of 192 segments, each 1¼ inches wide.

4. Combine the two types of segments into units, as shown in **Diagram 2C.** You will have a total of 192 units.

5. Make a strip set, as shown in **Diagram 3A,** combining two 1¼-inch-wide white print strips and one 1¼-inch-wide blue strip. Make six strip sets of this type. Cut the strip sets into 1¼-inch-wide segments, for a total of 192 segments.

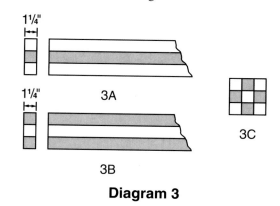

Diagram 3

6. Using two 1¼-inch blue strips and one 1¼-inch white print strip, make 12 **Diagram 3B** strip sets. Cut the strip sets into 1¼-inch-wide segments. You will need 384 segments.

7. Combine the two types of segments into Nine-Patch units, as shown in **Diagram 3C.** You will have a total of 192 units.

8. Make a strip set, as shown in **Diagram 4A,** combining two 2-inch-wide blue strips with one 1¼-inch-wide white strip. Make five of these strip sets. Cut the strip sets into 2-inch-wide segments, for a total of 96 segments.

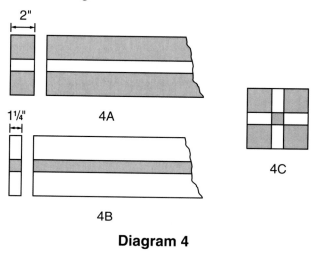

Diagram 4

9. Combine two 2-inch-wide white print strips and one 1¼-inch-wide blue strip to make a strip set as shown in **Diagram 4B.** Make a second strip set of this type. Cut the strip sets into 1¼-inch-wide segments, for a total of 48 segments.

10. Combine the two types of segments to make the block unit shown in **Diagram 4C.** Make a total of 48 units.

11. Lay out the pieced block units and the A and B rectangles as shown in **Diagram 5.** Join the units and rectangles into five vertical rows. Press the seams toward the rectangles.

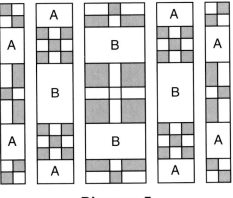

Diagram 5

12. Join the rows to form a block, as shown in **Diagram 6.** The block should measure approximately 11¾ inches from raw edge to raw edge. Repeat to make a total of 48 blocks.

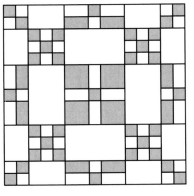

Diagram 6

Assembling the Quilt Top

1. Referring to the **Quilt Diagram** on page 84, lay out the blocks in eight horizontal rows of six blocks per row.

2. Join the blocks into rows; then join the rows.

3. Use the seventeen set-aside 2-inch-wide border strips to make the plain borders. Join eight pairs of strips, using diagonal seams.

4. Measure the length of the quilt top from raw edge to raw edge, measuring through the middle of the quilt. Cut segments from the remaining strip and sew them to two of the paired strips to make two side borders the length of the quilt (approximately 90½ inches). Sew the borders to the quilt, pressing the seams toward the borders.

5. Measure the width of the quilt top from raw edge to raw edge, measuring through the middle of the quilt. Trim two borders to this length (approximately 71 inches). Sew the borders to the top and bottom of the quilt. Press the seams toward the borders.

6. Use the remaining 1¼-inch-wide blue print and white print strips to make the checkerboard borders. Make seven **Diagram 7A** strip sets and seven **7B** strip sets. Cut the strip sets into 1¼-inch-wide segments; join the segments as shown in **7C.** You will need a total of 224 units.

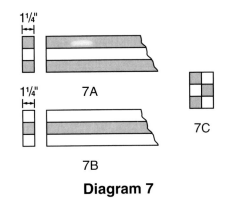

Diagram 7

7. Join 62 checkerboard units for each of the two side borders. Sew the borders to the sides of the quilt, pressing the seams toward the plain borders.

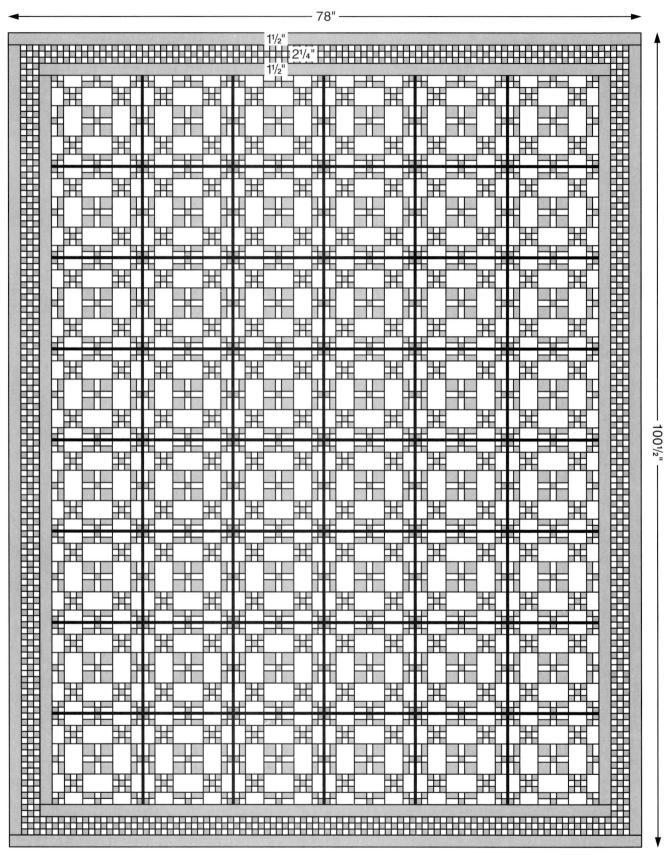

Quilt Diagram

8. Join 50 checkerboard units each for the top and bottom borders. Sew the borders to the top and bottom of the quilt; press.

9. To add the final plain borders, use the remaining four paired border strips. Add segments of the extra strip as needed to make the side borders the required length. Add the side borders first, then the top and bottom borders, as shown in the **Quilt Diagram.**

QUILTING AND FINISHING

1. Mark quilting designs. The quilt shown in the photo on page 80 has a diagonal X quilted through each block, as well as a fleur-de-lis in the areas between the Xs.

2. Piece the quilt back. Divide the backing fabric crosswise into two equal pieces. Cut one of the pieces in half lengthwise. Trim the selvages, and sew a narrow panel to each side of the full-width one.

3. Layer the backing, batting, and quilt top; baste. Quilt as desired.

4. From the fabric set aside for binding, make approximately 10½ yards (378 inches) of straight-grain or bias binding to bind the edges of the quilt. See page 13 in the "General Instructions" for details on making and attaching binding.

Prairie Stars

Star patterns abound in the history of quilt-making, their points of light created through clever use of triangles, diamonds, and other geometric shapes. Quilters of the past, their feet planted firmly on the ground, stitched heavenly beauties to warm their families on cold prairie nights.

The Bethlehem Star quilt, every inch of it covered with patchwork, quilting, and trapunto, is a masterpiece only an experienced quilter will rush to undertake. The Simple Star is one of the easiest quilts in the book. We used it for inspiration, adding a zigzag border for our new crib quilt, the Fenced Stars.

· Four Stars ·

Four stars per block, a hundred stars per quilt, and millions of stars sparkling in the skies above the great American prairie. Beautiful star quilts, like this classic example, were made by the quilters of long ago to keep their loved ones warm. This one displays the fabrics and colors common at the turn of the century, such as indigo blue, black, dark red, the distinctive "cheddar" yellow-orange, and muslin.

Because of the many set-in pieces, careful sewing is necessary to construct the Four-Stars block, also known as Old Maid's Patience. We recommend that you either piece this block by hand or use the machine piecing methods explained in the "General Instructions" on page 5.

SKILL LEVEL: *Challenging*

SIZE:

Finished quilt is approximately 77½ inches square
Finished block is 11 inches square (approximately 15½ inches on the diagonal)

NUMBER OF PIECED BLOCKS: 25

FABRICS AND SUPPLIES

■ 3½ yards of muslin or white fabric for setting squares and triangles
■ Approximately 3¼ yards total of assorted medium and dark print fabrics (red, brown, blue, navy, black, and green) for the stars. Each block uses two sets of 16 matching diamonds. (You can easily cut one set of 16 diamonds from a 12-inch-square fabric scrap.)
■ 2 yards of white print with tiny black dots for patchwork
■ ½ yard of "cheddar" yellow-orange fabric for patchwork
■ 4¾ yards of fabric for the quilt back

■ ¾ yard of fabric for binding
■ Batting, larger than 77½ inches square
■ Template plastic
■ Rotary cutter, ruler, and mat

CUTTING

Making the Four-Stars blocks requires careful piecing, whether by hand or machine. The instructions are written both for the traditional cutting method using templates and for hand piecing. Even though we suggest using templates to cut the patchwork pieces, we recommend using a rotary cutter and ruler to cut the setting squares and triangles. Measurements for the setting pieces include ¼-inch seam allowances.

Make templates for patterns A, B, C, D, and E on page 93. If you intend to hand piece the blocks, make finished-size templates by tracing the inner (dashed) lines on the patterns. Draw around the templates on the wrong side of the fabric, allowing at least ½ inch between pieces for seam allowances.

Add seam allowances around the pieces and cut them out.

If you intend to machine piece the blocks, make templates following the instructions in the "General Instructions" on page 5.

From the muslin or white fabric, cut:

■ 16 setting squares
  Quick-cut six 11½-inch-wide strips. From the strips, cut 11½-inch squares.
■ 16 side setting triangles
  Quick-cut two 16¾-inch-wide strips. From the strips, cut four 16¾-inch squares. Cut each square in half diagonally in both directions to make four triangles.
■ 4 corner setting triangles
  Quick-cut two 8⅝-inch squares. Cut each square in half diagonally to make two triangles.

From the assorted medium and dark print fabric scraps, cut:

■ 50 sets of 16 matching A diamonds (800 total)

From the white print fabric, cut:

■ 100 B squares
■ 100 C rectangles
■ 25 D squares
■ 200 E triangles

From the yellow-orange fabric, cut:

■ 100 B squares

MAKING THE BLOCKS

Because many pieces must be set in, avoid sewing into the seam allowances when you assemble the pieces. Stitch only on the sewing lines, indicated by dashed lines on the patterns on page 93. Secure the seams by backstitching or knotting threads.

1. Referring to the **Fabric Key** and the **Block Diagram** for correct placement, lay out two sets of 16 matching A diamonds (32 total), 4 yellow-orange B squares, and the following white print pieces: 4 B squares, 4 C rectangles, 1 D square, and 8 E triangles. When choosing the two fabrics for the diamonds, select fabrics with good contrast.

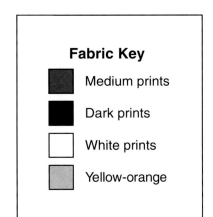

Fabric Key

Medium prints

Dark prints

White prints

Yellow-orange

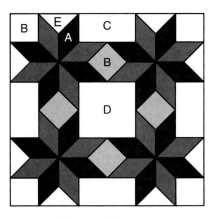

Block Diagram

2. Sew together pairs of A diamonds, as shown in **Diagram 1,** keeping the same fabric consistently on the left or right as you make pairs. Make 16 pairs.

Diagram 1

3. Referring to **Diagram 2,** set an orange B square into the opening between two pairs of diamonds. Make four units like this.

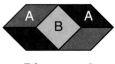

Diagram 2

4. Sew a Step 3 unit to two opposite sides of a D square, as shown in **Diagram 3.** Sew two more units to the remaining sides of the D square.

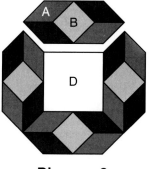

Diagram 3

5. Referring to **Diagram 4,** join two pairs of diamonds into a half star. Set E triangles and a B square into the openings around the outside of the partial star. Make four units like this.

Diagram 4

6. Sew half-star units onto the outside corners of the center unit, forming complete stars as shown in **Diagram 5.**

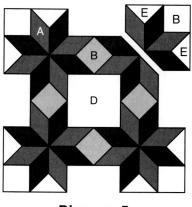

Diagram 5

7. To complete the block, set a C rectangle into the openings left along the sides. Press the completed block, pressing seams toward the darker fabric whenever possible.

8. Repeat to make a total of 25 blocks.

ASSEMBLING THE QUILT TOP

1. Referring to the **Quilt Diagram** on page 92, lay out the blocks on point in five rows with five blocks in each row. Place setting squares in the openings between blocks. Fill in around the outside edges with the side setting triangles and corner setting triangles.

2. Sew the blocks and setting pieces together in diagonal rows. The heavy lines in the diagram define the rows. Press the seams away from the blocks.

3. Join the rows.

QUILTING AND FINISHING

1. Mark quilting designs as desired. The blocks in the quilt shown are outline quilted around the patchwork pieces. The setting squares and triangles are quilted with a diamond grid, but you may wish to put a fancier motif in these spaces. Choose a quilting pattern designed to fit in an 11-inch or smaller square. Use half of the design or another compatible design for the setting triangles.

2. Divide the quilt back fabric crosswise into two equal lengths. Cut one piece in half lengthwise. Trim the selvages, and stitch a narrow panel to each long side of the full-width panel. Press the seam allowances away from the center panel.

3. Layer the quilt back, batting, and quilt top; baste. Quilt as desired.

4. Make approximately 10 yards (360 inches) of either bias or straight-grain binding. Sew the binding to the quilt. See page 13 in the "General Instructions" for details on making and attaching binding.

77½"

77½"

Quilt Diagram

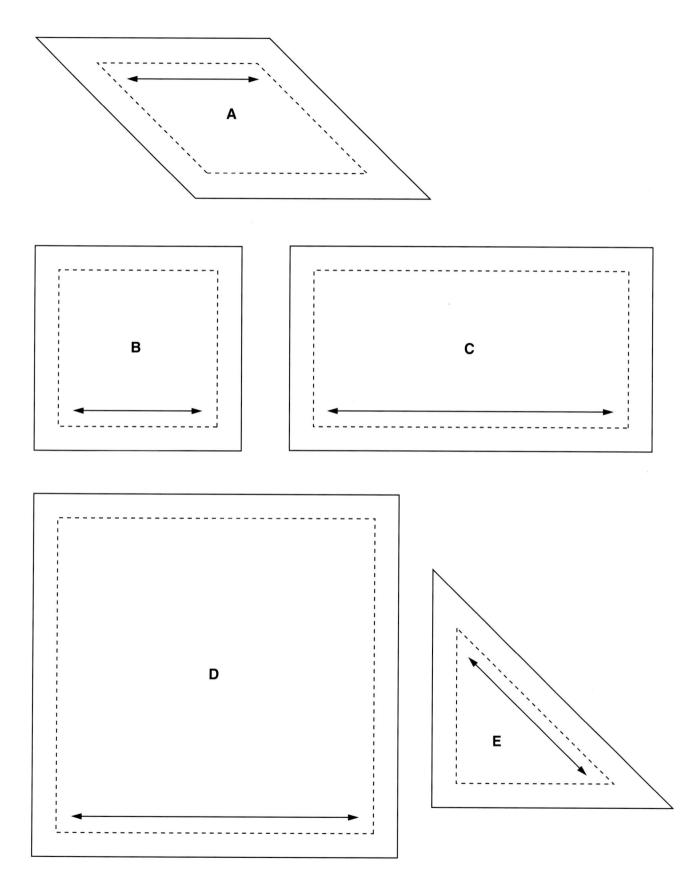

The dashed lines on the patterns indicate finished size.
The solid lines include seam allowances.

Twinkling Stars

This late-nineteenth-century quilt is a perfect example of beauty in simplicity. Purchased in Iowa by its present owner, it's a charmer that is still as good as new. The quiltmaker who crafted it had to use many scrap fabrics to create the stars (and in the process made stars that really twinkle), but she was blessed with enough red yardage for dynamic sashing. Our instructions give you the option of using either traditional template-style marking and cutting or quick rotary cutting.

SKILL LEVEL: *Easy*

SIZE:

Finished quilt is approximately 68 × 89½ inches
Finished block is 18 inches square

NUMBER OF PIECED BLOCKS: 12

FABRICS AND SUPPLIES

- 3 yards of muslin for patchwork
- 2½ yards of red fabric for sashing strips and borders
- 2¼ yards, or the equivalent in scraps, of medium and dark print fabrics (various reds and browns, purple, black, navy, tan) for small triangles
- 1¼ yards, or the equivalent in scraps, of light print fabrics (mostly white-background prints with small motifs in black, red, brown, and blue, some with stripes) for small triangles
- 5½ yards of fabric for the quilt back
- ¾ yard of brown-and-white check fabric for binding
- Batting, larger than 68 × 89½ inches
- Template plastic (optional)
- Rotary cutter, ruler, and mat

CUTTING

If you wish to cut the pieces using traditional methods, make templates for patterns A, B, C, and D on pages 98–99. If you prefer to quick-cut the pieces, follow the instructions below. All measurements include seam allowances. The borders are cut longer than necessary; trim to length when adding them to the quilt. Unless directed otherwise, cut strips across the fabric width.

From the muslin, cut:

- 48 B triangles
  Quick-cut four 5⅜-inch-wide strips. Cut the strips into 5⅜-inch squares; you will need 24 squares. Cut each square in half diagonally to make two triangles.
- 48 C squares
  Quick-cut six 5-inch-wide strips. Cut the strips into 5-inch squares.
- 48 D triangles
  Quick-cut three 10¼-inch-wide strips. Cut the strips into 10¼-inch squares; you will need 12 squares. Divide each square diagonally both ways to make four triangles.

From the red fabric, cut:

- Four 4 × 85-inch strips for lengthwise sashing and side borders
- Two 4 × 72-inch end border strips
- Nine 4 × 18½-inch sashing strips

From the medium and dark print fabrics, cut:

- 864 A triangles

  Quick-cut twenty-six 2⅜-inch-wide strips. Cut the strips into 2⅜-inch squares; you will need 432 squares. Cut each square in half diagonally to make two triangles.

From the light print fabrics, cut:

- 432 A triangles

  Quick-cut thirteen 2⅜-inch-wide strips. Cut the strips into 2⅜-inch squares; you will need 216 squares. Cut each square in half diagonally to make two triangles.

MAKING THE BLOCKS

1. Referring to the **Fabric Key** and **Diagram 1,** lay out six dark print A triangles and three light print A triangles. Sew the triangles together in rows, then join the rows to make pieced triangle units. Press the seams toward the dark fabric when possible. Make 144 of these units.

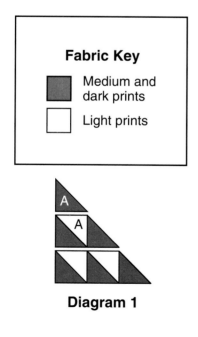

Diagram 1

2. To construct the center of the Twinkling Star block, combine four pieced triangle units with four muslin B triangles. The blocks of the quilt shown have two types of centers, as shown in **Diagram 2.** There are six blocks with Center I and six with Center II. Varying the center does not significantly affect the design of the quilt, so you may wish to construct the centers of all 12 blocks alike.

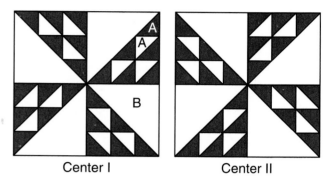

Center I   Center II

Diagram 2

3. Referring to **Diagram 3,** combine C squares, D triangles, pieced triangle units, and block centers to make the rows for the blocks. Rows 1 and 3 are identical. Make a total of 12 blocks.

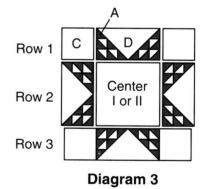

Diagram 3

ASSEMBLING THE QUILT TOP

1. Referring to the **Quilt Diagram,** combine completed blocks and red sashing strips to make three vertical rows with four blocks and three sashing strips per row. The heavy lines on the diagram help define the rows. Press the seams toward the sashing strips.

2. Measure the length of a row from raw edge to raw edge. Trim the four long sashing/border strips to this length (approximately 83 inches). Combine the long strips and the rows, as shown in the **Quilt Diagram.**

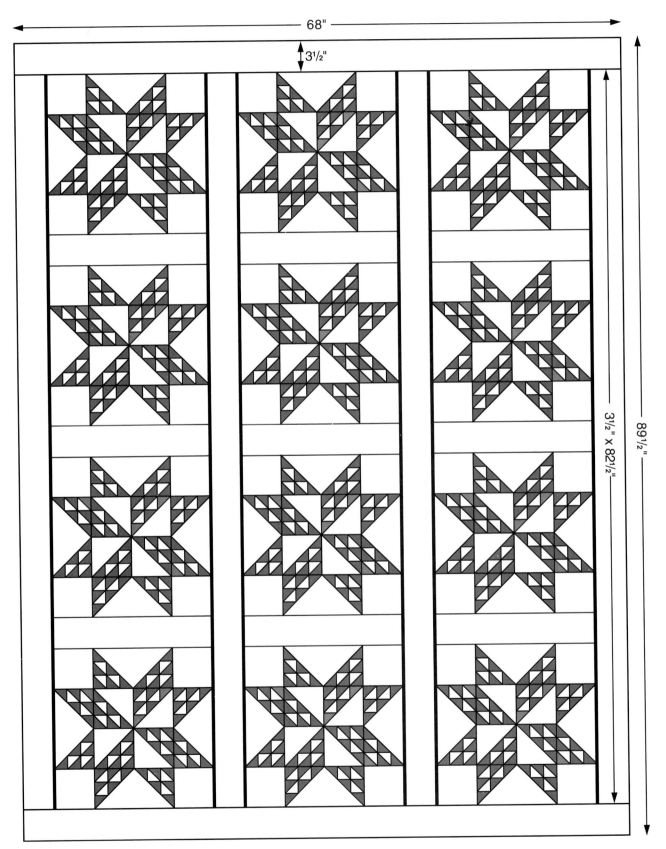

Quilt Diagram

3. Measure the width of the quilt. Trim the two remaining red border strips to length (approximately 68½ inches) and sew them to the top and bottom of the quilt top.

QUILTING AND FINISHING

1. Mark quilting designs as desired. On the quilt shown, the light print A triangles are quilted ⅛ inch away from the seams. The muslin squares have diagonal grid quilting, and the sashing strips and borders have diagonal line quilting. Suggested designs for the B and D triangles are included on the pattern pieces on the opposite page.

2. Piece the quilt back. Begin by dividing the backing fabric crosswise into two equal pieces. Cut one piece lengthwise into two narrow panels. Trim the selvages, and sew a narrow panel to each side of the full-width panel. Press the seams toward the narrow panels.

3. Layer the backing, batting, and quilt top; baste. Quilt as desired.

4. Make approximately 8½ yards (306 inches) of bias or straight-grain binding for the quilt. See page 13 in the "General Instructions" for details on making and attaching binding.

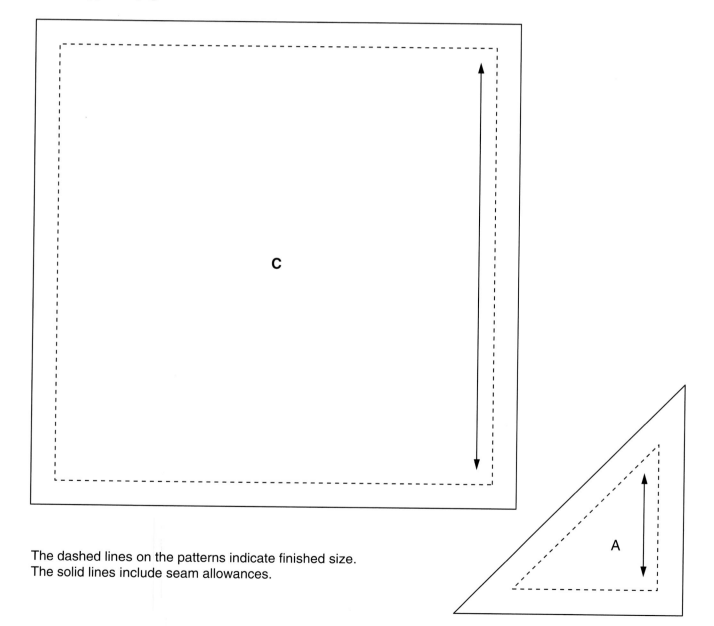

The dashed lines on the patterns indicate finished size.
The solid lines include seam allowances.

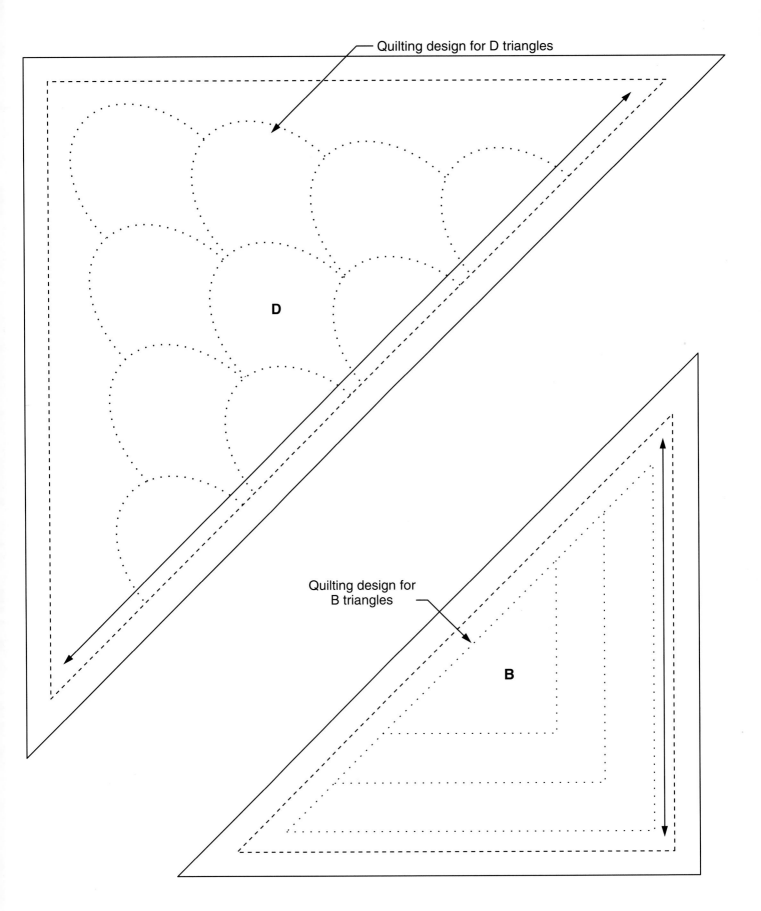

Quilting design for D triangles

D

Quilting design for
B triangles

B

· Simple Star ·

Ｎone of our pattern sources listed a name for this star block, so we were left to come up with our own. Because the blocks are so easy to piece and go together so quickly, we named it Simple Star. The random arrangement of light, medium, and dark fabrics from star to star gives this quilt a particularly scrappy look. A warm butterscotch gold print fabric for the setting squares ties together the diverse pink, red, gray, white, and brown fabrics used for the 21 Simple-Star blocks.

SKILL LEVEL: *Easy*

SIZE:

Finished quilt is approximately 66 × 77 inches
Finished block is 11 inches square

NUMBER OF PIECED BLOCKS: 21

FABRICS AND SUPPLIES

If you have lots of scrap fabrics, use them to make the star blocks; then purchase a print for the plain setting squares to tie the quilt together.

- 2½ yards of gold print fabric for the setting squares
- 1½ yards total of assorted medium print fabrics (red, medium brown, pink, and medium gray) for the stars
- 1½ yards total of assorted dark print fabrics (dark brown, black, and maroon) for the stars
- 1 yard total of assorted light print fabrics (white and light gray) for the stars
- 4¾ yards of fabric for the quilt back
- ¾ yard of fabric for binding (optional)
- Batting, larger than 66 × 77 inches
- Rotary cutter, ruler, and mat
- Template plastic (optional)

CUTTING

The placement of light, medium, and dark fabrics is random from block to block in the antique quilt shown. **Diagram 1** shows a few of the different fabric-value placements found in the blocks on the old quilt. For best results, plan the fabrics for your blocks so the stars created from the B triangles contrast with the background.

 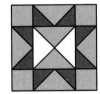 

Variation 1   Variation 2   Variation 3

Diagram 1

For each of the 21 blocks you will need eight A triangles (one set of four matching triangles for the outside of the block and two sets of two matching triangles for the block center), eight matching B triangles for the star points, and four matching C squares. **Diagram 2** on page 102 shows a drawing of the block with the pieces labeled. Refer to this as a guide when cutting pieces from the assorted light, medium, and dark fabric scraps.

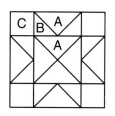

Diagram 2

If you wish to cut the pieces using traditional methods, make templates for patterns A, B, and C on page 104. If you prefer to quick-cut the pieces, follow the instructions below.

From the gold print fabric, cut:
■ Twenty-one 11½-inch setting squares

From the assorted fabrics, cut:
■ A triangles
  Quick-cut a 6¾-inch square. Cut the square diagonally in both directions. You will get four A triangles from each square.
■ B triangles
  Quick-cut a 3⅝-inch square. Cut the square diagonally into two triangles.
■ C squares
  Quick-cut 3¼-inch squares.

MAKING THE BLOCKS

1. Referring to **Diagram 2,** lay out the pieces for one block. You will need eight matching B triangles for the star points, four matching A triangles for the outside edges, two sets of two matching A triangles for the block center, and four matching C squares for the corners of the block.

2. Piece the center of the block by sewing two sets of two matching A triangles together to form a square, as shown in **Diagram 3.**

Diagram 3

3. Sew a B triangle to each side of the four matching A triangles, as shown in **Diagram 4.** Press the seam allowances away from the A triangles.

Diagram 4

4. Referring to **Diagram 5,** make Row 1 and Row 3 by adding a C square to opposite sides of an AB unit. Press the seams toward the C squares.

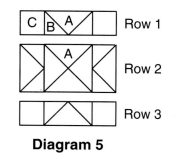

Diagram 5

5. To make Row 2, add AB units to two opposite sides of a center unit. Press the seams toward the center unit.

6. Join the three rows to complete the block. Repeat to make a total of 21 blocks.

ASSEMBLING THE QUILT TOP

1. Referring to the **Quilt Diagram,** lay out the blocks in seven horizontal rows with three star blocks and three setting squares in each row. The heavy lines on the diagram indicate the rows.

2. Join the stars and setting squares into rows. Press the seam allowances toward the setting squares.

3. Sew the rows together.

QUILTING AND FINISHING

1. Mark quilting designs as desired. The individual pieces within the star blocks on the antique quilt were outline quilted in the ditch. **Diagram 6** shows the quilting design used for the setting squares.

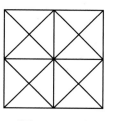

Diagram 6

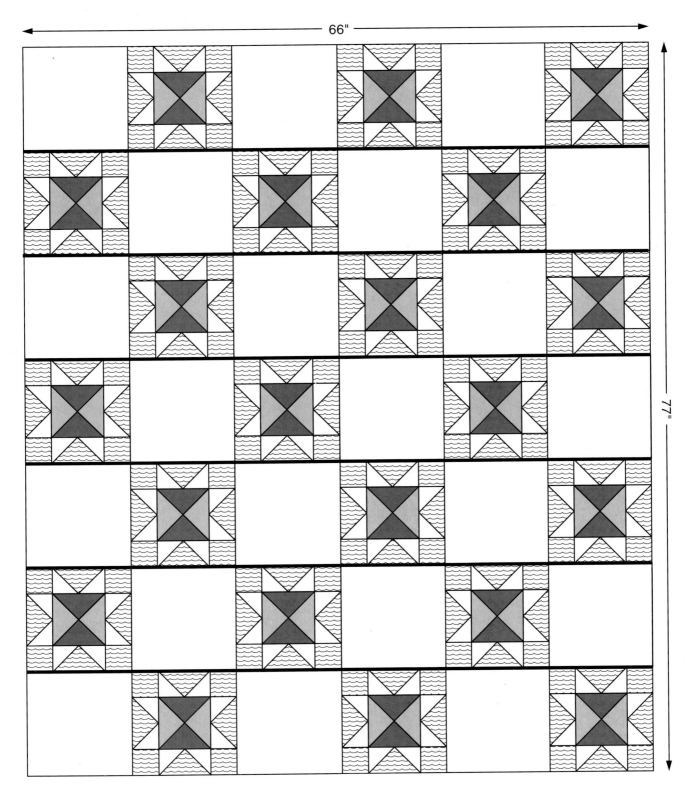

Quilt Diagram

2. To piece the quilt back, divide the backing fabric crosswise into two equal lengths. Cut one piece in half lengthwise. Trim the selvages, and sew a half panel to each side of the full-width panel. Press the seam allowances away from the center panel.

3. Layer the quilt back, batting, and quilt top; baste. Quilt as desired.

4. The quilt shown was finished by bringing the backing fabric over to the quilt front. If you desire to finish your quilt in this way, trim the excess batting even with the quilt top. Trim the quilt back so it is 1 inch larger than the quilt top. Turn in ½ inch on the quilt back. Bring the folded edge over to the front of the quilt and hand stitch in place.

If you prefer to finish your quilt with binding, make approximately 8½ yards (306 inches) of bias or straight-grain binding and sew it to your quilt. See page 13 in the "General Instructions" for details on making and attaching binding.

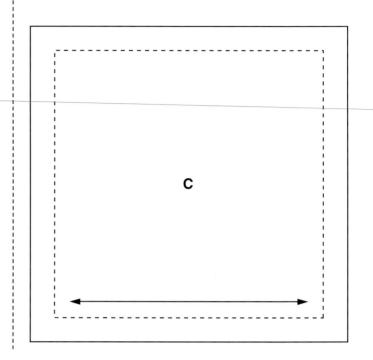

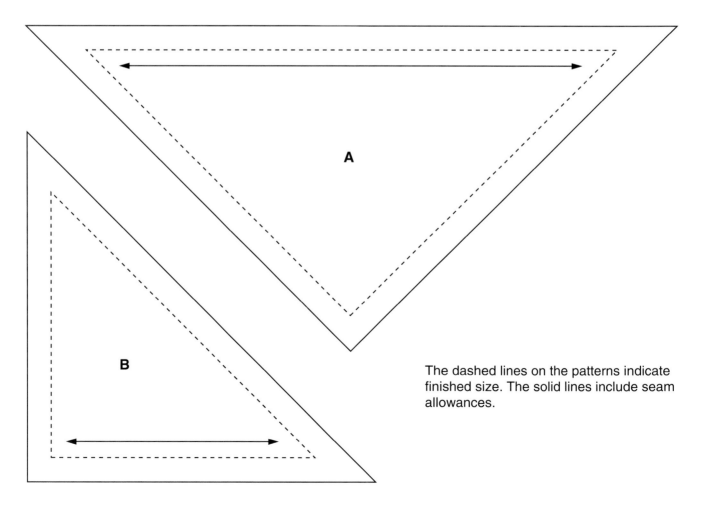

The dashed lines on the patterns indicate finished size. The solid lines include seam allowances.

Bethlehem Star

Quiltmakers throughout time have viewed a masterpiece such as this with awe and respect. An Iowa quiltmaker named Mary McCollister began this quilt at age 74, after her husband's death in 1876. It is a marvel how Mary could have conceived and executed such a stunning and sophisticated work of art without the advantages of the modern tools present-day quiltmakers have at their disposal. The quilting and trapunto are as expertly designed and executed as the patchwork and appliqué. Every inch of the light background areas is covered with close and intricate quilting, much of it stuffed meticulously with extra wisps of cotton wadding. Perhaps Mary filled up the empty hours after her husband's death by filling in every bit of space on her masterpiece quilt.

SKILL LEVEL: *Challenging*

SIZE:

Finished quilt is approximately 110½ inches square

NUMBER OF PIECED BLOCKS:

1 large center star
4 medium stars
32 small stars

FABRICS AND SUPPLIES

The fabric numbers in this list correspond to the fabric numbers used in the instructions and on all charts and diagrams.

- ⅛ yard of Fabric 1 (tan print)
- ⅛ yard of Fabric 2 (brown print)
- 2¼ yards of Fabric 3 (gold print)
- 2½ yards of Fabric 4 (red print)
- ¾ yard of Fabric 5 (pink print)
- 1½ yards of Fabric 6 (green print)
- 2½ yards of Fabric 7 (blue print)
- ⅞ yard of Fabric 8 (white print)
- ⅓ yard of Fabric 9 (black print)
- 1 yard of Fabric 10 (rust print)

- 1¼ yards of Fabric 11 (brown print)
- 10½ yards of Fabric 12 (muslin) if fabric has at least 43½ inches of usable width. If fabric is narrower, purchase 11¾ yards.
- 9¾ yards of fabric for quilt back
- 1 yard of fabric for binding
- Batting, larger than 110½ inches square
- Rotary cutter, ruler, and mat (ruler must have 45 degree angle guides)
- White three-ply heavyweight acrylic yarn and trapunto needle (optional)

CUTTING

Quick-piecing techniques are used for the large center star, the four medium stars, and the pieced borders. The large center star and the small stars are appliquéd onto the background fabric.

Follow the instructions on the opposite page to cut most of the pieces for the quilt. As you cut them, label the pieces with the fabric number. Some pieces, such as the muslin triangles for the middle and outer pieced borders and the diamonds for the small stars, will be cut as you need them. Use a rotary cutter and ruler to cut all pieces. Cut all strips across the fabric width. Measurements for all pieces include ¼-inch seam allowances.

From Fabric 1 (tan print), cut:
■ One 1½-inch-wide strip

From Fabric 2 (brown print), cut:
■ Two 1½-inch-wide strips

From Fabric 3 (gold print), cut:
■ Thirty 1¾-inch-wide strips
■ Eleven 1½-inch-wide strips

From Fabric 4 (red print), cut:
■ Thirty-two 1¾-inch-wide strips
■ Ten 1½-inch-wide strips

From Fabric 5 (pink print), cut:
■ Ten 1½-inch-wide strips

From Fabric 6 (green print), cut:
■ Fourteen 1¾-inch-wide strips
■ Nine 1½-inch-wide strips

From Fabric 7 (blue print), cut:
■ Thirty-six 1¾-inch-wide strips
■ Seven 1½-inch-wide strips

From Fabric 8 (white print), cut:
■ Twelve 1¾-inch-wide strips

From Fabric 9 (black print), cut:
■ Five 1¾-inch-wide strips

From Fabric 10 (rust print), cut:
■ Twelve 1¾-inch-wide strips

From Fabric 11 (brown print), cut:
■ Twenty 1¾-inch-wide strips

From Fabric 12 (muslin), cut:
■ One 43½-inch square for the quilt center. (If your fabric is too narrow to cut this square, cut two 43½-inch lengths and stitch them together. Then cut the square from the joined fabric.)

■ 4 A triangles for the quilt center
  Quick-cut two 31¼-inch squares. Cut each square in half diagonally to make two triangles.
■ 8 B triangles
  Quick-cut two 35¼-inch squares. Cut each square diagonally in both directions to make four triangles.
■ 4 C triangles
  Quick-cut two 17⅞-inch squares. Cut each square in half diagonally to make two triangles.
■ 16 D squares for the medium stars
  Quick-cut 7½-inch squares.
■ 16 E triangles for the medium stars
  Quick-cut four 11⅛-inch squares. Cut each square diagonally in both directions to make four triangles.
■ Twelve 1¾-inch-wide strips
■ Reserve remaining fabric to cut pieces for the middle and outer pieced borders

MAKING THE LARGE CENTER STAR

The large center star is composed of eight identical sections. Each section is made of three pieced diamond units: one center diamond and two identical outer diamonds. **Diagram 1** illustrates how the sections of the star fit together. **Diagram 2** on page 108 shows one section of the star.

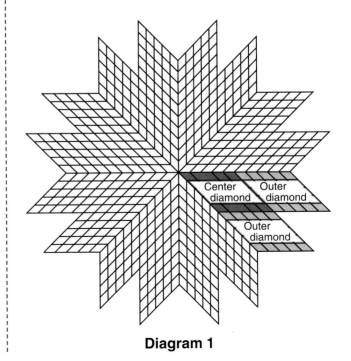

Diagram 1

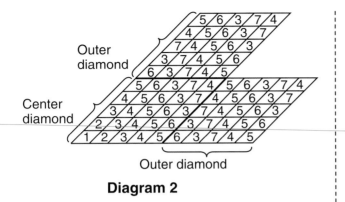

Outer diamond

Center diamond

Outer diamond

Diagram 2

Quick-piecing methods, using 1½-inch-wide strips, speed up the process of making the pieced diamonds. Sew strips together in the specified order to make strip sets. Cut the strip sets into rows of diamonds, then join the rows of diamonds into pieced diamond units.

Making the Center Pieced Diamonds

The center pieced diamonds are made up of five rows, with five diamonds in each row. Referring to **Diagram 3** and following the instructions below, make a strip set for each row. The heavy lines on the diagram define the rows (A, B, C, D, and E) that make up the diamond.

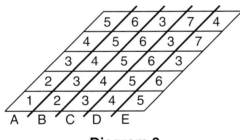

Diagram 3

1. To make the strip set for Row A, sew together 1½-inch-wide strips in the following order: Fabric 1, 2, 3, 4, and 5. Offset the strips by approximately 1½ inches, as shown in **Diagram 4.** (**Diagram 3** and

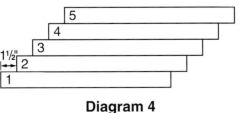

Diagram 4
Strip Set for Row A

Diagram 4 are drawn so that you are viewing the right side of the strips.) Press the seam allowances away from Fabric 1.

2. Using the 45 degree angle line on your ruler as a guide, trim the end of the strip at a 45 degree angle. Referring to **Diagram 5,** make a second cut parallel to the first cut and 1½ inches away, cutting a row of diamonds.

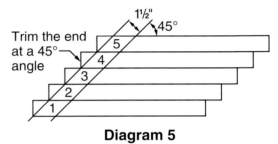

Trim the end at a 45° angle

Diagram 5

3. Cut a total of eight strips of Row A diamonds from the strip set, one for each center diamond in the large star. Label the Row A diamonds and set them aside.

4. In a similar manner, make one strip set for each remaining row in the center diamond (B, C, D, and E). Refer to **Diagram 3** to determine which strips to join and in what order. The bottom diamond in each row of the diagram is the bottom strip in the corresponding strip set. The second diamond is the second strip in the strip set. For example, for Row B, join strips in the following order, beginning with the bottom strip: 2, 3, 4, 5, and 6. Cut eight rows of diamonds from each strip set.

5. To make one center pieced diamond, lay out Rows A through E as shown in **Diagram 3.** Join the rows, taking care to match seams. Press the seams to one side.

6. Repeat Step 5 to make eight center pieced diamonds.

Making the Outer Pieced Diamonds

Make the outer pieced diamonds for the large center star using the same strip-piecing method used for the center pieced diamonds. The outer pieced diamonds are made up of Rows F, G, H, I, and J.

1. Study **Diagram 6** to determine the order to sew strips together for each of the strip sets. Make one strip set for each type of row.

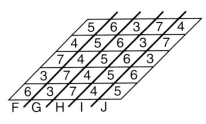

Diagram 6

2. Cut 16 rows of diamonds from each strip set.

3. Referring to **Diagram 6,** lay out the rows for one outer pieced diamond. Sew the rows together, carefully matching the seams. Press all of the seams to one side.

4. Repeat the directions in Step 3 to make 16 outer pieced diamonds.

COMPLETING THE LARGE CENTER STAR

1. To make one section for the large center star, lay out one center pieced diamond and two outer pieced diamonds, as shown in **Diagram 2.**

2. Sew the outer pieced diamonds to two adjacent sides of the center pieced diamond, carefully matching seams. As you join the units, leave the seam allowances free at the outer edges. The seam allowances will be turned under before appliquéing the large center star to the background.

3. Repeat to make a total of eight sections.

4. Join the sections together to form the center star. Begin by joining pairs of sections. Join pairs to pairs to make the two halves of the center star. Finally, join the halves. Press seams to one side.

5. Turn under the seam allowance around the outside of the center star and hand baste it in place.

6. Fold the 43½-inch muslin square in half vertically, horizontally, and diagonally in both directions; crease, determining the center and creating positioning guidelines.

7. Center and pin the large center star on the muslin square, aligning seam lines with creased positioning guides.

8. Appliqué the center star to the background square.

MAKING THE SMALL STARS

Each of the 32 small stars is made up of eight diamonds, two each of Fabrics 3, 4, 6, and 9. To cut the diamonds for the small stars, use five 1¾-inch-wide strips each of the four fabrics. Join the diamonds into stars as instructed, and then appliqué them to the quilt top as you construct it.

1. To cut the diamonds, begin by trimming one end of a 1¾-inch-wide strip at a 45 degree angle.

2. Make a second cut parallel to the first cut and 1¾ inches away, as shown in **Diagram 7.** Continue in this manner to cut approximately 15 diamonds from the strip. Check after cutting every three or four diamonds to make sure you are maintaining an accurate 45 degree angle. Correct the angle of the cut if necessary.

Diagram 7

3. Continue in this manner to cut a total of 64 diamonds each from Fabrics 3, 4, 6, and 9.

4. Referring to **Diagram 8** for correct fabric placement, lay out a set of eight diamonds for a star.

Diagram 8

5. Join sets of four diamonds into the two halves of a star, as shown in **Diagram 9.** As you join the diamonds, leave the seam allowances free around the outside of the star so they can be turned under for appliqué.

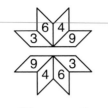

Diagram 9

6. Join the two halves to complete a star.

7. Turn under the seam allowance around the outside of the star and hand baste it in place.

8. Repeat Steps 4 through 7 to make 32 small stars.

COMPLETING THE CENTER PORTION OF THE QUILT

1. Sew a muslin A triangle to two opposite sides of the square that contains the center star. Press seams away from the square.

2. Sew muslin A triangles to the remaining two sides of the square and press.

3. Referring to the **Quilt Diagram** on page 112 and the photograph on page 105, appliqué small stars to the center of the quilt in the areas shown. You will have four small stars left to use in the pieced middle border.

MAKING THE SUGARLOAF MIDDLE BORDERS

The quick-piecing method for the pieced triangles in the middle border involves making pieced diamonds and then cutting pieced triangles from the ends of the diamonds. The pieced diamonds are constructed in a manner similar to the one you used to make the pieced diamonds for the large center star. Use 1¾-inch-strips to make the strip sets. Cut the rows of diamonds 1¾ inches wide.

1. Referring to **Diagram 10,** make two strip sets for Row K, using 1¾-inch-wide strips. The heavy lines on the diagram define the rows.

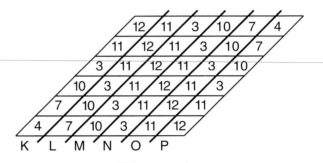

Diagram 10

2. Cut 18 rows of diamonds, each 1¾ inches wide, from the K strip sets.

3. Repeat to make two strip sets for each of the other rows (L, M, N, O, and P). Cut 18 rows of diamonds from each type of strip set.

4. Lay out the rows for one pieced diamond as shown in **Diagram 10.** Join the rows, pressing the seams to one side.

5. Make a total of 18 pieced diamonds.

6. Referring to **Diagram 11,** use a rotary cutter and ruler to cut two Sugarloaf triangles from each pieced diamond. To cut a triangle, position your ruler so it extends ¼ inch into the row of Fabric 12 diamonds, to allow for seams. Cut along the edge of the ruler. Repeat to cut a second triangle from the opposite end of the pieced diamond. Cut a total of 36 Sugarloaf triangles from the pieced diamonds.

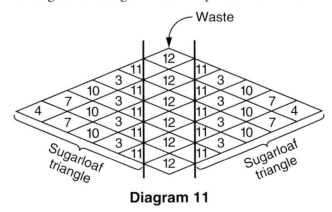

Diagram 11

7. From the remaining Fabric 12 (muslin), cut five 9-inch-wide strips.

8. Referring to **Diagram 12,** cut eight muslin triangles and one corner piece each from four of the muslin strips. The corner piece is left oversize to allow for mitered corners in a later step. You will have a total of 32 triangles and four corner pieces.

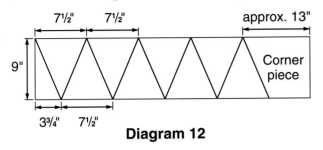

Diagram 12

9. Using a muslin corner piece as a guide, cut four more corner pieces from the fifth muslin strip so you have a total of eight corner pieces.

10. Refer to the **Quilt Diagram** to make the middle pieced borders. For each border join nine Sugarloaf triangles and eight muslin triangles into a long strip; add a corner piece to both ends. Be sure to sew the angled edge of the corner piece to the end. Make four middle pieced borders.

11. Sew a middle border to each side of the quilt top, adjusting seams along the middle borders as needed so the borders fit the sides of the quilt top; miter the corner seams. See page 9 in the "General Instructions" for details on mitering border corner seams.

12. Appliqué a small star at each corner, as shown in the **Quilt Diagram.**

MAKING THE MEDIUM STARS

Each medium star is made up of eight pieced diamonds, as illustrated by **Diagram 13.** The quick-piecing method for the diamonds is similar to that used for the pieced diamonds in the large center star. Unlike the center star and the small stars, which are appliquéd onto the background, the medium stars are squared off into blocks.

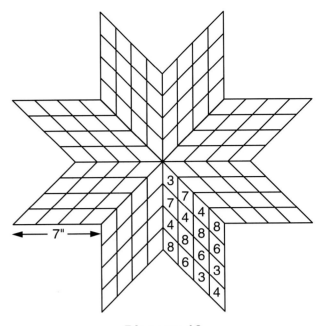

Diagram 13

1. Referring to **Diagram 14,** make three strip sets for Row Q, using 1¾-inch-wide strips.

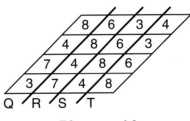

Diagram 14

2. Cut 32 rows of diamonds, each 1¾ inches wide, from the Row Q strip sets.

3. Repeat to make three strip sets each for Rows R, S, and T. Cut 32 rows of diamonds from each type of strip set.

4. Referring to **Diagram 14,** lay out the rows for one pieced diamond. Join the rows, pressing the seams to one side.

5. Make a total of 32 pieced diamonds.

6. To make one medium star, lay out eight pieced diamonds, as shown in **Diagram 13.**

7. Sew the pieced diamonds into pairs, join pairs to create half stars, then join the halves. As you join the diamonds, do not sew into the seam allowance at the ends of the seams; backstitch to secure the beginning and end of the seams.

8. To complete the star, you will need four muslin D squares and four muslin E triangles. Set a muslin triangle into alternate openings around the star. Press the seams away from the star. Set muslin squares into the remaining four openings. Press the seams away from the star.

9. Repeat Steps 6 through 8 to make a total of four medium stars.

ADDING THE MEDIUM STARS

1. Sew a muslin B triangle to two opposite sides of each medium star block, as shown in the **Quilt Diagram.** Press the seams toward the triangles.

2. Sew a muslin C triangle to a third side of each medium star, forming large corner triangles. Press the seams toward the triangles.

3. Referring to the **Quilt Diagram,** sew a large corner triangle containing a medium star to two opposite sides of the quilt top. Press the seams toward

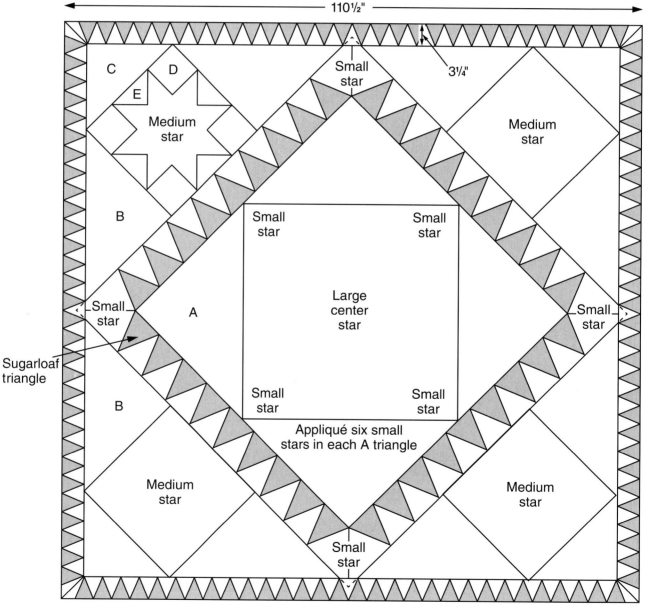

Quilt Diagram

the triangles. Then add triangles to the remaining two sides.

MAKING THE OUTER PIECED BORDERS

1. To make the pieced triangles for the outer borders, begin by making 11 strip sets like the one shown in **Diagram 15,** using 1¾-inch-wide strips of Fabric 4 and Fabric 7. Press the seams away from the Fabric 4 strips.

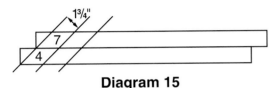

Diagram 15

2. Trim the ends of the strip set at a 45 degree angle. Cut pairs of joined diamonds by making cuts 1¾ inches apart and parallel to the first cut. You will need a total of 152 pairs of diamonds.

3. From 11 additional 1¾-inch-wide Fabric 7 strips, cut a total of 152 single diamonds. Trim the end of each strip at a 45 degree angle, and make cuts 1¾ inches apart.

4. Combine pairs of diamonds and single diamonds into 152 units, as shown in **Diagram 16.** Press the seams away from the Fabric 4 diamonds.

Diagram 16

5. Referring to **Diagram 17,** use a rotary cutter and ruler to trim excess Fabric 7 diamonds. Position the ruler ¼ inch from the tip of the Fabric 4 diamond to allow for seams, and trim along the edge of the ruler.

Diagram 17

6. From the remaining Fabric 12 (muslin), cut eight 4¼-inch-wide strips.

7. Cut muslin triangles from the strips as shown in **Diagram 18.** You will need a total of 156 muslin triangles.

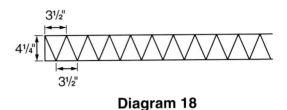

Diagram 18

8. Alternating types of triangles, join 38 pieced triangles and 39 muslin triangles into a long border strip. Make four of these borders.

9. Placing the strips so the pieced triangles point in toward the center of the quilt, sew the four borders to the quilt top, mitering the corner seams. See page 9 in the "General Instructions" for details on mitering border corner seams.

QUILTING AND FINISHING

1. Mark quilting designs on the quilt top. Some of the full-size quilting designs for the background areas on the quilt are provided on pages 114–116.

2. Divide the backing fabric crosswise into three equal lengths. Trim the selvages and join the three panels. Press the seams away from the center panel.

3. Layer the quilt back, batting, and quilt top; baste.

4. Quilt all marked designs, adding additional quilting as desired. Trapunto in some of the quilted areas gives the antique quilt in the photo extra appeal. If you wish to add trapunto to your quilt, follow the instructions in "Adding Trapunto" on page 114.

5. Make approximately 12¾ yards (460 inches) of either bias or straight-grain binding. Sew the binding to the quilt. See page 13 in the "General Instructions" for details on making and attaching binding.

Quilter's Schoolhouse

ADDING TRAPUNTO

The beauty of Mary McCollister's quilt is enhanced by the extra stuffing she added after the quilting was complete. This kind of padding is easiest when the quilt backing fabric is not too tightly woven, since you must insert a needle and yarn by spreading the threads.

Supplies for Trapunto
- 6-inch trapunto needle
- White, 100 percent acrylic yarn, such as the type used for package ties

Instructions

1. Cut a 15-inch length of yarn. If the yarn is three ply, separate it and thread the needle with only a single strand of yarn.

2. Turn the quilt to the back side. Choose an area to be stuffed and insert the needle between the threads by rubbing the blunt point against the threads. Run the needle between the layers of the quilt, across the area to be stuffed, and bring the point out.

3. Pull the yarn gently into the area to be filled. Clip the end of the yarn. If necessary, use your needle to poke the end of the yarn into the quilt. Continue to add lengths of yarn until the area is puffy but not tight. When stuffing large channels or circular channels, overlap the ends of the yarn by about ½ inch to help fill them uniformly.

4. Smooth the needle holes with your fingernail. The holes will largely disappear after the quilt is washed one time.

Single Daisy Quilting Design

Posy Quilting Design

Daisy Sprig Quilting Design

Teardrops and Daisy Quilting Design

One-half of Sunflower Quilting Design

Fenced Stars Crib Quilt

Inspired by the antique Simple Star quilt pictured on page 100, we scaled down the blocks to 8 inches for this rustic-looking quilt, suitable in size as either a wallhanging or a baby quilt. Ten light stars on a dark background alternate with ten dark stars on a light background in the body of the quilt. The zigzag, or rail fence, border that surrounds the Simple Star blocks is reminiscent of the log fences early pioneers built to enclose their farmsteads. We chose primitive-looking plaids, checks, and stripes in predominantly red, blue, and cream to give our quilt a warm homespun appeal that would make it fit into any country-style home.

SKILL LEVEL: *Easy*

SIZE:

Finished quilt is approximately 40 × 48 inches
Finished block is 8 inches square

NUMBER OF PIECED BLOCKS: 20

FABRICS AND SUPPLIES

Note: To allow freedom to arrange the fabrics for your quilt as you desire, we have given a generous approximate total amount of yardage needed of assorted light and assorted dark fabrics. All of the fabrics we used for the quilt shown were either plaids, checks, or stripes.

- 1¾ yards total of assorted light fabric scraps (cream, tan, and white) and medium-light fabric scraps (light blue and red-and-white check)
- 1¾ yards total of assorted dark fabrics (maroon, navy, and red-and-blue striped) and medium-dark fabrics (red, deep blue, black-and-tan check)
- 1½ yards of fabric for the quilt back
- ½ yard of fabric for binding
- Batting, larger than 40 × 48 inches

- Rotary cutter, ruler, and mat
- Template plastic (optional)

CUTTING

Twenty star blocks make up the center of the quilt. Dark stars on a medium or light background alternate with light stars on a dark background. The two variations are illustrated in **Diagram 1.** By playing with the relative values of the light, medium, and dark fabrics, you can create different illusions in the various star blocks.

For each block you will need eight A triangles (one set of four matching triangles for the outside of the block and two sets of two matching triangles for the

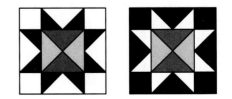

Diagram 1

block center), eight matching B triangles for the star points, and four matching C squares. **Diagram 2** shows a drawing of the block with the pieces labeled. Refer to this as a guide when cutting pieces from the assorted light, medium, and dark fabric scraps to make 20 star blocks.

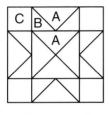

Diagram 2

If you wish to cut the pieces using traditional methods, make templates for patterns A, B, and C on page 121. If you prefer to quick-cut the pieces, follow the directions below.

From the assorted light and dark fabrics, cut the following pieces for the blocks:
■ A triangles
Quick-cut a 5¼-inch square. Cut the square diagonally in both directions. You will get four A triangles from each square.
■ B triangles
Quick-cut a 2⅞-inch square. Cut the square diagonally into two triangles.
■ C squares
Quick-cut 2½-inch squares.

From the assorted light and medium-light fabrics, cut the following pieces for the border:
■ 72 A triangles
Quick-cut a 5¼-inch square. Cut the square diagonally in both directions. You will get four A triangles from each square.
■ 12 B triangles
Quick-cut a 2⅞-inch square. Cut the square diagonally into two triangles.

From the assorted dark and medium-dark fabrics, cut the following pieces for the border:
■ 76 A triangles
Quick-cut a 5¼-inch square. Cut the square

diagonally in both directions. You will get four A triangles from each square.
■ 4 B triangles
Quick-cut a 2⅞-inch square. Cut the square diagonally into two triangles.
■ 4 C squares
Quick-cut 2½-inch squares.

MAKING THE BLOCKS

1. Referring to **Diagram 2,** lay out eight matching B triangles for the star points, four matching A triangles for the outside edges, two sets of two matching A triangles for the block center, and four matching C squares for the corners of the block.

2. Piece the center of the block by sewing two sets of two matching A triangles together to form a square, as shown in **Diagram 3.**

Diagram 3

3. Make four **Diagram 4** units by sewing a B triangle to adjacent sides of the four matching A triangles you have chosen for the outside of the block. Press the seam allowances away from the A triangles.

Diagram 4

4. Referring to **Diagram 5,** make Row 1 and Row 3 by adding a C square to opposite sides of an AB unit. Press the seams toward the C squares. To make Row 2, add AB units to two opposite sides of a center unit. Press the seams toward the center unit. Join the rows to complete a block.

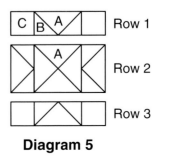

Diagram 5

5. Repeat to make a total of 20 blocks—10 with light stars on a dark background and 10 with dark stars on a light background.

ASSEMBLING THE QUILT TOP

1. Referring to the **Quilt Diagram,** lay out the blocks in five horizontal rows with four blocks in each row, alternating light stars and dark stars. The heavy lines on the diagram help define the rows.

2. Stitch the four blocks together into rows. Join the rows.

3. Piece and add the zigzag borders to the quilt in four steps. Begin by making a pieced inner border strip for the top and bottom edges of the quilt by sewing together eight dark A triangles, seven light A triangles, and two light B triangles for each border as shown in the **Quilt Diagram.** Stitch the borders to the quilt; press the seams toward the borders.

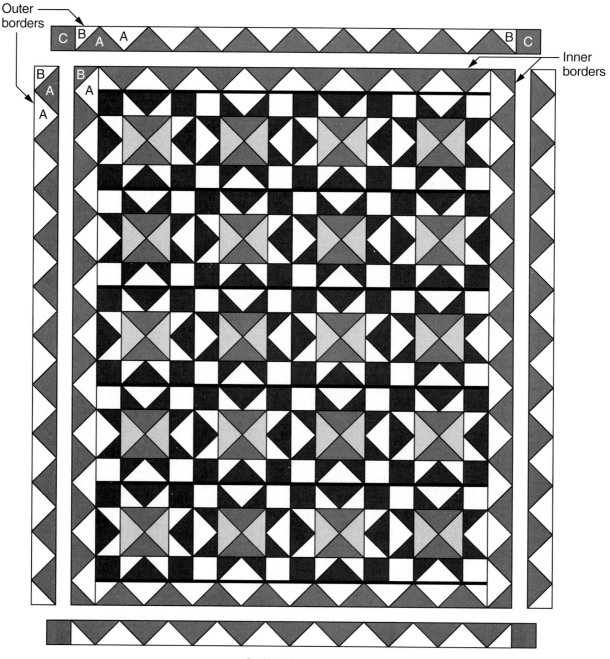

Quilt Diagram

4. Make pieced inner border strips for the sides of the quilt by joining 10 dark A triangles, 11 light A triangles, and 2 dark B triangles for each border as shown. Sew the borders to the sides of the quilt; press the seams toward the borders.

5. Piece the outer border strips for the sides of the quilt by joining 11 dark A triangles, 10 light A triangles, and 2 light B triangles for each border as shown. Sew the borders to the sides of the quilt; press the seams toward the borders.

6. Piece the outer border strips for the top and bottom edges by joining nine dark A triangles, eight light A triangles, two light B triangles, and two dark C squares for each border as shown. Stitch the borders to the quilt; press the seams toward the borders.

QUILTING AND FINISHING

1. Mark quilting designs as desired. **Diagram 6** shows the quilting pattern that was used for the blocks. The border was quilted by outline quilting in the ditch around the dark zigzag.

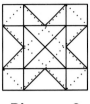

Diagram 6

2. Layer the quilt back, batting, and quilt top; baste. Hand or machine quilt as desired.

3. Make approximately 4½ yards of bias or straight-grain binding, and sew it to the quilt to finish the edges. See page 13 in the "General Instructions" for details on making and attaching binding.

The dashed lines on the patterns indicate finished size. The solid lines include seam allowances.

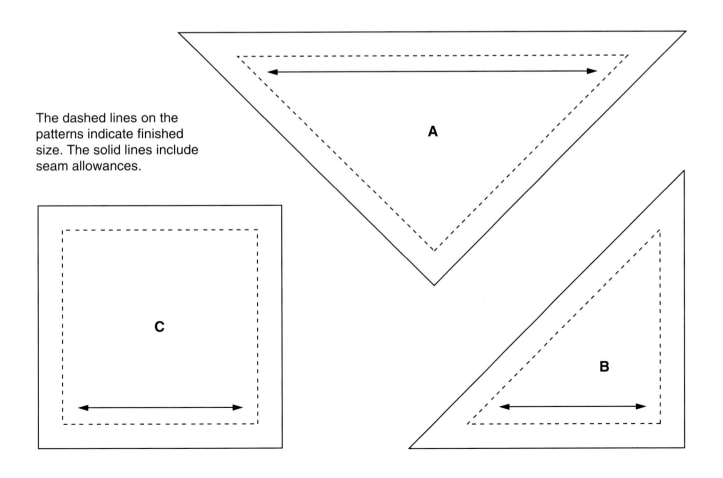

A Quilter's Garden

Old-time quilters created beautiful floral patterns surpassed only by nature itself. Their fresh arrangements of blossoms and buds are still vibrant today, and they provide unceasing inspiration for today's quiltmakers. Two of the antique quilts we chose, the Hexagon Posy and the Russian Sunflower, are for dedicated hand piecers. The Rose of Sharon is a classic that any lover of appliqué will enjoy. Our new project, a wallhanging in contemporary clear colors combined with black and white, was inspired by the simplest pattern in the chapter, the cheerful Spring Tulips quilt from the first half of this century.

· Spring Tulips ·

If you have a young daughter or granddaughter ready for her first "big girl bed," this charming quilt, with its clear, crisp colors and cheerful character, might be just the right coverlet for that little girl's room. Simple flower, leaf, and flowerpot shapes are easy to appliqué, and the straight setting and uncomplicated borders make it an ideal project for a beginning quilter.

SKILL LEVEL: *Easy*

SIZE:

Finished quilt is approximately 78 × 88½ inches
Finished block is 10½ inches square

NUMBER OF BLOCKS: 42

FABRICS AND SUPPLIES

Note: For best results, we recommend using a ½-inch-wide flat metal or heat-resistant plastic bias bar to prepare the stem strips for appliqué. Sets of bars in several widths used to prepare strips for Celtic and other appliqué are sold in quilt shops. The stem strips for the Spring Tulips block are cut on the straight of grain, but they are prepared in the same manner as bias strips.

- 5 yards of muslin for background squares and borders
- 1¾ yards of green fabric for borders, stems, and leaves
- 1 yard of green-and-white print for flowerpots
- 1 yard *each* of yellow, purple, and coral fabric for borders and appliqués
- 5½ yards of fabric for the quilt back
- ¾ yard of fabric for binding (optional)
- Quilt batting, larger than 78 × 88½ inches
- Rotary cutter, ruler, and mat

- Plastic-coated freezer paper (optional)
- Medium- or wide-tip black permanent marker
- 11-inch square of paper (tracing paper works well)
- ½-inch-wide bias bar

CUTTING

The instructions call for rotary cutting the border strips and the background squares. Measurements include ¼-inch seam allowances. Cut all strips across the fabric width.

For the appliqué pieces, make templates for the patterns on page 129. Follow the instructions in "Freezer Paper Appliqué," on page 126, or use your own favorite appliqué technique. Be sure to add seam allowances when cutting the pieces from the fabric.

From the muslin, cut:
- Nine 2-inch-wide border strips
- Forty-two 11-inch background squares
  Quick-cut fourteen 11-inch-wide strips. Cut the strips into 11-inch squares.

From the green fabric, cut:
- Nine 2-inch-wide border strips
- Sixteen 1¼-inch-wide strips for tulip stems
- 42 leaves and 42 reverse leaves

From the green-and-white print fabric, cut:
■ 42 flowerpots

From the yellow fabric, cut:
■ Nine 2-inch-wide border strips
■ 42 tulips

From the purple fabric, cut:
■ Nine 2-inch-wide border strips
■ 42 tulips

From the coral fabric, cut:
■ Nine 2-inch-wide border strips
■ 42 tulips

PREPARING THE STEMS

Each block requires one 6-inch-long piece and two 4½-inch-long pieces of prepared stem, a total of 630 inches of prepared stem for the quilt. Prepare the strips as described on the opposite page, then cut them into pieces as needed.

Quilter's Schoolhouse

FREEZER PAPER APPLIQUÉ

Freezer paper appliqué is ideally suited to the Spring Tulips pattern. Plastic-coated freezer paper is pressed to the appliqué pieces to create a guide for turning under the seam allowances as you stitch, and it is then pulled off later.

1. Make finished-size plastic templates for the appliqué pattern pieces.

2. Place templates on the smooth (not shiny) side of the freezer paper and draw around them. Do not add seam allowances. Cut out the patterns along the drawn outlines. Make a separate paper pattern for each appliqué piece. For example, for each Spring Tulips block, you would draw three tulips, a leaf and a reverse leaf, and one flowerpot.

3. Using a dry iron set on wool, press the paper patterns to the proper fabric, placing the shiny side of the paper on the right side of the fabric. Leave about ½ inch between pieces to allow for seam allowances.

4. Cut out the appliqués ⅛ inch to the outside of the paper edge to allow for seams. Leave the paper attached to the fabric.

5. Pin the appliqué in place on the background fabric with the paper still adhered to it. As you stitch the appliqué to the background, turn under the seam allowance along the edge of the freezer paper, aligning the fold of the fabric with the paper edge. Once the piece is stitched down completely, gently peel off the paper pattern.

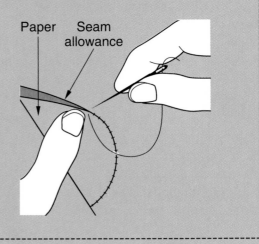

Paper   Seam allowance

1. Fold a 1¼-inch-wide strip in half lengthwise, wrong sides together.

2. Stitch along the aligned raw edges, taking a ⅛-inch seam.

3. Insert a ½-inch-wide bias bar in the fabric tube. Adjust the strip so the seam is centered along one flat side of the bar; press on both sides, pressing the seam allowances in one direction. Work the bar through the tube until the entire strip is pressed flat.

MAKING THE BLOCKS

Begin by making a master pattern for the appliqué blocks as described on page 4 in the "General Instructions." Refer to **Diagram 1** for placement of the appliqués. Follow the instructions below to make one block. Make a total of 42 blocks.

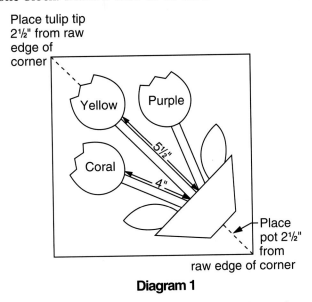

Place tulip tip 2½" from raw edge of corner

Yellow Purple

Coral

5½"

4"

Place pot 2½" from raw edge of corner

Diagram 1

1. Prepare one leaf and one reverse leaf, one flowerpot, and three tulips for appliqué. Use the freezer paper appliqué technique described in the box on the opposite page or the method you desire.

2. Fold a muslin background square in half diagonally and lightly crease to form a placement line.

3. Position and pin a 6-inch-long center stem and two 4½-inch-long side stems on the background square, using the master pattern as a guide. Position and pin a leaf and a reverse leaf in place. Remove the pattern and appliqué the pieces using thread that matches the appliqués.

4. In the same manner, position, pin, and appliqué the tulips and flowerpot in place.

ASSEMBLING THE QUILT TOP

1. Lay out the appliquéd blocks in seven horizontal rows of six blocks per row, as shown in the **Quilt Diagram** on page 128. Join the blocks into rows, pressing the seams in opposite directions from row to row; join the rows.

2. The borders are sewn together into sets, then added to the quilt as units. First, join pairs of 2-inch-wide strips of the same color end to end, making four long border strips of each color. Set aside two long strips of each color for the end borders. To make the longer side borders, cut the one remaining border strip of each color in half and sew a half-strip to each of the side border strips.

3. Fold each strip in half crosswise and finger press to form a center guideline. Match guidelines when joining strips. Make four border strip sets with five strips in each set. Join the strips in the following order: coral, purple, muslin, yellow, green. Press the seams toward the green strip.

4. Measure the length and width of your inner quilt top, measuring through the middle rather than along the edges, which may have stretched from handling. The quilt top should be approximately 63½ × 74 inches, including seam allowances. Sew the border sets to the quilt, mitering the corners. See page 9 in the "General Instructions" for tips on marking and sewing on borders for mitered corners.

QUILTING AND FINISHING

1. Mark quilting designs as desired. The quilt shown has outline quilting in the ditch next to all the appliqués. A grid of 1-inch squares is quilted in the background areas. The borders are quilted in the ditch along the seams.

2. Piece the quilt back. Begin by dividing the backing fabric crosswise into two equal pieces. Cut one of the pieces in half lengthwise to make two narrow panels. Sew a narrow panel to each side of the full-width panel. Press the seams away from the center panel.

Quilt Diagram

▪ Hexagon Posy ▪

3. Layer the backing, batting, and quilt top; baste. Quilt as desired.

4. The quilt shown was finished without binding by turning in the edges of the quilt top and backing. To finish the quilt this way, trim the backing and batting even with the edge of the quilt top. Separate the quilt top and backing from the batting and trim off an additional ½ inch of batting. Fold in ½ inch on the raw edges of the quilt top and the backing. Slip stitch the folded edges together.

If you prefer a separate binding, make approximately 10 yards (360 inches) of straight grain or bias binding. See page 13 in the "General Instructions" for details on making and attaching binding.

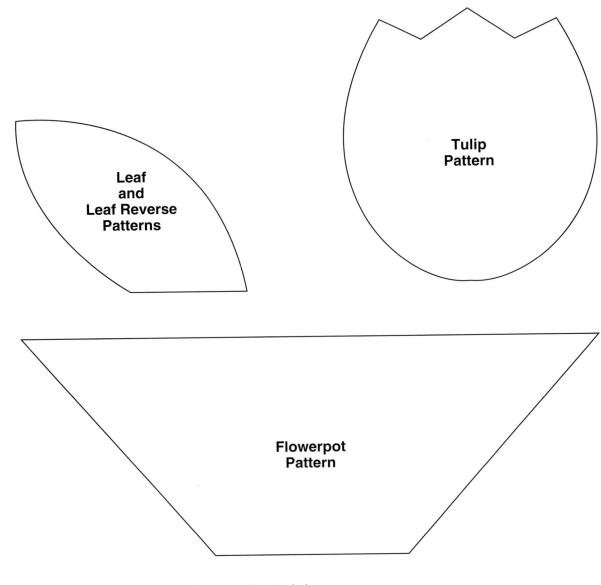

Pattern pieces are finished size.
Add seam allowances when cutting the pieces from fabric.

We love the simple charm of the cheery posies in this Depression-era quilt. The zigzagging border brings to mind neat and well-tended flower beds. The hexagon shape that makes up these purple posies appears much more often in the incredibly popular 1930s pattern, Grandmother's Flower Garden. We like to think that the long-ago maker of this quilt was a patchwork individualist, not content to make a quilt like everyone else's. She combined her pieced hexagons with appliqué leaves to make a one-in-a-million quilt!

SKILL LEVEL: *Intermediate*

SIZE:

Finished quilt is approximately 76¼ × 88¼ inches
Finished block is 8½ inches square (approximately 12 inches on the diagonal)

NUMBER OF BLOCKS: 72

FABRICS AND SUPPLIES

- 6 yards of white or off-white fabric for block backgrounds, side setting triangles, and corner setting triangles
- 3¼ yards of green fabric for flower stems, leaves, and binding
- 3 yards of purple fabric for hexagons and border strips
- ½ yard of gold fabric for posy centers
- 5½ yards of fabric for the quilt back
- Quilt batting, larger than 76¼ × 88¼ inches
- Template plastic
- Plastic-coated freezer paper (optional)

CUTTING

Make templates for pattern pieces A, B, C, and D on page 136. The patterns for the appliqué pieces B, C, and D are finished size. Add seam allowances when cutting them out. For tips on appliqué, see page 7 in the "General Instructions."

The technique described in the box "English Paper Piecing" on pages 132–133 works well for shapes like these hexagons. If you plan to use this method to piece the posies, follow the instructions in the box to make paper patterns and cut the hexagons.

The instructions below call for rotary cutting the setting triangles and border strips. Measurements given include seam allowances. Cut all strips across the fabric width.

From the white fabric, cut:

- Seventy-two 9-inch background squares
  Quick-cut eighteen 9-inch-wide strips. Cut the strips into 9-inch squares.
- 22 side setting triangles
  Quick-cut two 13¼-inch-wide strips. Cut the strips into six 13¼-inch squares. Divide the

Quilter's Schoolhouse

ENGLISH PAPER PIECING

The British technique of basting patchwork fabric pieces to paper templates and then whipstitching them together works well for shapes like hexagons.

You can make your own paper templates or purchase die-cut ones from your local quilt shop or a mail-order catalog. The hexagons for the Hexagon Posy quilt finish 1 inch on each side.

To make your own templates, you'll need template plastic, plastic-coated freezer paper, and a stapler or straight pins.

Preparing the Paper Templates

1. Begin by making a finished-size hard plastic template using the A hexagon pattern on page 136.

2. Tear a piece of freezer paper off the roll that is approximately 15 inches long by the width of the roll.

3. On the smooth (not shiny) side of the paper, draw around the hard-edged template, making as many hexagon outlines as possible.

4. Tear off three or four more pieces of freezer paper the same size as the first. Stack the extra sheets under the marked one.

5. Put a pin through the center of each hexagon to keep the layers from shifting. If you work with narrow sheets of freezer paper, you can staple through the hexagon centers to prevent shifting.

6. Use scissors to cut out the stacked paper hexagon templates.

7. Repeat the process to make enough paper templates for your patchwork. You need a total of 504 papers for the Hexagon Posy quilt.

---

squares diagonally both ways to produce four triangles per square. You will have two extra triangles.

■ 4 corner setting triangles
Quick-cut two 9⅛-inch squares. Cut each square in half diagonally ⊦o make a total of four triangles.

From the green fabric, cut:
■ 72 B stems
■ 72 C leaves
■ 72 D leaves
■ Reserve the remaining fabric for binding

From the purple fabric, cut:
■ 432 A hexagons
■ 46 border sashing strips
Quick-cut twelve 2-inch-wide strips. Cut the strips into 2 × 9-inch rectangles.
■ Two 2 × 12-inch corner border strips

From the gold fabric, cut:
■ 72 A hexagons

MAKING THE BLOCKS

1. Prepare the hexagons for joining using either the English paper piecing method described above or traditional hand-piecing methods.

Piecing the Hexagons

1. Use a dry iron set on wool to press paper templates to the *wrong* side of the fabric for the patchwork pieces. Place the shiny side of the paper against the fabric. Be sure to leave at least ½ inch between the papers for seam allowances.

2. Cut out the fabric shapes, adding seam allowances by cutting ¼ inch away from the edges of the paper templates.

3. To prepare the shapes for piecing, turn the raw edges of the fabric over the edges of the paper and thread baste, stitching through the fabric and the paper, as shown in **Diagram 1.**

4. To join shapes, place two prepared fabric pieces *right* sides together, aligning folded edges, as shown in **Diagram 2.** When joining hexagons, join one short side at a time. Sew aligned edges together with a whipstitch, keeping stitches small and sewing just through the folded edge. Begin and end with a knot.

5. When using this method for ordinary patchwork, remove the basting stitches and the papers after all the pieces are joined. For patterns such as the Hexagon Posy, first appliqué the posy unit and the other pieces to the background square. Cut away the background fabric from behind the posy unit; remove basting and papers.

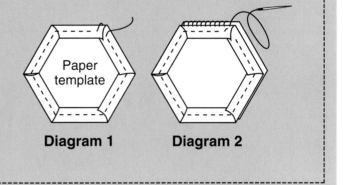

Diagram 1   **Diagram 2**

2. Lay out the following pieces for one block: a background square, six purple hexagons, one gold hexagon, one B stem, one C leaf, and one D leaf.

3. Referring to **Diagram 1,** stitch a purple hexagon to one side of a gold center hexagon.

4. Add a second purple hexagon, as shown in **Diagram 2,** setting it in at the side of the joined pieces from Step 3.

5. In the same manner, add the third, fourth, and fifth hexagons. Finally, set in the sixth hexagon between 1 and 5, as shown in **Diagram 3,** to complete the posy unit.

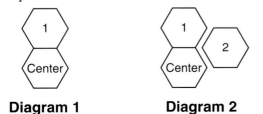

Diagram 1   **Diagram 2**

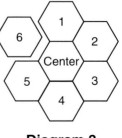

Diagram 3

6. If you pieced the block traditionally, prepare the posy unit for appliqué by turning under and basting the outer edges. Using your favorite appliqué method, prepare the leaves and stem for appliqué.

7. Lightly press a background square in half diagonally to form a center line. Referring to **Diagram 4,** position the posy unit on the background square. Align the seams of the hexagons with the center crease line. Position a stem and leaves as shown in the diagram.

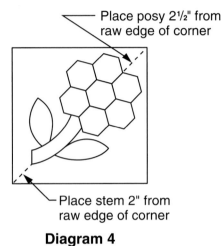

Place posy 2½" from raw edge of corner

Place stem 2" from raw edge of corner

Diagram 4

8. Stitch the leaves, stem, and posy in place. If you used the English paper piecing method, turn the block to the back, trim away the background fabric under the posy unit, and remove the basting stitches and the papers. Repeat to make 72 blocks.

ASSEMBLING THE QUILT TOP

Pay careful attention to the assembly directions. Wait until all rows are joined before adding the corner setting triangles.

1. Referring to **Diagram 5,** add the sashing strips to the blocks. Make ten units as shown in **5A,** ten

| A | B | C |
| Make 10 | Make 10 | Make 2 |

Diagram 5

units as shown in **5B,** and two units as shown in **5C.** Press the seams toward the purple strips.

2. Referring to **Diagram 6,** add sashing strips to the side setting triangles to make two types of side triangle units. Make ten units as shown in **6A** and 12 units as shown in **6B.**

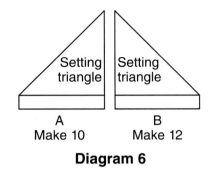

Setting triangle Setting triangle

A   B
Make 10   Make 12

Diagram 6

3. Referring to **Diagram 7,** lay out and join the blocks into 12 diagonal rows as shown, placing blocks with sashing strips at the ends of the rows. The numbers on the end blocks of each row correspond with the diagram number for the type of block you need. Lay out the rows as shown, but *do not* sew the rows to each other yet.

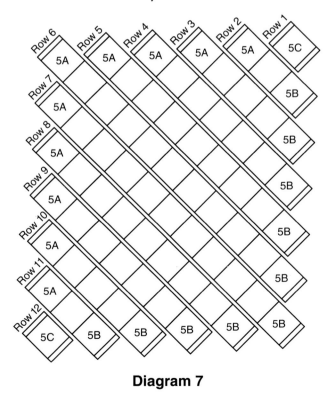

Diagram 7

4. Lay out **Diagram 6A** side setting triangles along the top and bottom edges of the quilt. Lay out **6B** triangles along the sides.

5. Referring to **Diagram 8,** sew a 2 × 12-inch purple strip to the outer side of Row 1. Then stitch the setting triangles to the ends of Row 1 as shown.

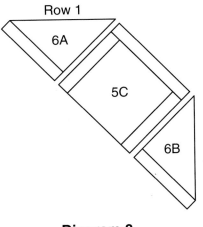

Diagram 8

6. Referring to **Diagram 9,** sew Row 2 to Row 1. Add the side setting triangles to the sides of the joined rows as shown.

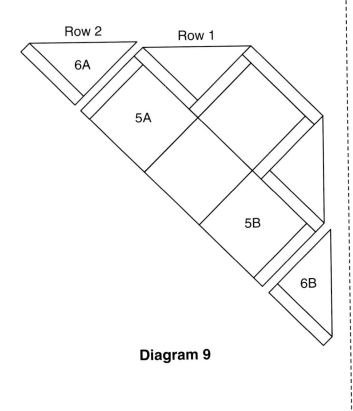

Diagram 9

7. Continue in this manner, joining a row to the quilt top and then adding setting triangles, until Row 5 has been added and the setting triangles sewn on. Add Row 6. Stitch a **Diagram 6B** setting triangle to the lower edge, but do not add the corner setting triangles at this time. Set this entire upper right portion of the quilt aside for now.

8. Assemble the lower left half of the quilt in the same manner. Begin by sewing a 2 × 12-inch purple strip to the outer edge of Row 12. Then add **Diagram 6A** and **6B** side setting triangles.

9. Join Row 11 to Row 12 and add side setting triangles. Continue in this manner until Row 7 has been added. Add a **Diagram 6B** setting triangle to the top edge of Row 7, but do not add the corner triangle at the lower edge.

10. Join the upper right and lower left quilt sections by stitching together Rows 6 and 7.

11. Sew corner setting triangles to the four corners of the quilt top. Trim any excess corner triangle even with the edges of the quilt top.

QUILTING AND FINISHING

1. Mark quilting designs as desired. The quilt shown has outline quilting a scant ¼ inch to the inside of the patchwork and appliqué pieces, as well as in the ditch around the appliqués. A grid of squares is quilted in the white background areas. The cable design for the purple strips is given full size on page 136.

2. Piece the quilt back. First, cut the backing fabric crosswise into two equal pieces. Cut one of the long pieces in half lengthwise. Sew a narrow panel to each side of the full-width panel. Press seams away from the center panel.

3. Layer the backing, batting, and quilt top; baste. Quilt as desired.

4. Make approximately 10 yards (360 inches) of bias or straight-grain binding. Sew the binding to the quilt top. Trim away excess backing and batting. Turn the binding to the back of the quilt and hand finish. See page 13 in the "General Instructions" for details on making and attaching binding.

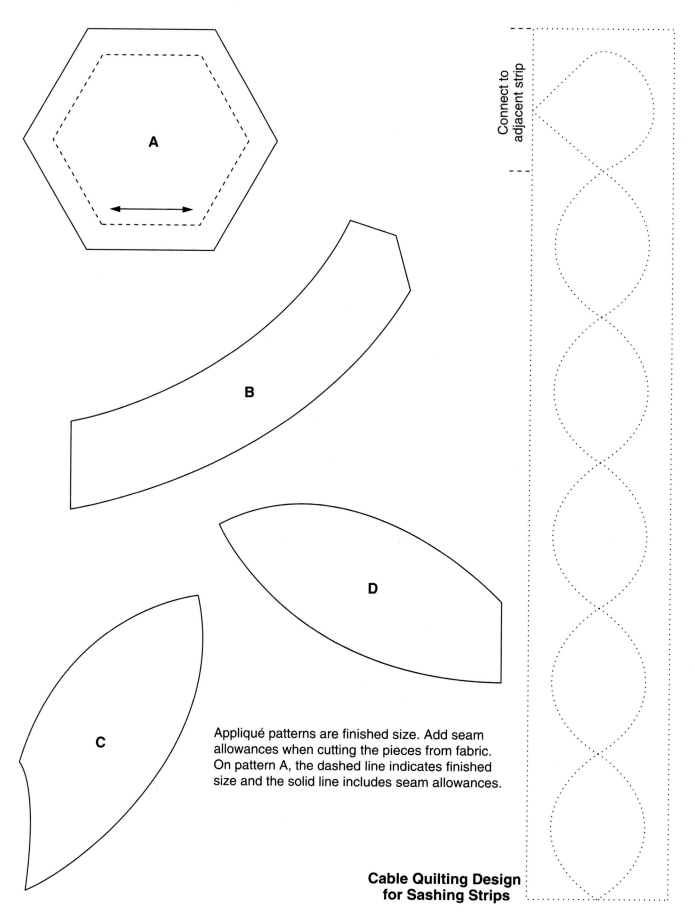

A

B

D

C

Appliqué patterns are finished size. Add seam allowances when cutting the pieces from fabric. On pattern A, the dashed line indicates finished size and the solid line includes seam allowances.

Connect to adjacent strip

Cable Quilting Design for Sashing Strips

▪ Rose of Sharon ▪

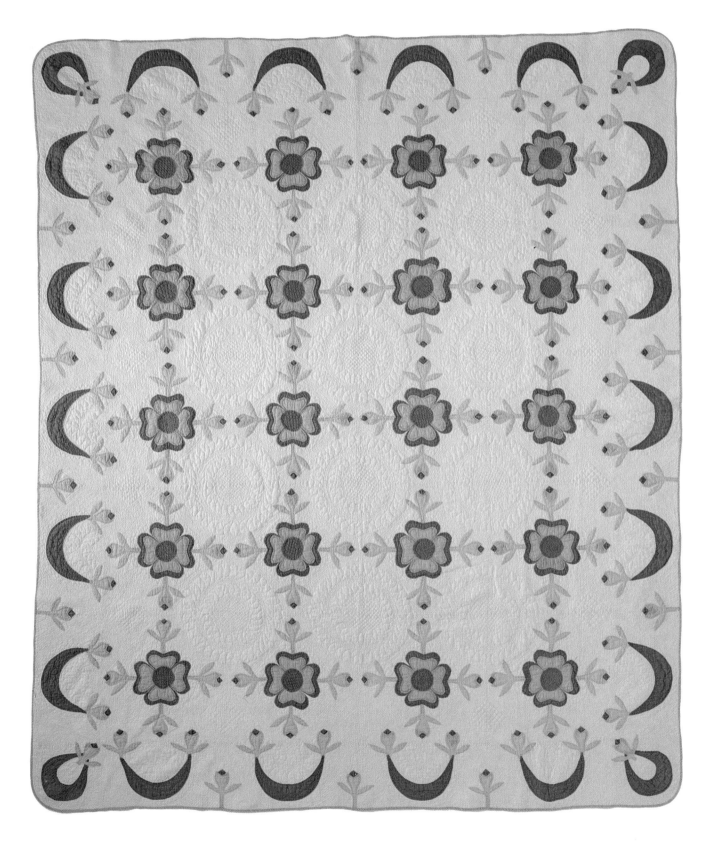

The number of hours of hand quilting invested in this floral beauty is astronomical! Unsigned and undated, its age is difficult to guess. The pattern and the heavy quilting suggest the mid-nineteenth century, but rose quilts of that era were almost always made in red and green. Perhaps the quilt's current colors have faded from more vivid ones, but they resemble in texture and hue the fabrics popular in the 1930s and 40s. If you devote the time it takes to make this Rose of Sharon, be sure to sign and date *your* work so future generations don't have to guess!

SKILL LEVEL: *Intermediate*

SIZE:

Finished quilt is approximately 80 × 96 inches
Finished block is 16 inches square

NUMBER OF BLOCKS: 20

FABRICS AND SUPPLIES

- 7½ yards of white or off-white fabric for background squares and borders
- 2¼ yards of dark blue fabric for appliqués
- 2 yards of light green fabric for appliqués
- 1 yard of light blue fabric for appliqués
- 6 yards of fabric for the quilt back
- ¾ yard of fabric for binding
- Quilt batting, larger than 80 × 96 inches
- Rotary cutter, ruler, and mat (optional)
- Plastic-coated freezer paper (optional)
- Tracing paper (16½-inch square)

CUTTING

The measurements given below for border strips and background squares include seam allowances. Measurements for border strips also include a few extra

inches in length. Trim them to size when adding them to the quilt top.

For the appliqué pieces, make templates for the patterns on pages 141–143. These patterns are finished size, so you will need to add seam allowances when cutting.

From the white fabric, cut:
- Four 8½ × 84-inch border strips
- Twenty 16½-inch-square background blocks

From the dark blue fabric, cut:
- 20 flower centers
- 80 large petals
- 18 border swags
- 4 corner swags
- 134 bud tips

From the light green fabric, cut:
- 80 block buds
- 36 swag buds
- 14 edge buds
- 4 corner buds

From the light blue fabric, cut:
- 80 small petals

Making the Blocks

Begin by making a master pattern as described in the "General Instructions" on page 4. Follow the instructions below to make one block. Make a total of 20 blocks.

1. Referring to the **Block Diagram,** lay out the following pieces for one block: 4 bud tips, 4 block buds, 4 large dark blue petals, 4 small light blue petals, 1 center circle. Using the technique described in "Freezer Paper Appliqué" on page 126 or your favorite method, prepare the pieces for appliqué.

Block Diagram

2. Fold a background square in half vertically, horizontally, and diagonally both ways, and lightly crease it, forming guidelines that will help you position the appliqués symmetrically.

3. Using your master pattern as a guide, position and appliqué the pieces in the following order: bud tips, block buds, large petals, small petals, and center circle. You may wish to trim the background fabric from behind the large petals before adding the small petals.

Assembling the Quilt Top

1. Lay out the blocks in five horizontal rows of four blocks per row, as shown in the **Quilt Diagram** on page 140. Join the blocks into rows, and then join the rows.

2. Measure the length of the completed inner quilt top (approximately 80½ inches), measuring through the center of the quilt. Trim two of the 8½-inch-wide borders to this length. Sew a border to each long side of the quilt.

3. Referring to the **Quilt Diagram,** position, pin, and appliqué the swag buds and swags to the side borders. Center each swag opposite the tip of a block bud. The lowest, or outer, edge of the swag should be approximately ¾ inch from the raw outer edge of the border. Appliqué the edge buds between the swags as shown.

4. Measure the width of the quilt top (approximately 80½ inches), measuring through the center of the quilt. Trim the two remaining borders to this length. Sew the borders to the top and bottom of the quilt top. Position, pin, and appliqué the swag buds and swags along the borders. Position and appliqué the corner swags and corner buds. Finally, appliqué the edge buds between the swags as shown.

Quilting and Finishing

1. Mark quilting designs. The quilt shown has lots of quilting. A classic double feather circle is quilted in the areas between the appliqués. One-quarter of the pattern for the feather circle is on page 142. See the **Quilt Diagram** for placement indications for the circle motif. The pattern for the feather spray that goes just inside the edge of the border swags is given on page 143. The quilt also has outline quilting on the appliqués and close straight-line quilting over the entire background.

Be aware that if you choose to do dense quilting such as this on a project, the amount of quilting must be fairly uniform over the entire quilt. Otherwise, the flat, heavily quilted portions will contrast too noticeably with the puffier, less quilted ones.

2. Piece the quilt back. Begin by dividing the backing fabric crosswise into two equal lengths. Cut one of the pieces in half lengthwise into two narrow panels. Sew a narrow panel to each side of the full-width panel. Press the seams away from the center.

3. Layer the backing, batting, and quilt top; baste. Quilt as desired.

4. Make approximately 10 yards (360 inches) of straight-grain or bias binding. See page 13 in the "General Instructions" for details on making and attaching binding.

Quilt Diagram

Patterns are finished size.
Add seam allowances when
cutting pieces from fabric.

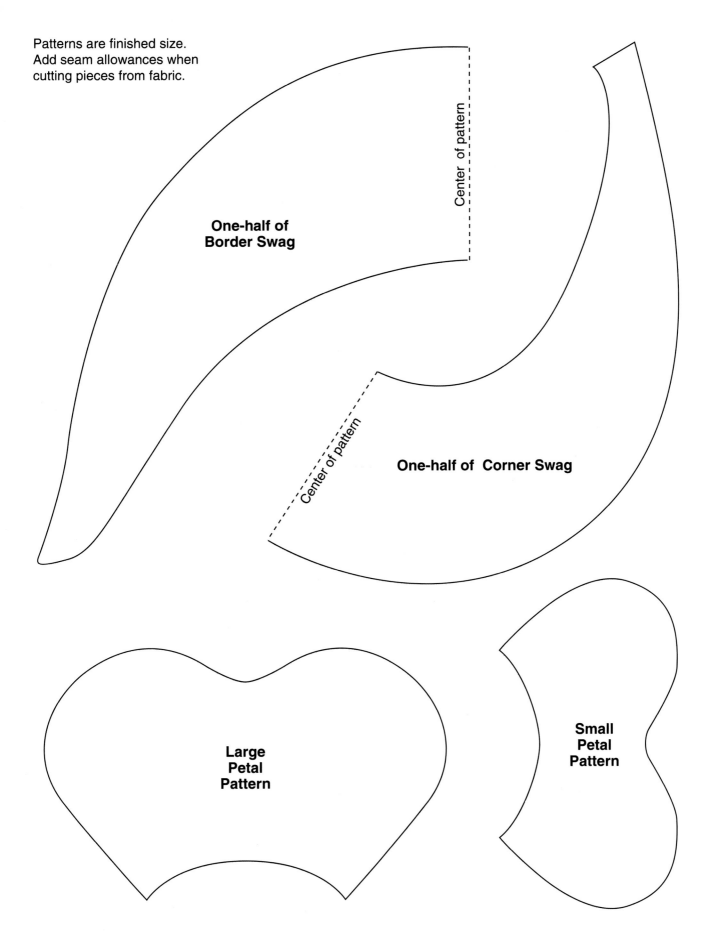

Center of pattern

**One-half of
Border Swag**

Center of pattern

One-half of Corner Swag

**Large
Petal
Pattern**

**Small
Petal
Pattern**

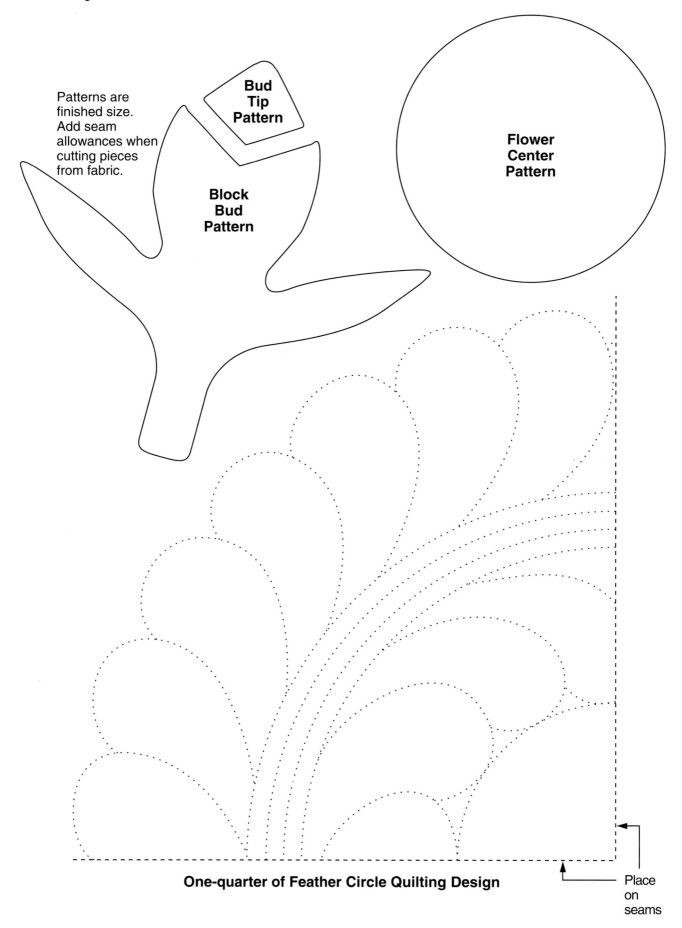

Patterns are finished size. Add seam allowances when cutting pieces from fabric.

Bud Tip Pattern

Block Bud Pattern

Flower Center Pattern

One-quarter of Feather Circle Quilting Design

Place on seams

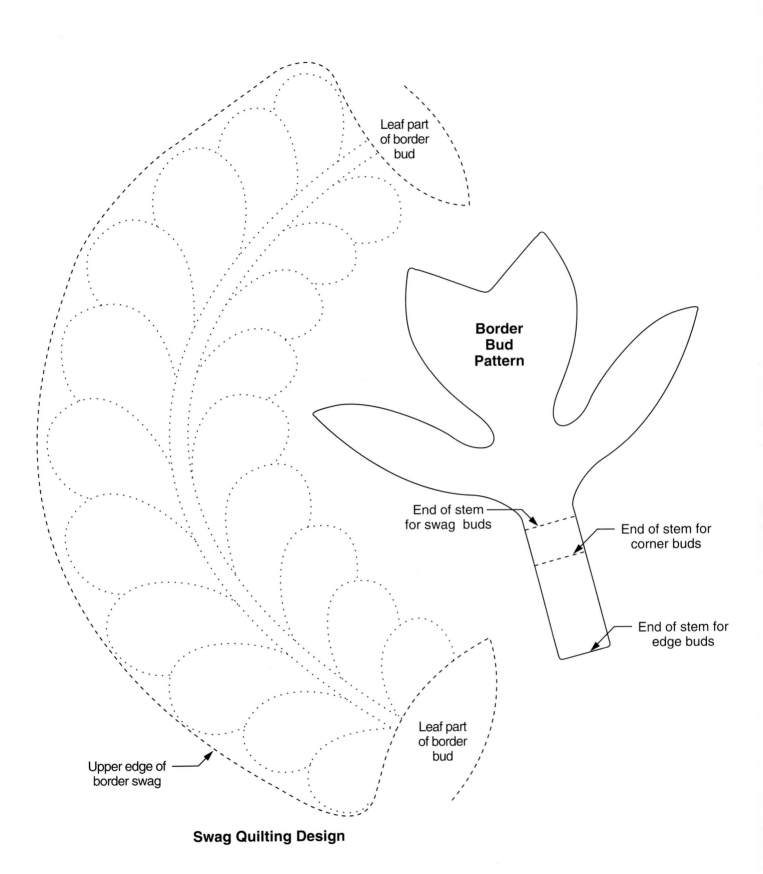

Leaf part
of border
bud

**Border
Bud
Pattern**

End of stem
for swag buds

End of stem for
corner buds

End of stem for
edge buds

Upper edge of
border swag

Leaf part
of border
bud

Swag Quilting Design

Russian Sunflower

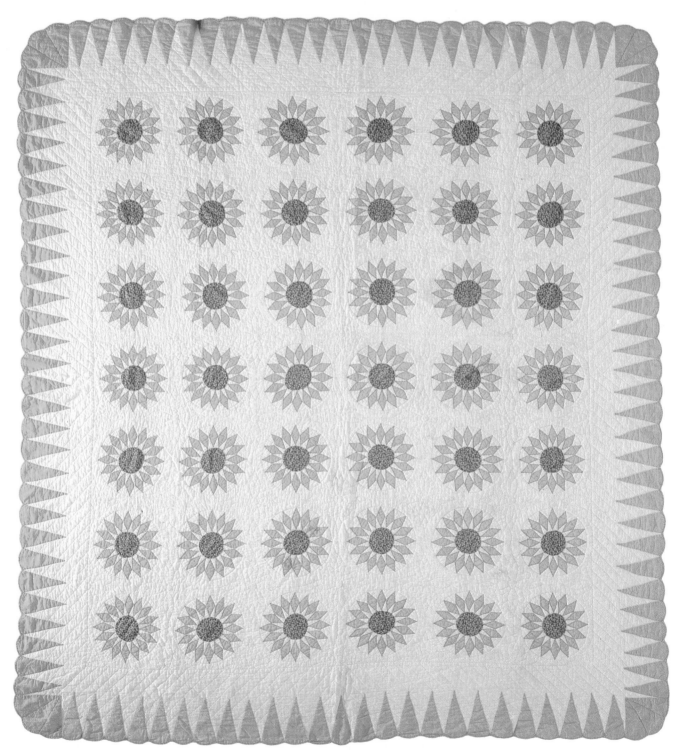

This quilt's sunflowers are as bright as when they took shape almost six decades ago. The pattern was published in the *Kansas City Star* newspaper in 1932, not surprising since the sunflower is the official state flower of Kansas. We have included it in our quilter's garden for the many quilters who take joy in intricate hand piecing. As readers of the *Star* were warned, this is not a pattern for amateurs. Each sunflower block contains 53 pieces, a total of 2,226 in the quilt, not counting the border wedges!

SKILL LEVEL: *Challenging*

SIZE:

Finished quilt is approximately 87½ × 99 inches
Finished block is 11½ inches square

NUMBER OF PIECED BLOCKS: 42

FABRICS AND SUPPLIES

- 11 yards of muslin or white fabric for patchwork and borders
- 5 yards of chrome yellow fabric for patchwork, border wedges, and binding
- 1 yard of brown print fabric for flower centers
- 9 yards of fabric for the quilt back
- Quilt batting, larger than 87 × 98½ inches
- Template plastic
- Rotary cutter, ruler, and mat (optional)

CUTTING

This quilt requires traditional template cutting and precise hand piecing. You may use a rotary cutter to cut the border strips. The measurements given for the borders include seam allowances and extra length. Trim them to size when adding them to the quilt top.

Make templates for patterns A, B, C, D, E, F, and G on pages 148–149. The patterns are finished size. Transfer the quarter-circle divisions on the pattern to your A template.

For patchwork pieces A through E, mark around the templates on the wrong side of the fabric to create a sewing line. Then cut out the pieces, adding seam allowances. Be sure to transfer the quarter-circle divisions onto the A fabric pieces.

For the appliqué pieces (F and G), mark lightly around the templates on the right side of the fabric. Add seam allowances when you cut out the fabric pieces.

From the muslin or off-white fabric, first cut off one 102-inch-long piece. From that piece, cut:
- Four 9¾ × 102-inch borders

From the remaining muslin, cut:
- 672 B pieces
- 672 D pieces
- 168 E pieces

From the chrome yellow fabric, cut:
- 672 C diamonds
- 108 F pieces

■ 4 G pieces
■ Reserve remaining fabric for binding

From the brown print fabric, cut:
■ 42 A circles

MAKING THE BLOCKS

When you join patchwork pieces, stitch on the sewing lines, without stitching into the seam allowances. Finger press as you go.

1. Referring to the **Block Diagram,** lay out the following pieces for one block: 1 A circle, 16 B pieces, 16 C diamonds, 16 D pieces, and 4 E pieces.

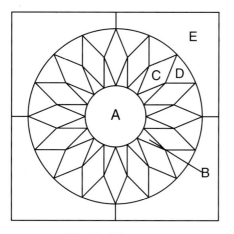

Block Diagram

2. Sew a B piece to one side of a C diamond, as shown in **Diagram 1.** Repeat to make a total of 16 BC units.

Diagram 1

3. Referring to **Diagram 2,** add a D piece to the opposite side of the C diamond. Repeat for each of the 16 BC units.

Diagram 2

4. Join four Step 3 units into a section, as shown in **Diagram 3.** Make four of these sections.

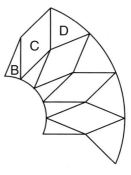

Diagram 3

5. Sew one of the sections to one quadrant of the A circle, as shown in **Diagram 4,** referring to the markings for correct placement.

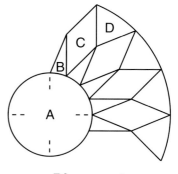

Diagram 4

6. In the same manner, sew the three remaining sections to the A circle; see **Diagram 5.** Join the sections together.

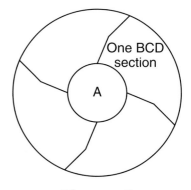

Diagram 5

7. Referring to the **Block Diagram,** sew four E pieces to the completed sunflower. Join the side seams. Press the finished block so that the seams lie neat and flat.

8. Repeat to make a total of 42 blocks.

Assembling the Quilt Top

We made one slight alteration to the borders of the quilt to make it more symmetrical. If you look closely, you'll notice that the quilt in the photo on page 144 has one extra appliquéd wedge in one of the side borders. These instructions are written so that the borders have an equal number of wedges.

1. Lay out the 42 blocks in seven vertical rows with six blocks in each row.

2. Join the blocks into rows, pressing the seam allowances in opposite directions from row to row. Sew the rows together.

3. Prepare the 108 chrome yellow F pieces by folding and basting back the seam allowances on the two straight sides. Leave the seam allowance on the curved edge unbasted. For the top and bottom borders, you will need 25 wedges per border. You will need 29 wedges per border for the two side borders. Prepare the four G corner pieces by folding and basting back the seam allowances on the two straight sides.

4. Press a border strip in half crosswise to create a center guideline. Referring to page 9 in the "General Instructions," measure and mark the four borders for mitered corner seams. Wait to trim off excess border until after you have sewn the borders to the quilt and completed the miter seam.

5. Referring to **Diagram 6,** appliqué the border wedges to the border strips. Start by centering one wedge on the fold at the center of the strip. Place the tips of the wedges 3½ inches away from the inside raw edge of the border strip as shown.

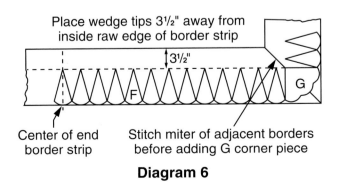

Place wedge tips 3½" away from inside raw edge of border strip

3½"

F

G

Center of end border strip

Stitch miter of adjacent borders before adding G corner piece

Diagram 6

For the end borders, place 12 wedges on each side of the center one. For the side borders, place 14 wedges on each side of the center one.

6. Sew the four borders to the quilt top, mitering the corner seams as described in the "General Instructions" on pages 9–10 and trimming away the excess border fabric at the miter seams. Press the seams toward the borders.

7. Appliqué a prepared G corner piece to each of the four corners.

Quilting and Finishing

1. Mark quilting designs as desired. The quilt shown has outline quilting around the patchwork pieces. A special quilting design for the E pieces is printed on pattern piece E on page 148. The quilt has diagonal quilting lines in the border area and in-the-ditch quilting along the sides of the border wedges.

2. Piece the quilt back. Begin by dividing the backing fabric into three equal lengths. Trim the selvages. Sew two of the lengths together along the long sides. Measure the width of the double panel. From the remaining length, cut off a lengthwise strip wide enough to make a backing that is 6 to 8 inches wider than your quilt top.

3. Layer the backing, batting, and quilt top; baste. Quilt as desired.

4. Wait to trim off excess border, batting, and backing until after the binding has been added. Make approximately 12 yards (432 inches) of 1½-inch-wide single-fold bias binding. Sew the binding to the completed quilt, aligning the raw edge of the bias with the raw edges of the border scallops and corner pieces.

5. Trim the outer edges of the white border fabric even with the scalloped edges.

6. Turn the binding to the back of the quilt and hand finish.

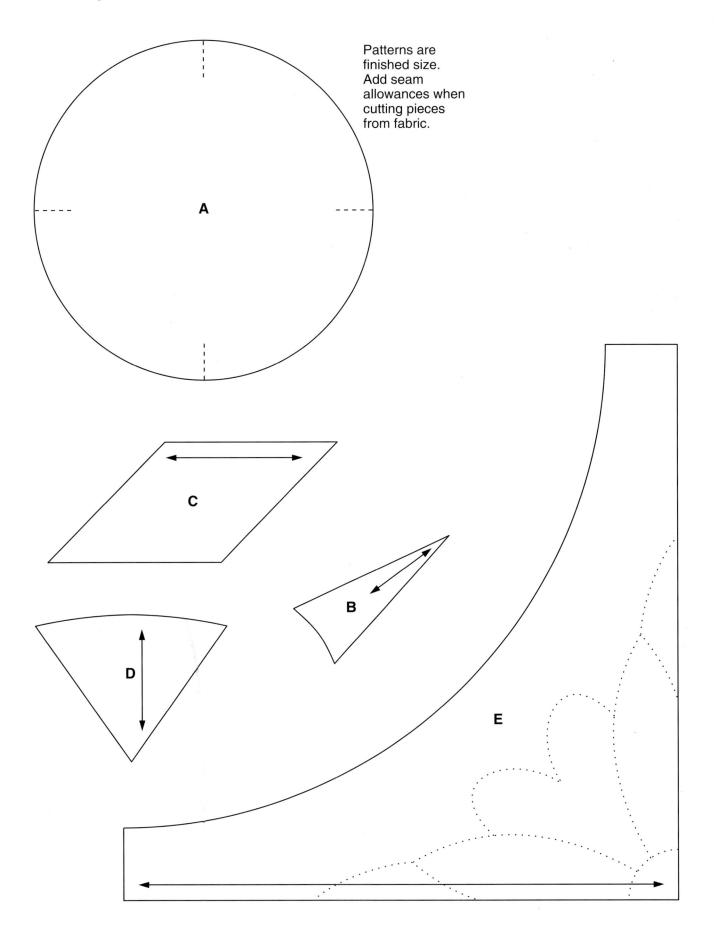

Patterns are
finished size.
Add seam
allowances when
cutting pieces
from fabric.

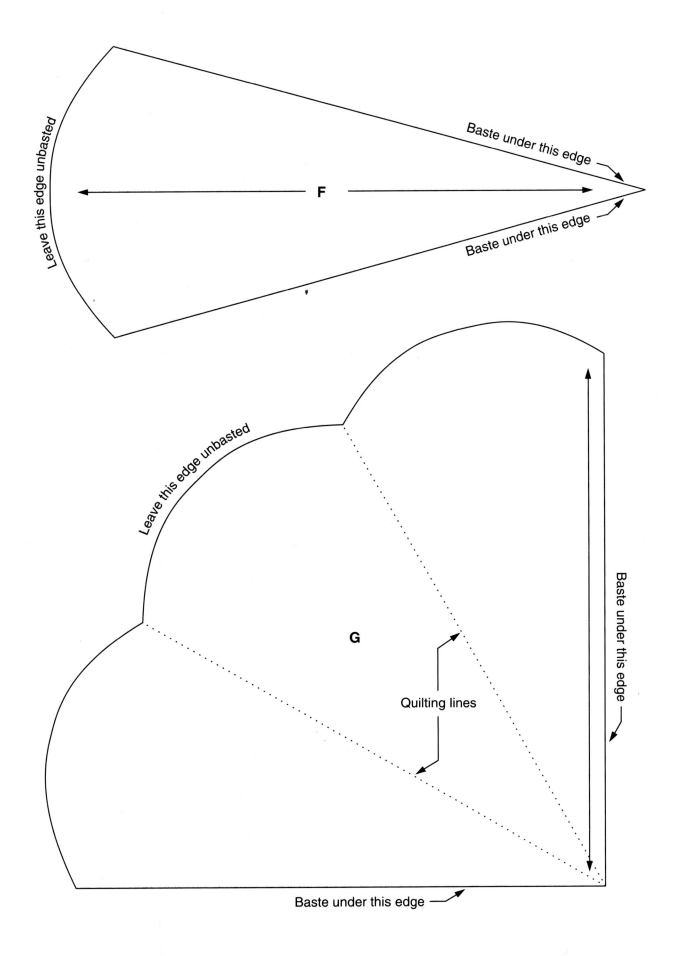

Spring Tulips
Wallhanging

We updated the Spring Tulips pattern by using bright, solid primary colors with contemporary black-and-white prints, and turning the simple block on point, which positions the flowerpots right side up. If you've always had a yen to do a project with an appliqué vine border, here's a fairly painless one, with only 16 flowers and 16 leaves. If you make this quilt, be sure to try the freezer paper appliqué method described on page 126. It's perfect for this pattern's simple shapes.

SKILL LEVEL: *Easy*

SIZE:

Finished quilt is approximately 51 inches square
Finished block is 10½ inches square (approximately 14⅞ inches on the diagonal)

NUMBER OF BLOCKS: 5

FABRICS AND SUPPLIES

Note: For best results, use a ½-inch-wide flat metal or heat-resistant plastic bias bar to prepare the stem strips and the long bias strip for the border vine. Sets of bars in several widths used to prepare strips for Celtic and other appliqué are sold in quilt shops. The stem strips for the Spring Tulips block are cut on the straight of grain, but they are prepared in the same manner as bias strips.

- 1¾ yards of black-and-white woven plaid fabric for background squares and borders
- 1½ yards of red fabric for tulips, sashing, inner borders, and binding
- 1 yard of black fabric for side setting triangles and corner setting triangles
- ¾ yard of green fabric for stems, leaves, and vine
- ½ yard of white-and-black dotted fabric for flowerpots and border squares
- ¼ yard or scraps of blue fabric for tulips

- ¼ yard or scraps of yellow fabric for tulips
- 3⅛ yards of fabric for the quilt back
- Quilt batting, larger than 51 × 51 inches
- Rotary cutter, ruler, and mat
- Plastic-coated freezer paper (optional)
- ½-inch-wide bias bar
- Medium- to wide-tip black permanent marker
- Tracing paper for master patterns. You will need the following size pieces: One 11-inch square, one 6 × 19½-inch strip, and one 6 × 51-inch strip.

CUTTING

The instructions call for rotary cutting the borders, setting pieces, and background squares. Measurements include seam allowances. Cut all strips across the fabric width.

If you use a woven plaid for the block background squares and for the wide outer border, as we did, you may need to cut the fabric with scissors to keep the lines of the plaid as straight as possible.

For the appliqué pieces, make templates for the patterns on page 129. Follow the instructions in "Freezer Paper Appliqué," on page 126, to prepare and cut out the appliqué pieces, or use your favorite appliqué technique.

From the black-and-white plaid fabric, cut:
■ Four 6½-inch-wide outer border strips
■ Five 11-inch background squares

From the red fabric, cut:
■ Four 2-inch-wide inner border strips
■ Four 2-inch-wide sashing strips. From these strips, cut eight 2 × 11-inch strips and two 2 × 14-inch strips.
■ Two 2 × 38-inch strips
■ 5 tulips
■ Reserve the remaining fabric for binding

From the black fabric, cut:
■ 4 side setting triangles
   Quick-cut one 18¼-inch square. Divide the square in half diagonally both ways to produce four triangles.
■ 4 corner setting triangles
   Quick-cut two 10½-inch squares. Divide each square in half diagonally one way to produce four triangles.

From the green fabric, cut:
■ Two 1¼-inch-wide strips for tulip stems
■ One 16½-inch square to make bias strip for vine
■ 13 leaves and 13 reverse leaves

From the white-and-black dotted fabric, cut:
■ Four 6½-inch border squares
   Quick-cut one 6½-inch-wide strip. Cut four squares from the strip.
■ 5 flowerpots

From the blue fabric, cut:
■ 13 tulips

From the yellow fabric, cut:
■ 13 tulips

PREPARING THE STEMS
The stems for the five blocks are made from strips cut on the straight of grain. Each block requires one 6-inch piece and two 4½-inch pieces of prepared straight stem, a total of 75 inches. Using the two 1¼-inch-wide strips, prepare as described, then cut into pieces as needed.

1. Fold the strip in half lengthwise, wrong sides together.

2. Stitch along the aligned raw edges, taking a ⅛-inch seam.

3. Insert a ½-inch-wide bias bar in the fabric tube. Adjust the strip so the seam is centered along one flat side of the bar; press on both sides, pressing the seam allowances in one direction. Work the bar through the tube until the entire strip is pressed flat.

PREPARING THE VINE
Referring to the tips on making bias binding on page 13 in the "General Instructions," make a continuous bias strip from the 16½-inch square of green fabric. Mark and cut the strip 1¼ inches wide. You will need approximately 202 inches of prepared bias vine.

Fold the long strip in half lengthwise, wrong sides together. Stitch along the aligned raw edges as described above for the straight strips, and press with a ½-inch bias bar.

MAKING THE BLOCKS
Make a master pattern as described in the "General Instructions" on page 4. Refer to **Diagram 1** for placement of the appliqués; the placement is the

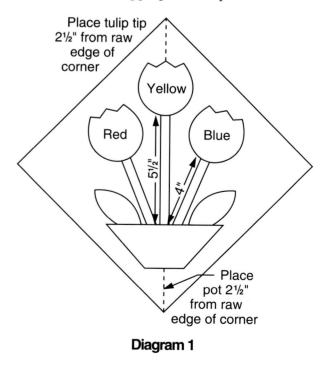

Diagram 1

same as for the antique Spring Tulips quilt pictured on page 124.

1. Prepare one leaf and one reverse leaf, one flowerpot, and three tulips for appliqué.

2. Fold a background square in half diagonally, and lightly crease it to form a placement line.

3. Lay the master pattern under or over the background square. Use a few pins to hold the pattern in place.

4. Position and pin a 6-inch-long center stem and two 4½-inch-long side stems on the background square, using the paper pattern as a guide. Position and pin a leaf and a reverse leaf in place. Remove the

pattern and appliqué the pieces using thread that matches the appliqués.

5. In the same manner, position, pin, and appliqué the tulips and flowerpot in place. Trim the background fabric from behind the appliqués if it shadows through, as described on page 8 in the "General Instructions." Repeat to make five blocks.

ASSEMBLING THE INNER QUILT TOP

1. Referring to the **Quilt Diagram,** lay out the five completed blocks, the sashing pieces, the side setting triangles, and the corner setting triangles. The heavy lines on the diagram indicate the sections for setting the quilt top together.

Quilt Diagram

2. Join the three blocks and the four 11-inch-long sashing strips that make the center diagonal section of the quilt. Press the seams toward the sashing strips. Sew a 38-inch-long sashing strip to the two sides of the three-block strip to complete the center diagonal section. Press the seams toward the sashing.

3. Refer to **Diagram 2** to make the two large corner sections. The numbers on the diagram show the order in which to add the pieces. Begin by adding an 11-inch-long sashing strip to the top left and bottom right sides of the two remaining blocks (2). Add a 14-inch-long sashing strip to the top right side of one of the blocks, and to the bottom left side of the second block (3). Press the seams toward the sashing.

Sew side setting triangles to opposite sides of the sashed blocks (4). Press the seams toward the sashing. Sew a corner setting triangle to the remaining sashed side of each block to complete each corner section (5). Press the seams toward the sashing.

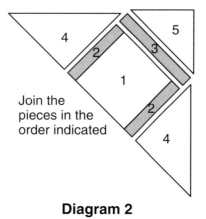

Diagram 2

4. Referring to the **Quilt Diagram,** join the two corner sections to the center section. Add the two remaining corner triangles to opposite ends of the center diagonal section to complete the inner quilt top. Press the seams toward the sashing.

5. Measure the length of the quilt from raw edge to raw edge, measuring through the center (approximately 36¾ inches). Cut two of the red border strips to this length. Sew the strips to the two opposite sides of the quilt top. Press the seams toward the border strips.

6. Measure the width of the quilt from raw edge to raw edge, measuring through the center (approximately 39¾ inches). Cut the remaining two red bor-

der strips to this length. Sew the strips to the top and bottom of the quilt. Press seams toward the borders.

7. Trim the four black-and-white border strips to the size of the quilt including seam allowances (approximately 39¾ inches). Sew two borders to two opposite sides of the quilt. Press the seams toward the borders.

8. Sew two corner squares to the two opposite ends of the two remaining border strips. Press the seams toward the border strips. Sew the two border strips with corner squares to the remaining two opposite sides of the quilt.

MAKING THE MASTER PATTERN FOR THE FLORAL VINE

1. To make the pattern for the vine repeat, fold the 6 × 19½-inch strip of tracing paper into quarters, as shown in **Diagram 3.**

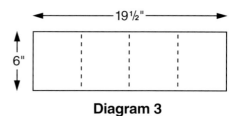

Diagram 3

2. Trace the repeat curve pattern on page 157 onto the A section of the paper strip, as shown in **Diagram 4.**

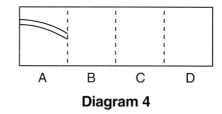

Diagram 4

3. Rotate the paper strip 180 degrees, and trace the curve onto the B section of the paper strip, as shown in **Diagram 5.**

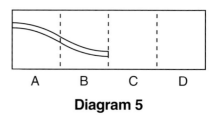

Diagram 5

4. Fold the paper strip in half, with the penciled surface facing *out,* and trace the mirror image of the curve onto the C and D sections of the strip, as shown in **Diagram 6.** The completed pattern should look like the one shown in **Diagram 7.**

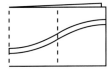

Diagram 6

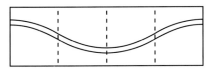

Diagram 7

5. Fold the 6 × 51-inch strip of tracing paper in half crosswise. Referring to **Diagram 8,** fold in a 6-inch segment on each end to form the corners of the repeat.

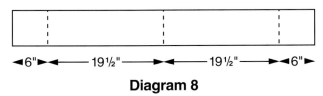

◄6"►◄——— 19½" ———►◄——— 19½" ———►◄6"►

Diagram 8

6. Trace the completed vine repeat pattern onto the two long segments of the paper strip. Trace the corner curve pattern from page 156 onto the corners, as shown in **Diagram 9.**

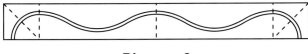

Diagram 9

7. Use the tulip and leaf templates to trace outlines for the appliqués onto the master pattern, as shown in **Diagram 10.** Darken all the outlines with permanent marker.

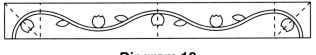

Diagram 10

ADDING THE FLORAL VINE

1. Pin the master pattern to one of the four sides of the quilt top. Line up the bias vine with the master pattern and baste it to the border. You may want to cut the paper pattern apart along the edge that is toward the inner quilt, and then pin the pattern to the borders in turn, using the cut edge to help you position and baste the vine in place. Remove and repin the paper pattern on each side of the quilt in order to position and baste the vine.

2. Where the two ends of the vine meet, trim off excess vine at a 45 degree angle, allowing ¼ inch on each end to sew the ends together and to make a smooth connection. You will need to remove some of the stitching on the ⅛-inch seam that forms the bias tube so that the strip ends can be opened out. Place the opened-out ends right sides together and stitch, taking a ¼-inch seam; press seam open. Fold the joined section in half and resew the ⅛-inch seam across that section. Position the joined section properly on the border and complete the basting.

3. Use the paper pattern to help position and pin the border leaves and tulips in place.

4. Using matching threads, appliqué the vine, leaves, and tulips to the borders. If the background fabric shadows through any of the appliqués, trim it away before layering the quilt.

QUILTING AND FINISHING

1. Mark quilting designs as desired. The quilt shown has outline quilting in the ditch next to all the appliqués and radiating straight lines in the black setting pieces.

2. Piece the quilt back. Begin by dividing the backing fabric crosswise into two equal lengths. Cut a 16-inch-wide panel from one of the two lengths. Sew the narrow panel to one side of the full-width panel to complete the quilt backing.

3. Layer the backing, batting, and quilt top; baste. Quilt as desired.

4. Use the remaining red fabric to make approximately 6 yards (216 inches) of straight grain or bias binding. See page 13 in the "General Instructions" for details on making and attaching binding. See page 15 for tips on making hanging sleeves for wallhangings.

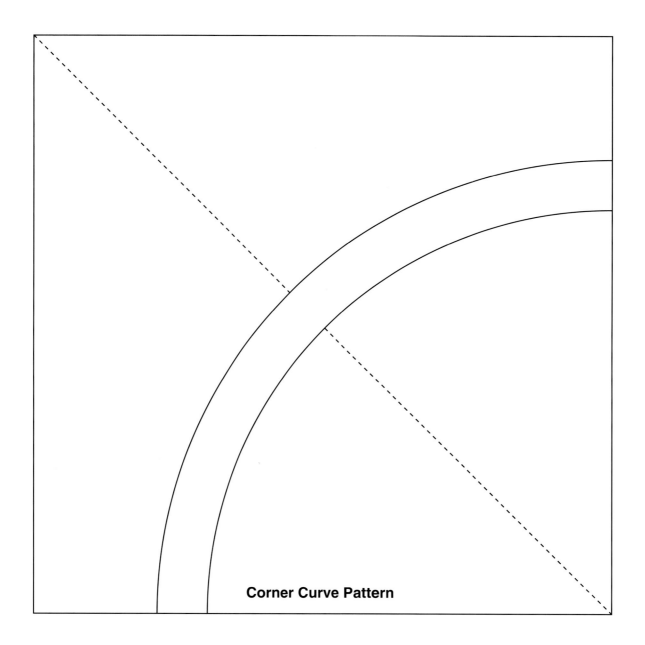

Corner Curve Pattern

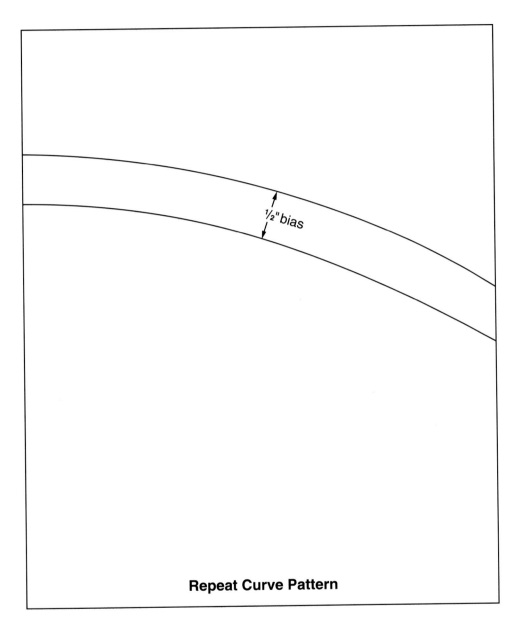

½"bias

Repeat Curve Pattern

Super
Scrap
Quilts

The vast majority of quilts from the past are scrap quilts, and it's that practice of making quilts from small pieces of cloth left over from other sewing that has given quiltmakers their unbeatable reputation as frugal recyclers. We'll never know whether, given the choice of plenty of yardage, a nineteenth-century quilter would have stuck to quilts combining only a few fabrics. Today's quilters buy their scraps at quilt shops and revel in the pleasure of combining dozens upon dozens of prints in a single quilt, trying, often with success, to capture the spontaneity of yesteryear.

The old quilts in this chapter are virtual albums of printed fabrics. The instructions for each quilt give the option of traditional, template-style cutting or modernized, quick, rotary-cutting methods. The Heartland Schoolhouse Medallion, one of our all-time favorite quilts, was a star attraction during an Iowa quilt exhibit in 1990. Our new project, Katie's Grand Graduation Quilt, was inspired by the antique Grand Right and Left.

Diamond
Four Patch

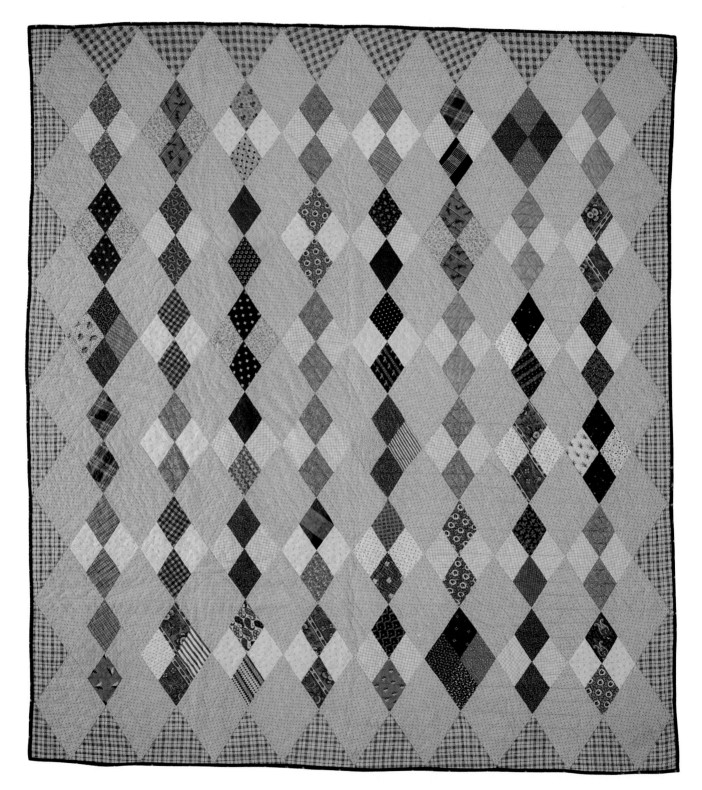

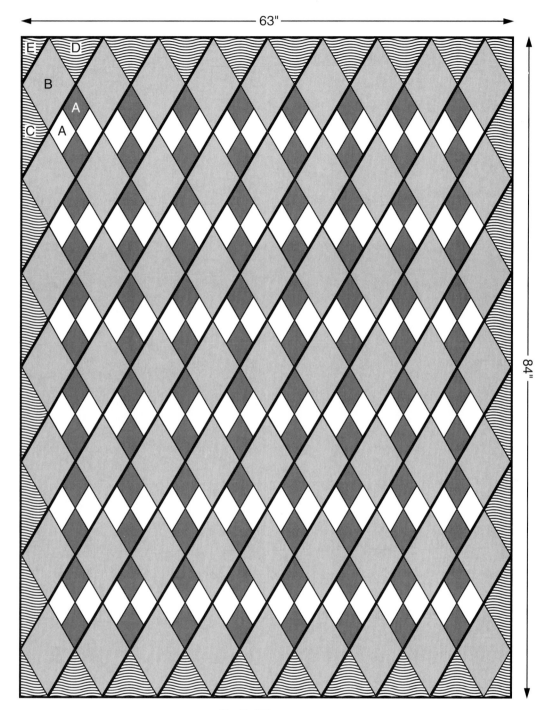

Quilt Diagram

QUILTING AND FINISHING

1. Mark quilting designs as desired. The quilt shown has parallel straight lines running horizontally across it.

2. Divide the backing fabric crosswise into two equal lengths. Cut one piece in half lengthwise. Trim the selvages, and stitch a half panel to each long side of the full-width panel. Press the seam allowances away from the center panel.

3. Layer the quilt back, batting, and quilt top; baste. Quilt as desired.

4. Make approximately 9 yards (324 inches) of either bias or straight-grain binding. Sew the binding to the quilt. See page 13 in the "General Instructions" for details on making and attaching binding.

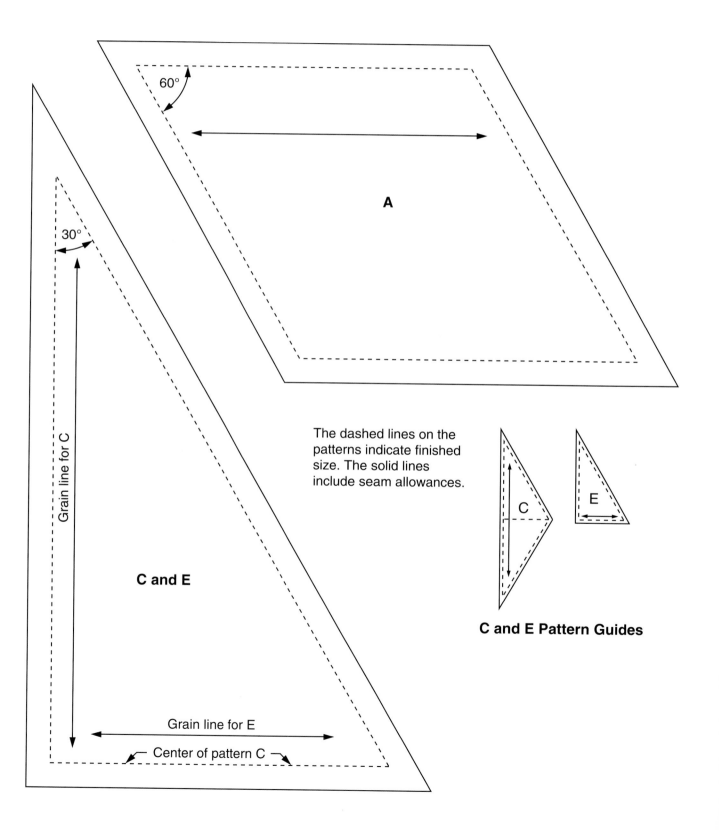

60°

A

30°

Grain line for C

C and E

The dashed lines on the patterns indicate finished size. The solid lines include seam allowances.

C

E

C and E Pattern Guides

Grain line for E

Center of pattern C

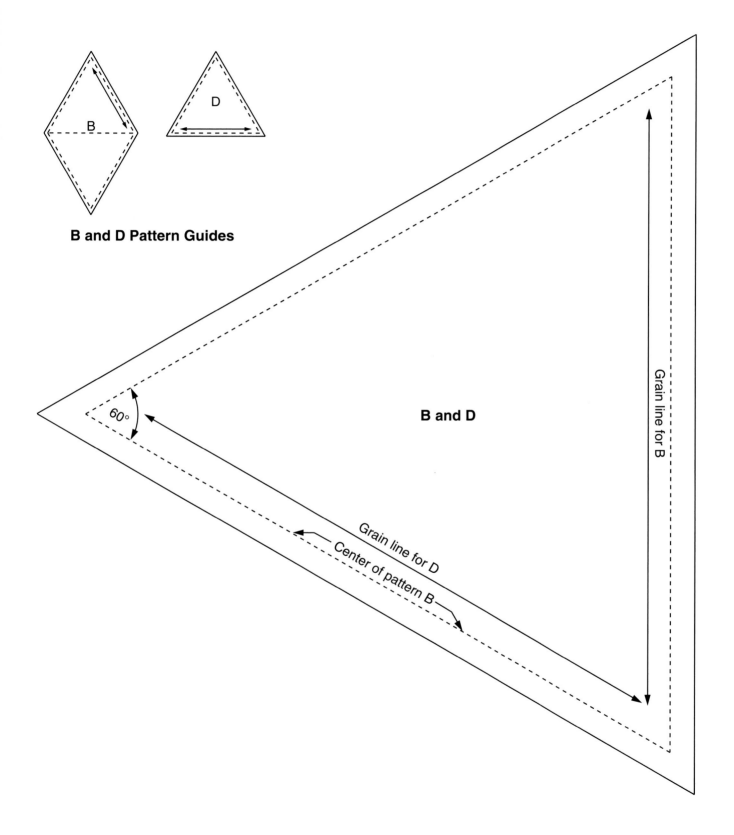

B and D Pattern Guides

B

D

60°

B and D

Grain line for B

Grain line for D

Center of pattern B

Grand Right and Left

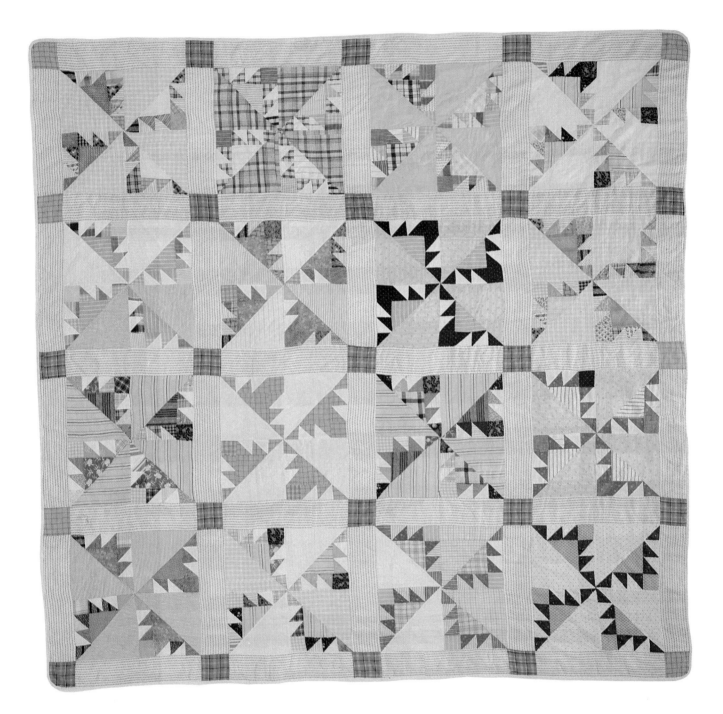

his humble scrap quilt contains a collection of fabrics used for everyday clothing at the turn of the century. The many light fabrics may have begun their lives as men's shirts, pajamas, or underwear, and the darker fabrics as ladies' aprons or housedresses. The maker of the quilt blocks made do with what she had available. Although the blocks are all the same basic construction, they are not shaded consistently. The placement of light, medium, and dark fabrics varies from block to block, giving the quilt individual character. In contrast to the block fabrics, the orange plaid fabric in the sashing squares is more typical of quilts made during the Depression. This combination of fabrics from the late 1800s and the 1930s makes it easy to imagine that some quiltmaker discovered a stack of these old blocks, left unjoined by the original quiltmaker, and stitched them into a quilt.

SKILL LEVEL: *Easy*

SIZE:

Finished quilt is approximately 84 inches square
Finished block is 16 inches square

NUMBER OF PIECED BLOCKS:

16 blocks made of 4 sections each

FABRICS AND SUPPLIES

The amounts of fabric listed are generous to allow you freedom to arrange the light, medium, and dark fabrics in a variety of ways within the blocks, just as in the quilt shown.

- 3¾ yards total of assorted light print, striped, and plaid fabrics (white, tan, lavender, light blue, and pale pink)
- 3 yards of white shirting fabric with narrow black stripes for the sashing strips
- 2¼ yards total of assorted medium and dark print,

striped, or plaid fabrics (red, pink, brown, black, and medium and dark blue)
- ¾ yard of orange plaid fabric for the sashing squares
- 8¼ yards of fabric for the quilt back
- Batting, larger than 84 inches square
- Rotary cutter, ruler, and mat
- Template plastic (optional)

CUTTING

The placement of light, medium, and dark fabrics is very random from block to block in the antique quilt shown. **Diagram 1** shows three examples of the fabric value placements found in the blocks on the old quilt. The one constant in almost all blocks is that light fabrics were used consistently for the large D triangles and for the small A triangles on the outer edges of the four sections of the blocks.

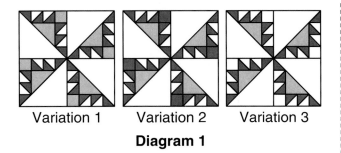

Variation 1   Variation 2   Variation 3

Diagram 1

If you wish to cut the pieces using traditional methods, make templates for patterns A, B, and C on page 171. You will also need to make a template for D; it is a right triangle with 8-inch legs. To include seam allowances on the template, draw the triangle with 8⅞-inch legs. Cut the D triangles with the legs on the straight of grain. If you prefer to quick-cut the pieces, follow the instructions below.

Each block is made up of four sections. **Diagram 2** shows one section with the pieces labeled. Refer to the diagram when cutting the pieces for the 16 blocks. For each block you will need: 16 light A triangles, 24 medium or dark A triangles, 4 light, medium, or dark B squares, 4 medium or dark C triangles, and 4 light D triangles.

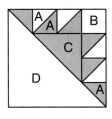

Diagram 2

From the assorted light fabrics, cut:

- 256 A triangles
  Quick-cut 2⅞-inch squares; you will need 128 squares. Cut each square in half diagonally to make two triangles.
- B squares
  Quick-cut 2½-inch squares. You will need a total of 64 B squares. The number you cut from light fabrics will depend on how you arrange the light, medium, and dark fabrics in the blocks.
- 64 D triangles
  Quick-cut 8⅞-inch squares; you will need 32 squares. Cut each square in half diagonally to make two triangles.

From the white fabric with black stripes, cut:

- 40 sashing strips with the stripes running parallel to the long sides
  Quick-cut five 16½-inch-wide strips across the fabric width. Cut the strips into 4½ × 16½-inch rectangles.

From the assorted medium and dark fabrics, cut:

- 384 A triangles
  Quick-cut 2⅞-inch squares; you will need 192 squares. Cut each square in half diagonally to make two triangles.
- B squares
  Quick-cut 2½-inch squares. You will need a total of 64 B squares. The number you cut from medium and dark fabrics will depend on how you arrange the light, medium, and dark fabrics in the blocks.
- 64 C triangles
  Quick-cut 4⅞-inch squares; you will need 32 squares. Cut each square diagonally to make two triangles.

From the orange plaid fabric, cut:

- 25 sashing squares
  Quick-cut three 4½-inch-wide strips across the fabric width. Cut 4½-inch squares from the strips.

MAKING THE BLOCKS

Each Grand Right and Left block is made up of four sections that are joined, as shown in **Diagram 3.** Begin by making the 64 sections; then, join them into 16 blocks.

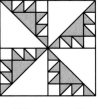

Diagram 3

1. Referring to **Diagram 2,** lay out the following pieces for one section: four light A triangles, six medium or dark A triangles, one light, medium, or

dark B square, one medium or dark C triangle, and one light D triangle.

2. Make four triangle-square units by joining light A triangles with either medium or dark A triangles to form squares. Press the seam allowances toward the darker triangles.

3. Referring to **Diagram 4,** sew pairs of triangle-squares into two strips. Add an A triangle to one end of each strip as shown. Press the seam allowances toward the darker pieces.

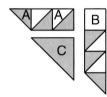

Diagram 4

4. Sew a strip of triangles to one side of a C triangle. Press the seam toward the C triangle.

5. Sew a B square to the end of the second strip of triangles as shown in the diagram. Press the seam allowance toward the square. Sew the strip to the adjacent side of the C triangle. Press the seam allowance toward the C triangle.

6. To complete the section, sew the Step 5 unit to a D triangle as shown in **Diagram 5.** Press the seam allowance toward the D triangle.

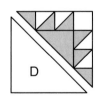

Diagram 5

7. When you have made all the sections, join them into blocks as shown in **Diagram 6.**

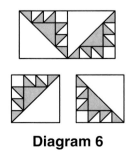

Diagram 6

ASSEMBLING THE QUILT TOP

1. Referring to the **Quilt Diagram** on page 170, lay out the blocks, sashing strips, and sashing squares. Sew the blocks and sashing strips together in four horizontal rows with four blocks and five strips in each row. Press the seam allowances toward the sashing strips.

2. Make five horizontal sashing rows with five sashing squares and four sashing strips in each row. Press the seam allowances toward the squares.

3. Join the rows, alternating sashing rows with block rows. Press the seams toward the sashing rows.

QUILTING AND FINISHING

1. Mark quilting designs as desired. The quilt shown was quilted with diagonal lines spaced approximately 2 inches apart.

2. To piece the quilt back, divide the backing fabric crosswise into three equal lengths. Trim the selvages and join two of the lengths. Measure the two-panel backing to see how wide it is. Cut a strip from the remaining panel wide enough to make the backing 99 inches wide. Use the remaining fabric from the third panel for binding if you choose to finish your quilt in this manner.

3. Layer the quilt back, batting, and quilt top; baste. Quilt as desired.

4. The antique quilt was finished by turning the back over to the front. If you wish to finish your quilt in this manner, trim the excess batting even with the quilt top. Trim the excess quilt back so that the back is 1 inch larger than the quilt top on all sides. Turn in ½ inch on all sides of the quilt back. Bring the folded edge over to the front of the quilt and blindstitch in place.

If you prefer to finish the edges of your quilt with separate binding, make approximately 8 yards (288 inches) of bias or straight-grain binding and sew it to the quilt. See page 13 in the "General Instructions" for details on making and attaching binding.

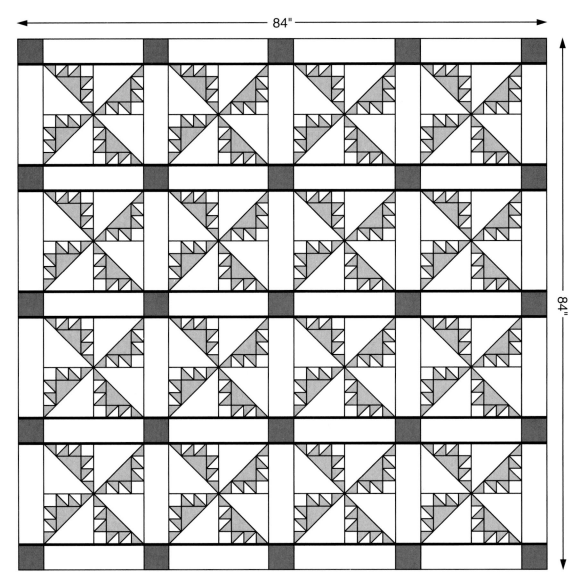

Quilt Diagram

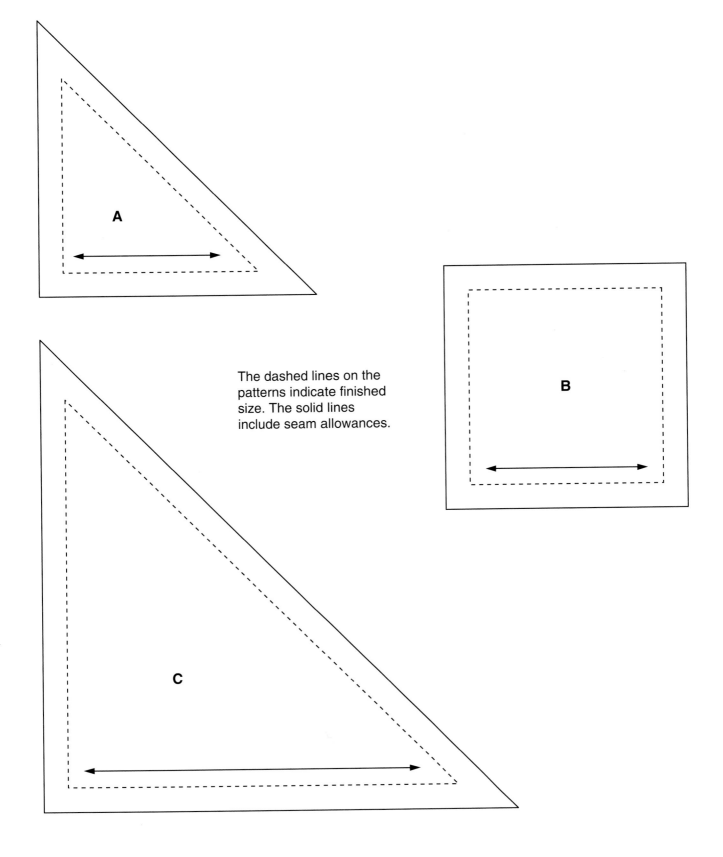

The dashed lines on the patterns indicate finished size. The solid lines include seam allowances.

· Churn Dash ·

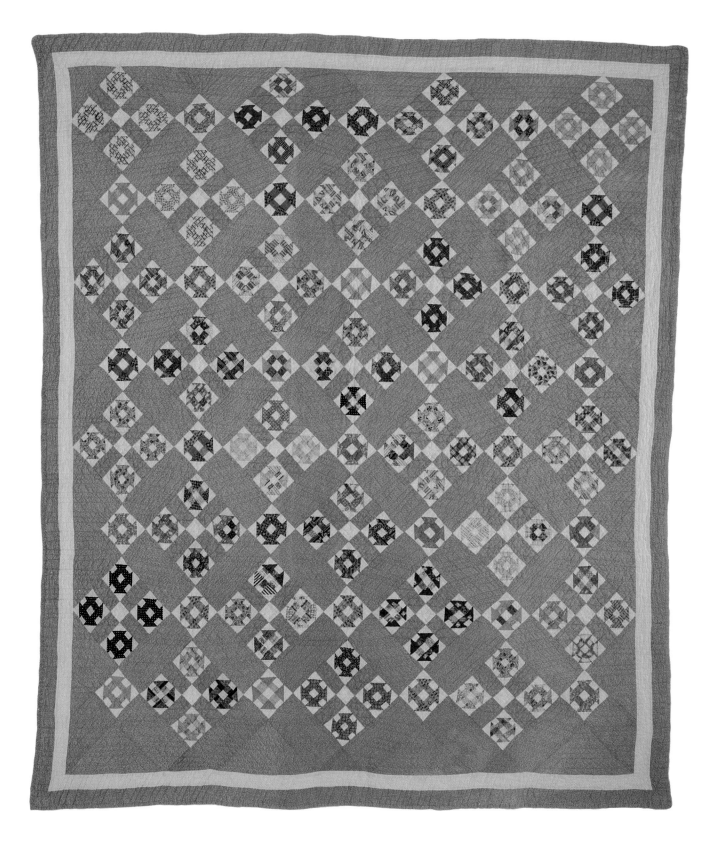

Because pink printed fabrics were plentiful, inexpensive, and relatively colorfast, pink became a popular color scheme for quilts during the late 1800s and early 1900s. Quilters have given many names to these distinctive "pink-on-pink" print fabrics, including double pink, bubblegum, seaweed, Pepto-Bismol, and strawberry. One of the more interesting names is Merrimack pink, named after the textile mills along the Merrimack River in New England that printed thousands of variations for many years. In this very pink quilt, what at first appears to be a single block turns out to be two: the Tiny Churn Dash blocks and the Hole in the Barn Door blocks, which are almost identical. Only the sizes of some of the pieces are different.

SKILL LEVEL: *Easy*

SIZE:

Finished quilt is approximately 70¼ × 87 inches

Finished Quadruple Churn Dash block is 8¼ inches square (approximately 11⅝ inches on the diagonal)

Finished Tiny Churn Dash block is 3¼ inches square

Finished Hole in the Barn Door sashing block is 3¾ inches square

NUMBER OF PIECED BLOCKS:

32 Quadruple Churn Dash blocks

31 Hole in the Barn Door sashing blocks

FABRICS AND SUPPLIES

You'll need to study **Diagram 5** on page 177 to understand this quilt's construction, which is hidden by the abundance of double pink. Four Tiny Churn Dash blocks (**Diagram 2** on page 175) are joined with pink strips and a muslin center square to form a larger Quadruple Churn Dash block (**Diagram 3** on page 175). The blocks are set on point with wide pink sashing strips broken up by small Hole in the Barn Door sashing blocks (**Diagram 4** on page 175).

The two small blocks, the Tiny Churn Dash block and the Hole in the Barn Door block, are so similar you may not notice the differences at first. Basically, the four triangle-squares are the same size in both blocks, while the center piece and the connecting squares and rectangles are different sizes.

Also, if you compare the photo of the quilt on the opposite page with the **Quilt Diagram** on page 176, you'll notice that we've added a row of blocks at the bottom of the quilt to make the quilt symmetrical and easier to piece.

■ 6¼ yards of pink print fabric for patchwork, sashing strips, setting triangles, outer border, and binding

■ Approximately 4 yards total of assorted medium and dark print fabrics (brown, tan, rust, medium blue, navy blue, and gray) for patchwork. A 6-inch-square fabric scrap is large enough to cut the pieces for one Tiny Churn Dash or Hole in the Barn Door block.

■ 3½ yards of muslin or white fabric for patchwork and inner border

■ 5½ yards of fabric for the quilt back

- Batting, larger than 70¼ × 87 inches
- Rotary cutter, ruler, and mat
- Template plastic (optional)

CUTTING

The patchwork pieces can be cut using traditional template methods or by following the quick-cutting instructions below. For traditional piecing, make templates for patterns A, B, C, D, E, F, G, and H on page 178.

Cut all strips across the fabric width unless instructed otherwise. Measurements include ¼-inch seam allowances. Borders are cut longer than needed; trim them to length before adding them to the quilt top.

All the medium or dark pieces for a single Tiny Churn Dash block or Hole in the Barn Door block can be cut from a 6-inch square. **Diagram 1** shows the most efficient way to cut the pieces.

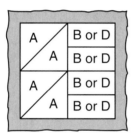

Diagram 1
Cutting Guide

From the pink print fabric, cut:
- Nine 2½-inch-wide border strips
- 128 G rectangles
  Quick-cut eight 3¾-inch-wide strips. Cut the strips into 2¼ × 3¾-inch rectangles.
- 62 sashing strips
  Quick-cut sixteen 4¼-inch-wide strips. Cut the strips into 4¼ × 8¾-inch rectangles.
- 14 side setting triangles
  Quick-cut four 18¼-inch squares. Cut each square diagonally both ways to make four side triangles. You will have two extra triangles.
- 4 corner setting triangles
  Quick-cut two 6¾-inch squares. Cut each square in half diagonally to make two corner triangles.
- Reserve the remaining fabric for binding

From the medium and dark fabric scraps, cut:
- 636 A triangles
  Quick-cut three hundred eighteen 2⅛-inch squares. Cut each square in half diagonally to make two triangles. You will need four triangles for each small block.
- 512 B squares
  Quick-cut 1¼-inch squares. You will need four for each Tiny Churn Dash block.
- 124 D rectangles
  Quick-cut 1¼ × 1¾-inch rectangles. You will need four for each Hole in the Barn Door block.

From the muslin or white fabric, cut:
- Nine 2½-inch-wide border strips
- 636 A triangles
  Quick-cut seventeen 2⅛-inch-wide strips. Cut the strips into 2⅛-inch squares. You will need 318 squares. Cut each square in half diagonally to make two triangles.
- 128 B squares
  Quick-cut four 1¼-inch-wide strips. Cut the strips into 1¼-inch squares.
- 512 C rectangles
  Quick-cut sixteen 1-inch-wide strips. Cut the strips into 1 × 1¼-inch rectangles.
- 124 E rectangles
  Quick-cut six 1-inch-wide strips. Cut the strips into 1 × 1¾-inch rectangles.
- 31 F squares
  Quick-cut two 1¾-inch-wide strips. Cut the strips into 1¾-inch squares.
- 32 H squares
  Quick-cut two 2¼-inch-wide strips. Cut the strips into 2¼-inch squares.

MAKING A TINY CHURN DASH BLOCK

1. Referring to **Diagram 2,** lay out the following pieces for one block: four muslin and four medium or dark A triangles, one muslin and four medium or dark B squares, and four muslin C rectangles. The medium or dark pieces for one block can be all the same fabric or a combination of fabrics.

2. Make four triangle-squares by sewing a dark A triangle to a muslin A triangle. Press the seam allowances toward the dark triangles.

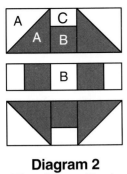

Diagram 2
Tiny Churn Dash
Block Assembly

3. Sew a muslin C rectangle to each dark B square. Press the seams toward the B squares.

4. Referring to **Diagram 2,** join the pieces into three rows. Join the rows to complete the block. The block should measure 3¾ inches, including seam allowances.

5. Repeat to make a total of 128 blocks.

MAKING THE QUADRUPLE CHURN DASH BLOCKS

1. Lay out four Tiny Churn Dash blocks, four pink G rectangles, and one muslin H square, as shown in **Diagram 3.**

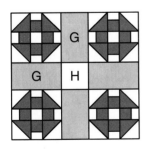

Diagram 3
Quadruple Churn Dash
Block Assembly

2. Piece the block in three rows. To piece the first and third rows, stitch a Tiny Churn Dash block to each long side of a G rectangle. Press the seams toward the G rectangles.

3. To make the middle row, sew the short side of a G rectangle to opposite sides of the H square. Press the seams toward the G rectangles.

4. Join the three rows. Press the seams toward the middle row. The completed block should measure 8¾ inches square, including seam allowances.

5. Repeat to make a total of 32 blocks.

MAKING THE HOLE IN THE BARN DOOR SASHING BLOCKS

1. Referring to **Diagram 4,** lay out the following pieces for one block: four muslin and four medium or dark A triangles, four medium or dark D rectangles, four muslin E rectangles, and one muslin F square. The dark pieces for one block can be all the same fabric or a combination of fabrics.

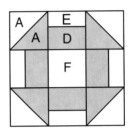

Diagram 4
Hole in the Barn Door
Block Assembly

2. Make four triangle-squares by sewing a dark A triangle to a muslin A triangle. Press the seam allowances toward the dark triangles.

3. Sew a muslin E rectangle to each dark D rectangle. Press the seams toward the D rectangles.

4. Sew the pieces together in three rows as shown. Join the rows. The block should measure 4¼ inches, including seam allowances.

5. Repeat to make a total of 31 blocks.

ASSEMBLING THE QUILT TOP

Note: Assembling this quilt top is somewhat tricky, so read through all of the instructions in this section and study **Diagrams 5, 6, 7,** and **8** on page 177 and the **Quilt Diagram** on page 176 before beginning. As you join the pieces, press the seam allowances toward the sashing strips.

1. Referring to the **Quilt Diagram,** lay out the Quadruple Churn Dash blocks, sashing strips, Hole in the Barn Door sashing blocks, and side setting triangles in a pleasing arrangement. You will not need the corner setting triangles at this time.

2. Study **Diagram 5,** which shows the five main sections you will make to assemble the quilt top. The heavy lines on the diagram designate the diagonal rows. Follow the directions to make each section, then join the sections.

3. Rows 1 and 9 are identical. To make a row, sew 4¼ × 8¾-inch pink sashing strips to opposite sides

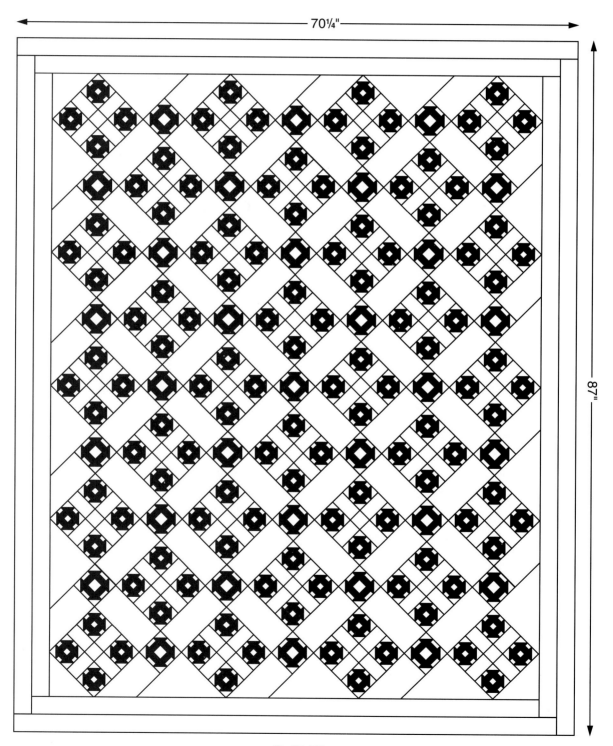

Quilt Diagram

of a block (see **Diagram 6**). Sew Hole in the Barn Door sashing blocks to the ends of a sashing strip. Sew this strip to the bottom of the block.

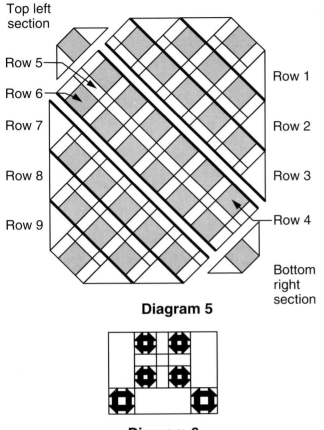

Diagram 5

Top left section

Row 5
Row 6
Row 7
Row 8
Row 9

Row 1
Row 2
Row 3
Row 4

Bottom right section

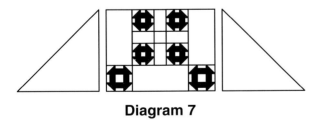

Diagram 6

4. Sew side setting triangles to the sides of the sashed block (see **Diagram 7**). Make two rows.

Diagram 7

5. Rows 2 and 8 are identical. Referring to **Diagram 5,** join three blocks and four sashing strips into a row. Sew four sashing squares and three sashing strips together; add to the bottom of the three-block row. Add side setting triangles to the ends.

6. Rows 3 and 7 are identical. Join five blocks and six sashing strips into a row. Make a sashing row by sewing together six sashing squares and five sashing strips; add to the row of blocks. Referring to **Diagram 5,** add a side setting triangle to the lower right end of Row 3 and the top left end of Row 7.

7. Rows 4 and 6 are identical. To make each row, join six blocks and seven sashing strips.

8. To make Row 5, join seven sashing squares and six sashing strips.

9. Join Rows 1, 2, and 3 to form the top right section of the quilt. Join Rows 7, 8, and 9 to form the lower left section of the quilt.

10. Sew Rows 4, 5, and 6 together to make the center section of the quilt.

11. Join the three main sections of the quilt by sewing Row 3 to Row 4 and Row 6 to Row 7.

12. The top left and bottom right sections of the quilt are identical. To make one section, sew a setting triangle to opposite sides of a block, as shown in **Diagram 5**. Trim excess triangle points even with the block. Repeat to make a second section. Sew the sections to the quilt top.

13. Press the quilt top well. Trim off excess sashing strips and setting triangles before adding the corner setting triangles and the borders. Referring to **Diagram 8,** use a rotary cutter and ruler to trim off the excess so that a ¼-inch seam allowance extends beyond the corners of the Quadruple Churn Dash blocks.

14. Sew a corner setting triangle to each corner of the quilt top.

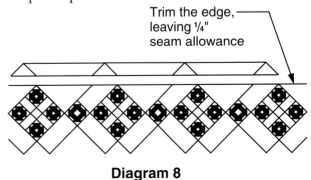

Trim the edge, leaving ¼" seam allowance

Diagram 8

15. Piece four muslin borders by joining pairs of 2½-inch-wide muslin border strips with diagonal seams. For the side borders, cut the remaining muslin strip in half, and sew one half each to two of the pieced borders. Repeat to make four pink borders.

16. Measure the length of the quilt top from raw edge to raw edge. Trim two muslin borders to this length (approximately 79½ inches). If necessary, cut segments from the extra strip and add them to the long strips to get the needed length. Sew the borders to the sides of the quilt top as shown in the **Quilt Diagram.** Press the seams toward the borders.

17. Measure the width of the quilt top, including the side borders. Trim the remaining two muslin borders to this length (approximately 66¾ inches). Sew the borders to the top and bottom of the quilt top. Press the seams toward the borders.

18. In a similar manner, add the pink borders to the quilt. Press the seams toward the pink borders.

QUILTING AND FINISHING

1. Mark quilting designs as desired. The quilt shown is quilted in parallel diagonal lines.

2. Divide the quilt back fabric crosswise into two equal pieces. Cut one piece in half lengthwise. Trim the selvages, and sew a half panel to each side of the full-width panel. Press the seam allowances away from the center panel.

3. Layer the quilt back, batting, and quilt top; baste. Quilt as desired.

4. From the reserved binding fabric, make approximately 9 yards (324 inches) of bias or straight-grain binding. See page 13 in the "General Instructions" for details on making and attaching binding.

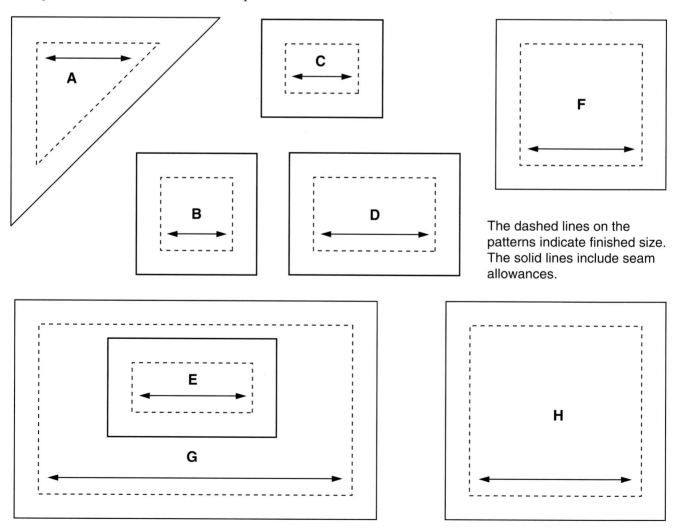

The dashed lines on the patterns indicate finished size. The solid lines include seam allowances.

Heartland Schoolhouse Medallion

This humble, yet powerful, folk art masterpiece epitomizes pre-1900 quiltmaking in America's great Midwest, where ordinary people made do with their scraps of color and, in making do, created a legacy of simple yet singular beauty. In this quilt, the classic one-room schoolhouse stands proudly in the middle of patchwork fabric farmlands. The varied colors of the pieced borders resemble the dormant corn and soybean fields of early spring, dotted with graying patches of leftover snow. Though all the stitching on the antique quilt was done by hand, we've applied modern cutting and sewing methods in our instructions.

SKILL LEVEL: *Intermediate*

SIZE:

Finished quilt is approximately 68 × 81½ inches
Finished Schoolhouse block is 12 inches square
Finished Broken Dishes block is 4 inches square

NUMBER OF PIECED BLOCKS:

1 Schoolhouse block
4 Broken Dishes blocks

FABRICS AND SUPPLIES

- 1 yard of gray striped fabric for three outer borders
- ½ yard of brown plaid fabric for one outer border
- ⅓ yard of red solid fabric for Schoolhouse block
- ⅓ yard of blue-and-white striped or other blue print fabric for background of Schoolhouse block and borders on the sides of block
- ⅛ yard of muslin or off-white solid fabric for Schoolhouse block
- ⅛ to ⅔ yard *each* of approximately 25 to 30 scrap fabrics for pieced and plain fabric borders and binding. (Use fabrics that are a full 44 to 45 inches wide. Colors used in the quilt shown include brown, blue, red, tan, gray, black, pink, and white. Plaids, checks, stripes, and printed fabrics were used.)

- Four red print fabric scraps (at least 3 × 6 inches) for Broken Dishes blocks
- Four white print fabric scraps (at least 3 × 6 inches) for Broken Dishes blocks
- Brown embroidery floss or pearl cotton
- 5 yards of fabric for the quilt back
- Batting, larger than 68 × 81½ inches
- Rotary cutter, ruler, and mat
- Template plastic

CUTTING

Cut all strips across the fabric width unless instructed otherwise. Begin by cutting the outer fabric borders. Label them and set aside. For the Schoolhouse block, make templates for patterns J, K, L, M, and N on pages 185–186. These pieces are for Row 2 (the roof section) of the block. When making and using the templates, label them just as the patterns are labeled. When marking the pieces, turn templates K, L, and M over so that the labeled side is against the wrong side of the fabric; otherwise, all your shapes will be reversed. For pattern N, you'll need to make one regular and one reverse piece. Use the template label-side down for N, then flip it over to mark the N reverse piece.

Cut pieces A to I and O to R by referring to the cutting directions below.

From the gray striped border fabric, cut:
■ Six 5-inch-wide strips

From the brown plaid border fabric, cut:
■ Two 6½-inch-wide strips

From *each* of the four red print scrap fabrics for the Broken Dishes blocks, cut:
■ 4 triangles
  Quick-cut two 2⅞-inch squares. Cut each square in half diagonally to make two triangles.

From *each* of the white print scrap fabrics for the Broken Dishes blocks, cut:
■ 4 triangles
  Quick-cut two 2⅞-inch squares. Cut each square in half diagonally to make two triangles.

Cutting for the Schoolhouse Block
From the red fabric, cut:
■ 1 J piece
■ 1 M piece (position the template so labeled side is against wrong side of fabric as you mark and cut)
■ 1 G piece (2 × 7 inches)
■ 1 C piece (2 × 4½ inches)
■ 1 E piece (2 × 3 inches)
■ 2 P pieces (1¾ × 2¼ inches)
■ 1 H piece (1½ × 7 inches)
■ 2 B pieces (1½ × 4½ inches)
■ 2 F pieces (1½ × 3 inches)

From the blue-and-white striped fabric, cut:
■ 1 N piece and 1 N reverse piece
■ 1 R piece (2¼ × 12½ inches)
■ 1 Q piece (2¼ × 5½ inches)
■ 2 O pieces (2¼ × 2¾ inches)

From the muslin, cut:
■ 1 K piece (reverse template so labeled side is against wrong side of fabric as you mark and cut)
■ 2 L pieces (reverse as for K piece)
■ 2 E pieces (2 × 3 inches)
■ 1 I piece (1 × 7 inches)
■ 3 D pieces (1 × 6 inches)

From the brown fabric, cut:
■ 1 A piece (2½ × 4½ inches)

A SPECIAL NOTE BEFORE YOU START
We've redesigned the central block slightly to make it a 12-inch square and substituted a patchwork door and windows for the appliqué ones on the original. As you can see in the photograph on page 179, the quilt is oriented horizontally rather than in the usual vertical manner for bed quilts. Once you complete the quilt out to the four red and white Broken Dishes blocks, you can turn that section to orient your quilt vertically if you desire. The directions will remind you when to turn the section.

MAKING THE SCHOOLHOUSE BLOCK
1. Referring to the **Block Piecing Diagram,** lay out the pieces for the Schoolhouse block. As you join pieces and sections, press the seams toward the darker fabric whenever possible.

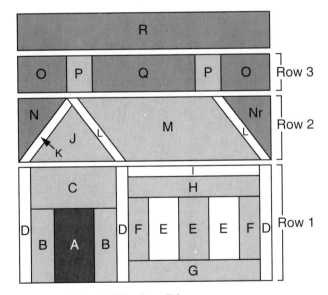

Block Piecing Diagram

2. To make Row 1, begin by making the door section of the house front. Sew red B pieces to the two long sides of the brown A door. Sew the red C piece to the top of the door section. Add white D strips to the two long sides of the unit to complete the door section.

3. To make the window section, join the one red and two white E pieces for the windows. Sew a red F piece to each of the two white E pieces. Sew the red H piece and then the white I piece to the top of the window strip. Sew the red G piece to the bottom. Add the remaining white D piece to the right-hand side of the unit to complete the window section. Join the door section and the window section to complete Row 1.

4. To make Row 2, sew the white K piece to the upper left side of the red J triangle (the house peak). Be sure to position the J piece so that the longest side is at the bottom.

Sew the white L pieces to the sides of the M piece (roof). Sew the roof section to the peak section. Add N and N reverse pieces to complete the row.

5. To make Row 3, sew red P pieces (the chimneys) to the two short ends of the blue Q piece. Sew blue O pieces to the two opposite sides of the chimney unit to complete the row.

6. Sew the three rows together, as shown in the **Block Piecing Diagram.** Sew the blue R strip to the top of the block. The block should measure 12½ inches square, including seam allowances.

7. Use embroidery floss and a simple outline stitch to indicate the panes of glass on the white E window pieces.

MAKING THE INNER QUILT

Refer to the **Inner Quilt Diagram** as you cut and add the plain borders to the central Schoolhouse block. Press seams away from the center. Dimensions on the illustration give both cut and finished sizes, with the cut size in parentheses. Numbers 1 through 11 indicate the order in which to add borders. Colors used on the antique quilt are also indicated.

1. From a brown print or other scrap fabric, cut a 2½ × 12½-inch Border 1 strip. Sew the strip to the bottom of the Schoolhouse block.

2. From the same blue print you used for the sky area of the Schoolhouse block, cut two 3 × 14½-inch Border 2 strips. Sew the strips to the right and left sides of the Schoolhouse block.

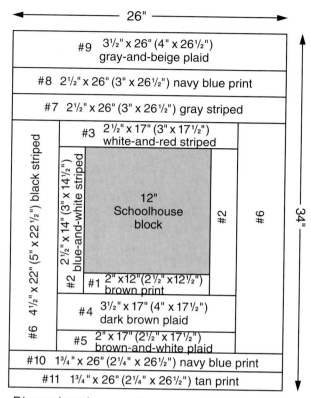

Dimensions in parentheses are cut size of strips

Inner Quilt Diagram

3. From a white-and-red striped or other scrap fabric, cut a 3 × 17½-inch Border 3 strip. Sew it to the top of the block.

4. From a dark brown plaid or other scrap fabric, cut a 4 × 17½-inch Border 4 strip. Sew the strip to the bottom of the block as in the diagram.

5. From a brown-and-white plaid or other fabric, cut a 2½ × 17½-inch Border 5 strip. Sew the strip to the bottom of the Border 4 strip.

6. From a black striped or other scrap fabric, cut two 5 × 22½-inch Border 6 strips. Sew the Border 6 strips to the two long sides of the bordered block.

7. Cut 26½-inch-long strips of scrap fabrics in the following colors and widths: From gray striped, 3 inches wide (Border 7); from navy blue print, 3 inches wide (Border 8); from gray-and-beige plaid, 4 inches wide (Border 9); from navy blue print, 2¼ inches wide (Border 10); and from tan print, 2¼ inches wide (Border 11).

Join the first three strips (Borders 7, 8, and 9) along the long sides. Sew the joined strips to the top of the bordered block, with Border 9 on the outside edge. Join the remaining two strips (Borders 10 and 11) with one long seam. Sew the joined strips to the bottom of the bordered block, with Border 11 on the outside edge.

8. Measure the completed inner quilt. It should measure 26½ × 34½ inches including seam allowances. If your quilt is a different size, trim as needed, or add additional strips to achieve the correct size before continuing.

MAKING THE BROKEN DISHES BLOCKS

1. Referring to **Diagram 1,** join the red print and white print triangles to make a total of 16 triangle-square units. Press the seams toward the red print triangles. You will need four units per block.

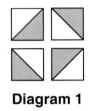

Diagram 1

2. Join the triangle-square units into two rows of two units per row, as shown in **Diagram 2A.** Join the rows as shown in **2B** to complete a block. Make four blocks. The finished blocks should measure 4½ inches square, including seam allowances.

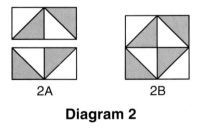

2A   2B

Diagram 2

PIECING THE RANDOM BORDERS

1. Cut two to six strips of assorted widths from each of the 25 to 30 scrap fabrics. Cut across the fabric width, in strips varying from 2 to 5 inches wide.

2. Make five to six strip sets similar to the one illustrated in **Diagram 3,** using five or six strips in each set. Vary the fabrics and strip widths from set to set. Cut segments from the strip sets according to the directions that follow.

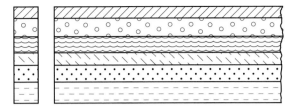

Diagram 3

ADDING THE PIECED BORDERS

1. Cut enough 4½-inch-wide segments from the various strip sets to make two 4½ × 26½-inch pieced borders. Piece the cut segments together as needed, and trim to the right length.

2. Sew a Broken Dishes block to each end of the two pieced borders. Note that on the antique quilt, the dark and light triangles of the Broken Dishes blocks are not positioned symmetrically at the corners. Position the blocks as you desire. Sew the borders to the right and left sides of the inner quilt.

Note: Before going on to Step 3, decide which way you want your quilt oriented. If you want it to be longer than it is wide, so it is more like a typical bed quilt, you can turn the section you have constructed so far, since it is square. Add borders as described below, but when referring to the **Quilt Diagram** on page 184, remember that the section that includes the Broken Dishes corner blocks is turned 90 degrees.

3. Using the measurements on the **Quilt Diagram,** cut, join, and trim strip segments to make the various borders the correct width and length. The numbers 1 through 12 on the diagram indicate the order in which to add borders. The dimensions are given both for finished size and cut sizes, with cut size given in parentheses. Sew the borders to the growing medallion center, pressing the seams away from the center as you go. Note that one side of the quilt has four pieced borders and the opposite side has five.

4. Complete the quilt top by adding the plain borders as described below.

ADDING THE OUTER BORDERS

1. Join pairs of the 5-inch-wide gray striped fabric strips to make three long outer borders. Trim two of the borders so they are 71½ inches long. Sew these Border 10 strips to the top and bottom of the quilt top. Press the seams toward the borders.

2. Trim the remaining gray-striped border so it is 68½ inches long. Sew this Border 11 strip to the quilt top on the right-hand side.

3. Join the two 6½-inch-wide brown plaid border strips to make one long Border 12 strip. Trim the strip so it is 68½ inches long. Sew the border to the quilt top.

QUILTING AND FINISHING

1. Mark quilting designs as desired. The quilt shown has Baptist Fan quilting over the whole surface. A pattern for this design is on page 31.

2. Piece the quilt back. Begin by dividing the backing fabric crosswise into two equal pieces. Cut one of the pieces in half lengthwise into two narrow panels. Trim the selvages, and sew a narrow panel to each side of the full-width panel. Press the seams toward the narrow panels.

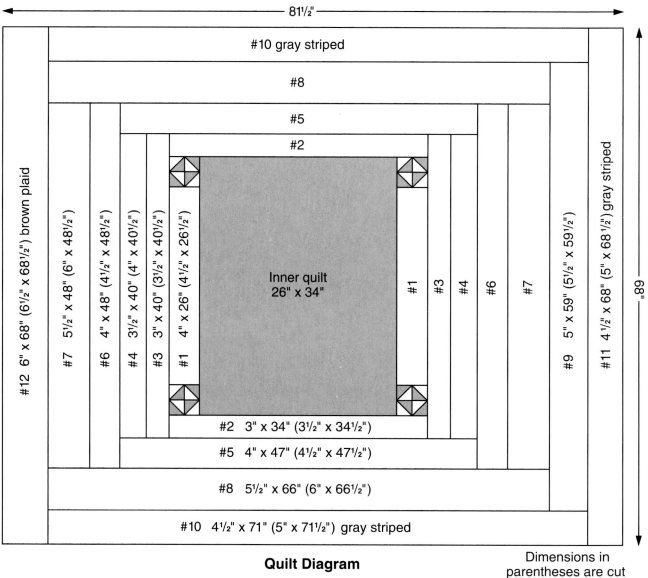

Quilt Diagram

Dimensions in parentheses are cut size of pieced strips

3. Layer the backing, batting, and quilt top; baste. Quilt as desired.

4. The binding on the quilt shown is pieced from various scrap fabrics. Make an 8½-yard-long continuous strip. Sew the binding to the quilt and hand finish. See page 13 in the "General Instructions" for details on making and attaching binding.

The dashed lines on the patterns indicate finished size. The solid lines include seam allowances.

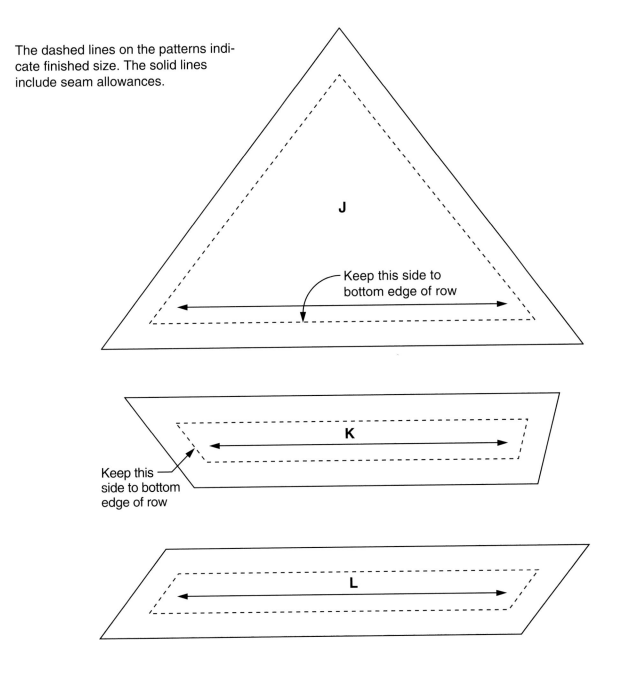

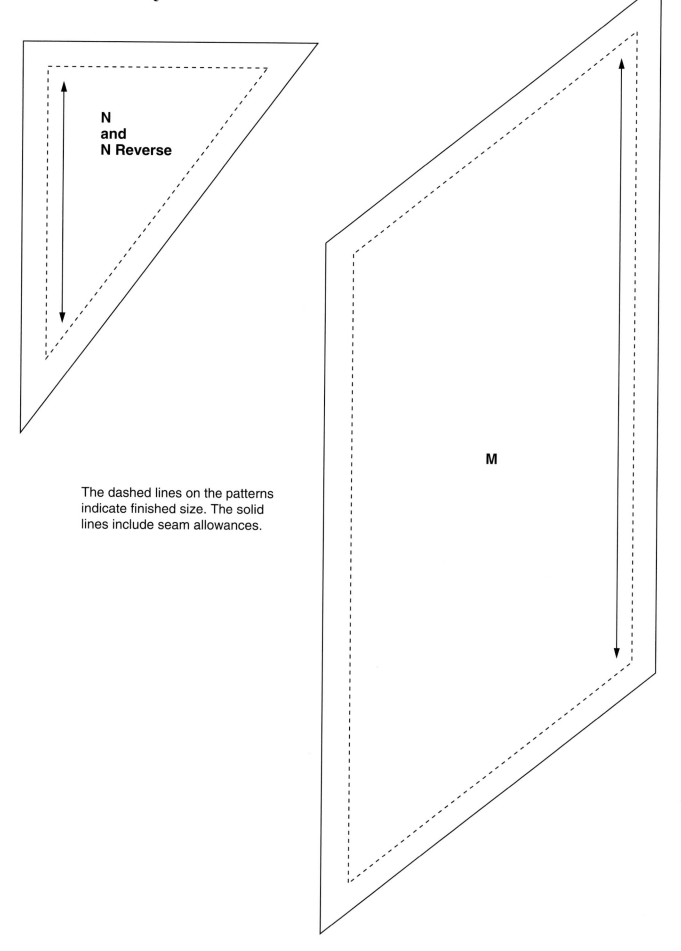

N
and
N Reverse

M

The dashed lines on the patterns indicate finished size. The solid lines include seam allowances.

Katie's Grand
Graduation Quilt

Send your child off to college with a quilt filled with child-hood and high school memories. The colorful patchwork quilt in the photograph is a veritable autograph album containing good wishes, words of wisdom, and shared memories from 88 friends and relatives of Liz's daughter, Katie Porter.

SKILL LEVEL: *Intermediate*

SIZE:

Finished quilt is 72 × 96 inches
Finished block is 8 inches square

NUMBER OF PIECED BLOCKS: 88

FABRICS AND SUPPLIES

The quilt shown was made as a scrap quilt using a variety of madras plaids for the medium and dark fabrics and an assortment of soft, discreetly printed pastel prints for the light fabrics. If you plan to make this as an album quilt and have people write in the open, unpieced triangles, choose light fabrics that will not detract from the writing.

If you prefer to make this quilt from just two fabrics, rather than as a scrap quilt, you will need approximately 5½ yards of light fabric and 4½ yards of dark fabric (this includes sufficient dark fabric for matching binding).

- ¾ yard *each* of 13 different light print fabrics for patchwork and borders
- ½ yard *each* of 13 different medium and dark plaid fabrics for patchwork and borders
- 6 yards of fabric for the quilt back
- ¾ yard of fabric for binding
- Batting, larger than 72 × 96 inches
- Fine tip, permanent marking pen. (Micron Pigma 01 pens and Pilot SC UF pens all come in a

variety of colors and work for writing on fabric.)
- Rotary cutter, ruler, and mat
- Plastic-coated freezer paper
- Template plastic (optional)

CUTTING

This quilt uses the same patterns as the Grand Right and Left on page 166. If you wish to cut the pieces using traditional methods, make templates for patterns A, B, and C on page 178. You will also need a template for piece D; it is a right-angle triangle with 8-inch legs. To include seam allowance on the template, draw the triangle with 8⅞-inch legs. Cut the D triangles with the legs on the straight of grain. If you prefer to quick-cut the pieces, follow the instructions on the opposite page. All measurements include ¼-inch seam allowances. Cut all fabric strips across the fabric width.

Note: When cutting the medium and dark A triangles, cut sets of six A triangles to match each C triangle, then cut extra assorted triangles for the sawtooth border.

If you are making an album quilt, cut freezer paper triangles to stabilize each of the D triangle signature patches. Cut fifty-two 7-inch squares of paper, then cut each square in half diagonally to make two triangles.

From the light print fabrics, cut:

- 512 A triangles
  Quick-cut two 2⅞-inch-wide strips from each of the 13 fabrics. Cut twenty 2⅞-inch squares from each pair of matching strips. Cut each square diagonally to make two triangles. You will have 40 triangles from each fabric. There will be 8 extra triangles.

- 88 B squares
  Quick-cut one 2½-inch-wide strip from each of the 13 fabrics. Cut seven 2½-inch squares from each strip. You will have 3 extra squares. Save the remaining approximately 22 inches of each strip to use for the pieced inner border.

- 88 D triangles
  Quick-cut one 8⅞-inch-wide strip from each of the 13 light fabrics. Cut four 8⅞-inch squares from each strip. Cut each square in half diagonally to make two triangles. You will have 104 triangles, but only need 88 for the quilt. Save the extra triangles to use as replacements for any that are not returned, or to send an extra to someone who made an error and needs a new one.

From the medium and dark plaid fabrics, cut:

- 88 C triangles
  Quick-cut one 4⅞-inch-wide strip from each of the 13 fabrics. Cut four 4⅞-inch squares from each strip. Cut each square in half diagonally to make two triangles. You will have 16 extra triangles; this will give you more flexibility in arranging the blocks.

- 688 A triangles
  Quick-cut two 2⅞-inch-wide strips from 12 of the fabrics and three strips from 1 of the fabrics. Cut thirteen 2⅞-inch squares from each of the strips for a total of 351 squares. Cut each square in half diagonally to make two triangles. You will have 14 extra triangles.

- 4 B squares for the sawtooth border corners
  Quick-cut 2½-inch squares.

MAKING THE BLOCKS

Follow the instructions below to make 88 blocks like the one shown in **Diagram 1.** You will make the pieced portion for all the blocks first, and then join each pieced portion to a D triangle to complete the blocks.

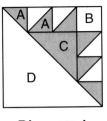

Diagram 1

1. If you are making a signature quilt, center and press the shiny side of a freezer paper triangle to the wrong side of each large D triangle. This will stabilize the fabric and make it easier to write on. Use a dry iron set on wool to do the pressing.

2. Obtain signatures on the D triangles. After the triangles are signed, remove the paper backing and press the pieces with a dry iron set on cotton. This will set the ink and make it more permanent.

3. Referring to **Diagram 1,** lay out the following pieces for the pieced portion of one block: four assorted light A triangles, six A triangles and one C triangle from the same medium or dark fabric, and one light B square.

4. Make four triangle-squares by joining light and dark A triangles. Referring to **Diagram 2,** stitch pairs of triangle-squares together, paying careful attention to the slant of the triangle-square seams.

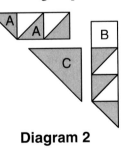

Diagram 2

5. Add a dark A triangle to one end of each of the triangle-square strips as shown. Sew one strip to the short side of a C triangle; press the seam toward the C triangle. Sew a light B square to the end of the other triangle-square strip; sew the strip to the adjacent short side of the C triangle. Press the seam toward the C triangle.

6. To complete a block, sew the pieced portion to a D triangle, as shown in **Diagram 3.**

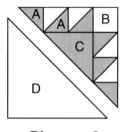

Diagram 3

ASSEMBLING THE QUILT TOP

1. Referring to the **Quilt Diagram,** lay out the blocks in 11 horizontal rows with eight blocks in each row. The heavy lines on the diagram help define the rows.

2. Join the blocks in each row; press the seams toward the D triangles. Then, join the rows.

3. To make the pieced inner border, cut the leftover portions of the 2½-inch-wide light fabric strips into segments ranging from 4 to 22 inches long. Join the segments into one long strip, arranging the fabrics and pieces randomly. Cut and add additional light segments until the strip is approximately 340 inches long.

4. Measure the length of the quilt, measuring through the center rather than along the sides, which may have stretched. From the long pieced strip, cut two borders to this length (approximately 88½ inches). Sew the borders to the sides of the quilt top; press the seams toward the borders.

5. Measure the width of the quilt top, again measuring through the center of the quilt. From the remaining pieced strip, cut borders to this length (approximately 68½ inches) for the top and bottom. Sew the borders to the top and bottom edges of the quilt; press the seams toward the borders.

6. To make the sawtooth outer borders, begin by making 160 triangle-squares by joining light A triangles and medium or dark A triangles.

7. Piece two side borders by joining 46 triangle-square units for each border. Refer to the **Quilt Diagram** for the correct angle of the triangle-square

seams for each border. Press the seams toward the dark fabrics. It may be necessary to adjust the fit by taking slightly wider or narrower seams between some of the triangle-squares. Sew the borders to the sides of the quilt, with the dark triangles toward the inner quilt; press the seams toward the inner borders.

8. Piece the top and bottom borders by joining 34 triangle-square units for each border. Refer to the **Quilt Diagram** for the correct angle of the triangle-square seams. Add a dark B square to the end of each border. Press the seams toward the dark fabrics. Adjust the fit as needed, and sew the borders to the top and bottom edges of the quilt, with the dark triangles toward the inner quilt. Press the seams toward the inner borders.

QUILTING AND FINISHING

1. Mark quilting designs as desired. A suggested quilting design for the blocks is shown in **Diagram 4.** On the quilt shown, the outer borders are quilted in the ditch along the diagonal seams that join the triangles. This line is continued into the light inner borders.

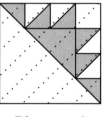

Diagram 4

2. To piece the quilt back, divide the backing fabric crosswise into two equal lengths. Cut one piece in half lengthwise. Trim the selvages, and sew a half panel to each side of the full-width panel; press the seams away from the center panel.

3. Layer the quilt back, batting, and quilt top; baste. Hand or machine quilt as desired. The quilt shown is machine quilted.

4. Make approximately 10 yards (360 inches) of bias or straight-grain binding. Finish the edges of the quilt with binding. See page 13 in the "General Instructions" for details on making and attaching binding.

72"

96"

Quilt Diagram

Reflections
of
Daily Life

A basket, a bowl, a house on a hill, a tree, a fence, a bird in the sky— everyday objects in the lives of nineteenth-century women found their way into quilts. Patterns inspired by daily life are a rich history lesson for quilters today. They allow us nostalgia for times gone by, when life took place in a farm cottage rather than in an apartment building. Each of the old quilts in this chapter has a special charm, whether it's the appeal of demure baskets or grass-roots patriotism. Our new project, Country Schools, combines the house pattern with the Chimneys and Cornerstones block from the next chapter.

Little Red
·Schoolhouses·
and Birds

Duuring the nineteenth and early twentieth centuries, when so much of life in our land was rural, the country schoolhouse was a familiar sight in every township in the heartland of America. More often white than red, one-room schools dotted the hillsides and prairies. Toward these humble wooden or brick structures children walked or rode ponies daily, perhaps with redbirds flying overhead. It is only fitting that the schoolhouse, which played such an important part in every child's life, became the subject for quilts. Although this quilt was made in the traditional red and white fabrics, it rises above the ordinary with the addition of birds pieced from Drunkard's Path units, elegant feather quilting, and the clever mirror-image arrangement of the house blocks. Blocks placed this way allowed the quilt to be turned more than one way on a bed, a prudent plan designed to extend wear.

SKILL LEVEL: *Intermediate*

SIZE:

Finished quilt is approximately 72 × 83 inches
Finished Schoolhouse blocks are 9 × 10 inches
Finished Bird blocks are 6 inches square

NUMBER OF PIECED BLOCKS:

20 Schoolhouse blocks
12 Bird blocks

FABRICS AND SUPPLIES

- 4½ yards of white solid fabric for patchwork, sashing strips, and border
- 3½ yards of red solid fabric for patchwork, border, and binding
- 5 yards of fabric for the quilt back
- Batting, larger than 72 × 83 inches
- Template plastic
- Rotary cutter, ruler, and mat

CUTTING

The instructions for the Schoolhouse blocks are written to give you the option of template-style cutting for traditional piecing or quick-cutting and quick-piecing for most of the house sections. If you plan to quick-piece the sections, you will only need to make templates for patterns E, F, G, and H on page 203. If you plan to use template-style cutting and traditional piecing, then you must also make templates for A, B, C, D, I, and J on page 202.

You could also make the schoolhouses from a variety of scrap fabrics rather than from the simple red and white fabrics. See "Making Scrap Schoolhouses," on page 196, for details and cutting information.

For the Drunkard's Path Bird blocks, make templates for patterns X and Y on page 201. Include the register marks on the X and Y patterns on your templates. These marks indicate the centers of the curves. As you mark the fabric pieces, transfer these center marks to the fabric to help you align the curved edges when pinning and sewing.

Choose one of the piecing methods and cut all of the pieces listed for that method. Use a rotary cutter and ruler to cut the sashing strips and borders. Measurements for all pieces include ¼-inch seam allowances. Cut all strips across the fabric width.

Cutting for Quick-Piecing

Use these cutting instructions if you will be quick-piecing the Schoolhouse blocks.

From the white fabric, cut:
- 31 sashing strips
  Quick-cut eight 6½-inch-wide strips. From each strip, cut two 9½-inch-long strips and two 10½-inch-long strips. You will have one extra 9½-inch-long strip.
- Eight 4-inch-wide strips for borders

- Two 3½-inch-wide strips for strip sets
- Four 2½-inch-wide strips for strip sets
- Eight 2¼-inch-wide strips for borders
- Nine 1½-inch-wide strips for strip sets
- 20 D rectangles
  Quick-cut three 1½-inch-wide strips. Cut the strips into 1½ × 5½-inch rectangles.
- 20 E and 20 E reverse triangles
- 20 G pieces
- 24 X pieces
- 24 Y pieces

From the red fabric, cut:
- 20 C rectangles
  Quick-cut two 2½-inch-wide strips. Cut the strips into 2½ × 3½-inch rectangles.
- Eight 2¼-inch-wide strips for borders

Quilter's Schoolhouse

MAKING SCRAP SCHOOLHOUSES

If you prefer to make the schoolhouses from many different scrap fabrics, rather than all from the same red fabric, use templates to cut pieces E, F, G, and H, then quick-cut pieces A, B, C, D, I, and J by referring to the dimensions in the cutting chart below. Measurements for all pieces include ¼-inch seam allowances. Referring to the **Block Piecing Diagram** on the opposite page, piece the scrap blocks using the traditional piecing method.

CUTTING CHART FOR SCRAP SCHOOLHOUSE BLOCKS

Pattern Piece	Dimensions	Number to Cut per Block
A rectangle	1½ × 2½ inches	5 for house, 2 for windows, 1 for door, 2 for chimneys
B rectangle	1½ × 3½ inches	1 for house
C rectangle	2½ × 3½ inches	1 for house
D rectangle	1½ × 5½ inches	2 for house, 2 for background
E and E reverse triangles	see pattern	1 each for background
F triangle	see pattern	1 for house
G piece	see pattern	1 for background
H piece	see pattern	1 for roof
I square	2½ × 2½ inches	2 for background
J rectangle	2½ × 3½ inches	1 for background

- Seventeen 1½-inch-wide strips for strip sets
- 20 B rectangles
  Quick-cut two 1½-inch-wide strips. Cut the strips into 1½ × 3½-inch rectangles.
- 20 D rectangles
  Quick-cut three 1½-inch-wide strips. Cut 1½ × 5½-inch rectangles.
- 20 F triangles
- 20 H pieces
- 24 X pieces
- 24 Y pieces
- Reserve the remaining fabric for binding

Cutting for Traditional Piecing

Use these cutting instructions for template-style cutting and traditional piecing.

From the white fabric, cut:

- 31 sashing strips
  Quick-cut eight 6½-inch-wide strips. From each strip, cut two 9½-inch-long strips and two 10½-inch-long strips. You will have one extra 9½-inch-long strip.
- Eight 4-inch-wide strips for borders
- Eight 2¼-inch-wide strips for borders
- 60 A rectangles
- 40 D rectangles
- 20 E and 20 E reverse triangles
- 20 G pieces
- 40 I squares
- 20 J rectangles
- 24 X pieces
- 24 Y pieces

From the red fabric, cut:

- Eight 2¼-inch-wide strips for borders
- 140 A rectangles
- 20 B rectangles
- 20 C rectangles
- 40 D rectangles
- 20 F triangles
- 20 H pieces
- 24 X pieces
- 24 Y pieces
- Reserve the remaining fabric for binding

MAKING THE SCHOOLHOUSE BLOCKS

Refer to the **Block Piecing Diagram** as you assemble the Schoolhouse blocks. The quick-pieced units and the pattern pieces are labeled; heavier lines frame the quick-pieced units. If you have chosen to piece the blocks using traditional methods, skip this section and begin with Traditional Piecing Method on page 199.

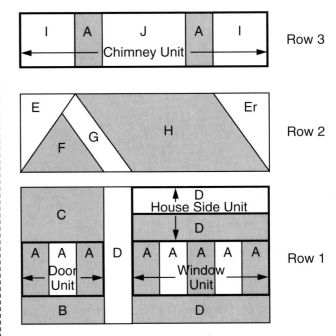

Darker lines frame quick-pieced units
Block Piecing Diagram

Quick-Piecing Method

1. To make the Door Units, sew together 1½-inch-wide red and white strips to make two strip sets, as shown in **Diagram 1**. Press the seams toward the red strips. Cut 2½-inch-wide segments from the strip sets. You will need 20 segments. Each Door Unit should measure 2½ × 3½ inches, including seam allowances.

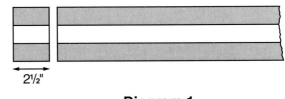

Diagram 1
Door Unit Strip Set

2. Referring to **Diagram 2,** add a red C rectangle to the top of each Door Unit and a red B rectangle to the bottom. Press the seams away from the Door Unit. The house front should measure 3½ × 5½ inches, including seam allowances. Make 20 house fronts.

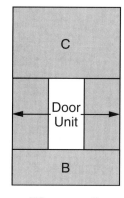

Diagram 2

3. To make the Window Units, sew together 1½-inch-wide red and white strips to make two strip sets as shown in **Diagram 3.** Press the seams toward the red strips. Cut 20 segments, each 2½ inches wide, from the strip sets. Each Window Unit should measure 2½ × 5½ inches, including seam allowances.

2½"

Diagram 3
Window Unit Strip Set

4. To make the House Side Units, sew together 1½-inch-wide red and white strips to make three strip sets as shown in **Diagram 4.** Press the seams toward the red strips. Cut 20 segments, each 5½ inches wide, from the strip sets. Each House Side unit should measure 2½ × 5½ inches, including seam allowances.

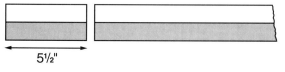

5½"

Diagram 4
House Side Unit Strip Set

5. Referring to **Diagram 5,** sew a House Side Unit to the top of each Window Unit and a red D rectangle to the bottom of each unit. Press the seams away from the Window Unit. Make 20 house sides. Each house side should measure 5½ inches square, including seam allowances.

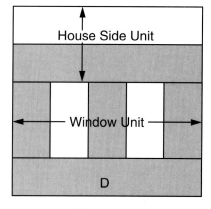

Diagram 5

6. To assemble Row 1 of the Schoolhouse block, stitch a **Diagram 2** house front to the left side of a white D rectangle, and a **Diagram 5** unit to the right side of the rectangle. Press the seams toward the white D rectangle. Make 20 of Row 1.

7. To make Row 2 of the Schoolhouse block, refer to the **Block Piecing Diagram.** Begin by stitching a G piece to the right edge of an F triangle. Press the seam toward the G piece. Sew an E triangle to the left edge this unit. Press the seam toward the E triangle. Sew the EFG unit to the left side of an H piece (house roof); press the seam toward the H piece. Sew an E reverse triangle to the other side of the H piece, pressing the seam toward the H piece. Make 20 of Row 2.

8. Refer to **Diagram 6** to make the Chimney Units (Row 3). Sew two 1½-inch-wide red strips, two 2½-inch-wide white strips, and one 3½-inch-wide white strip into a strip set. Press seams toward the red strips. Make two of these strip sets. Cut 20 segments, each 2½ inches wide, from the strip sets.

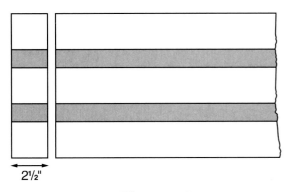

Diagram 6
Chimney Unit Strip Set

9. Join sets of three rows to complete the blocks. Make 20 blocks.

Traditional Piecing Method

1. Referring to the **Block Piecing Diagram,** lay out the following pieces for one block: three white A and seven red A rectangles, one red B rectangle, one red C rectangle, two red and two white D rectangles, one white E and one white E reverse triangle, one red F triangle, one white G piece, one red H piece, two white I squares, and one white J rectangle. As you join the pieces for the house, press the seams toward the red fabric whenever possible.

2. Make the house front by starting with a Door Unit. Join a red A rectangle to each side of one white A rectangle.

3. Add a C rectangle to the top and a B rectangle to the bottom of the Door Unit.

4. To piece the house side, begin by making a Window Unit. Sew together three red A rectangles and two white A rectangles, alternating colors.

5. Make a House Side Unit by joining a red D rectangle to a white D rectangle along the long sides.

6. Sew the House Side Unit to the top of the Window Unit. Sew a red D rectangle to the lower edge of the Window Unit.

7. Sew a white D rectangle to the right edge of the house front. Sew the side of the house to the opposite side of the white D rectangle to complete Row 1.

8. To make Row 2, begin by stitching a G piece to the right edge of an F triangle. Press the seam toward the G piece. Sew an E triangle to the left edge of this unit. Press the seam toward the E triangle. Sew the EFG unit to the left side of an H piece (house roof); press the seam toward the H piece. Sew an E reverse triangle to the other side of the H piece, pressing the seam toward the H piece.

9. To make Row 3, combine two white I squares, two red A rectangles, and one white J rectangle as shown in the **Block Piecing Diagram.**

10. To complete the block, join the three rows. The block should measure $9\frac{1}{2} \times 10\frac{1}{2}$ inches, including seam allowances. Make 20 blocks.

MAKING THE DRUNKARD'S PATH BIRD BLOCKS

1. Referring to **Diagram 7,** pin the curved edge of a white Y piece to the curved edge of a red X piece, matching center register marks and outer edges. To make pinning along the curved edges easier, start at the corners and center of the curve, taking up only a few threads with each pin. Stitch the curved seam. Press the seam away from the X piece, clipping the seam if needed. Make 24 units.

Diagram 7

2. In the same manner, make 24 Step 1 units using red Y pieces and white X pieces.

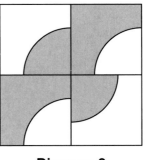

Diagram 8

3. Referring to **Diagram 8,** combine the two types of units to make 12 Drunkard's Path Bird blocks.

ASSEMBLING THE QUILT TOP

1. Referring to the **Quilt Diagram,** lay out the Schoolhouse blocks, Drunkard's Path Bird blocks, and sashing strips, paying careful attention to the direction of the houses and birds.

2. Join the Schoolhouse blocks in four vertical rows, each with five blocks and four 10½-inch-long

sashing strips between the blocks. The heavier lines in the diagram define the rows.

3. Join the Drunkard's Path Bird blocks in three vertical rows, each with four birds and five 9½-inch-long sashing strips.

4. Join the rows.

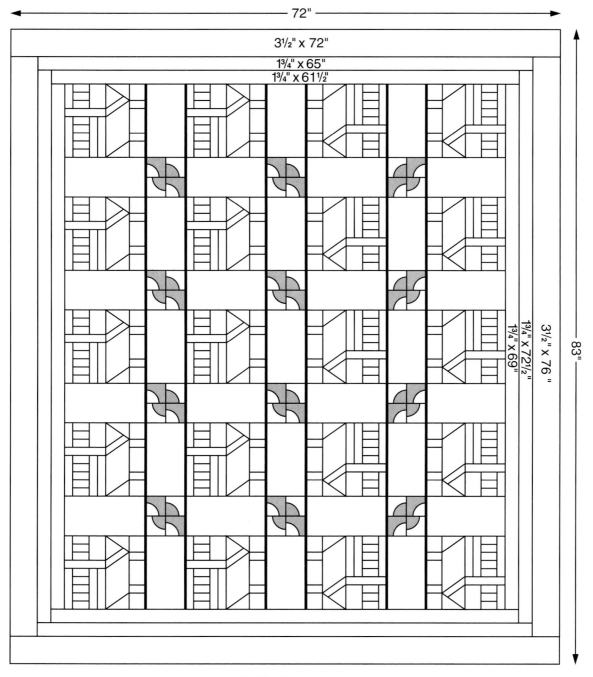

Quilt Diagram

5. Taking diagonal seams, join pairs of 2¼-inch-wide white border strips into four long borders. Repeat for the wider white border strips and the red border strips. Instructions for joining border strips are on page 9 in the "General Instructions."

6. Measure the length of your quilt, measuring through the middle rather than along the edges. Trim two narrow white borders to this length (approximately 69½ inches). Sew the borders to the sides of the quilt; press the seams toward the borders. Measure the width of your quilt, measuring through the middle and including the side borders. Trim the remaining two narrow white borders to this length (approximately 62 inches). Sew the borders to the top and bottom of the quilt.

7. In a similar manner, sew the red borders and then the wide white borders to the quilt top.

QUILTING AND FINISHING

1. Mark quilting designs as desired. The quilt shown has feather quilting in the borders and sashing, and diagonal straight-line quilting in the Schoolhouse blocks. Patterns to make templates for drawing the feather quilting designs are shown at right.

To draw the feathered quilting design for a sashing strip, begin by cutting a piece of tracing paper the finished size of a sashing strip. Fold the paper in half lengthwise to determine the center. Draw two parallel lines spaced approximately ¼ inch apart along the center of the paper. Use the feather template to draw the feathered design on the paper. Trace the design onto the fabric by placing the paper pattern underneath.

To mark the feathered design on the border, use the large template to draw feathers on both sides of the seam joining the outer and middle borders.

2. Divide the backing fabric crosswise into two equal lengths. Cut one piece in half lengthwise. Stitch a half panel to each long side of the full-width panel. Press the seams away from the center panel.

3. Layer the quilt back, batting, and quilt top; baste. Quilt as desired.

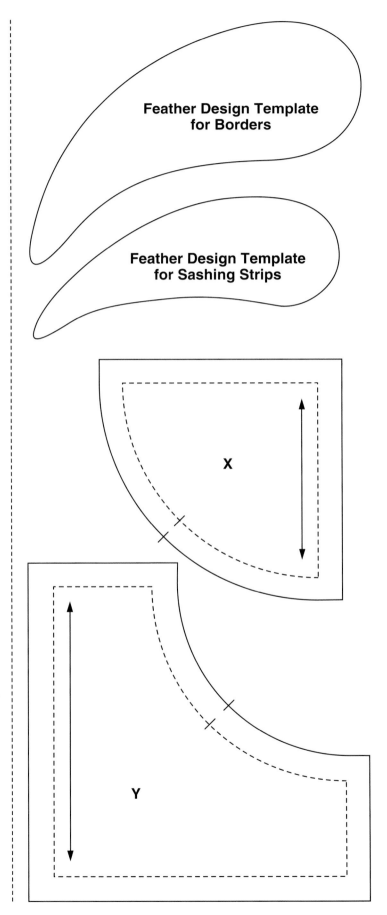

Feather Design Template for Borders

Feather Design Template for Sashing Strips

X

Y

4. Make approximately 9 yards (324 inches) of straight-grain or bias binding from the remaining red fabric. Sew the binding to the quilt. See page 13 in the "General Instructions" for details on making and attaching binding.

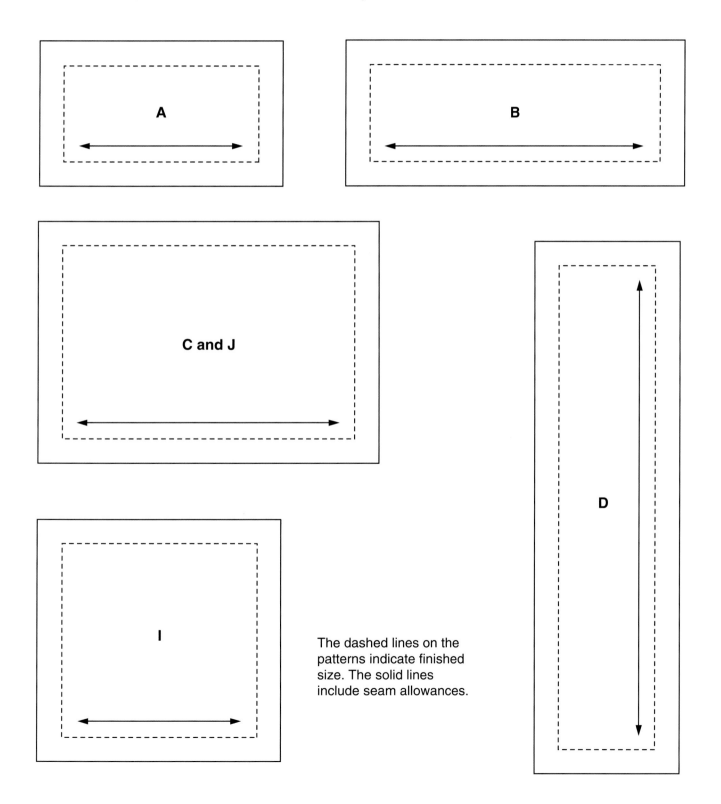

The dashed lines on the patterns indicate finished size. The solid lines include seam allowances.

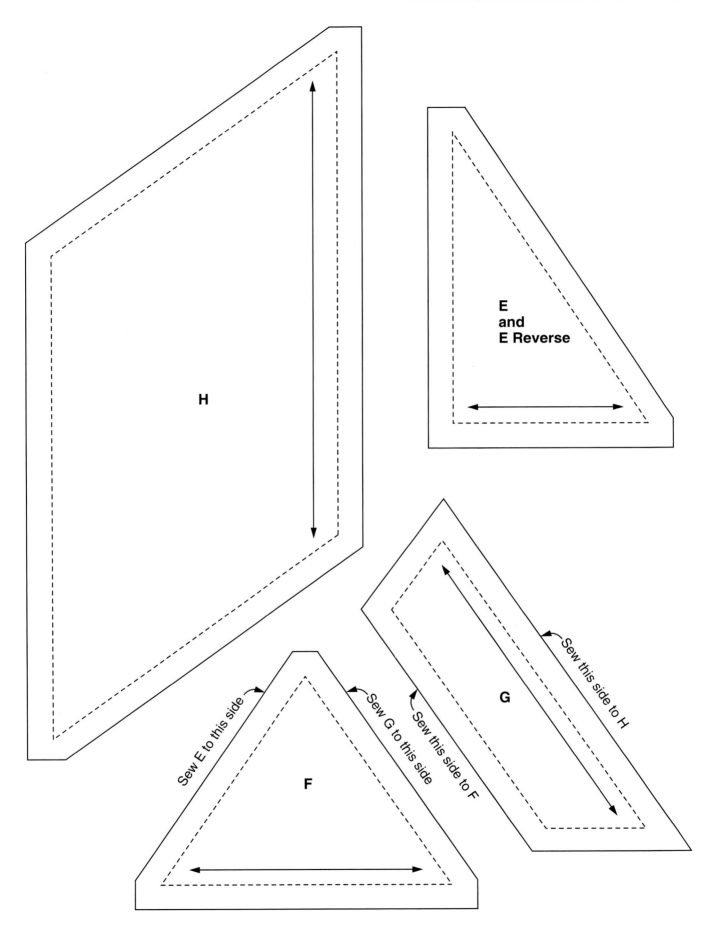

· Bow Tie ·

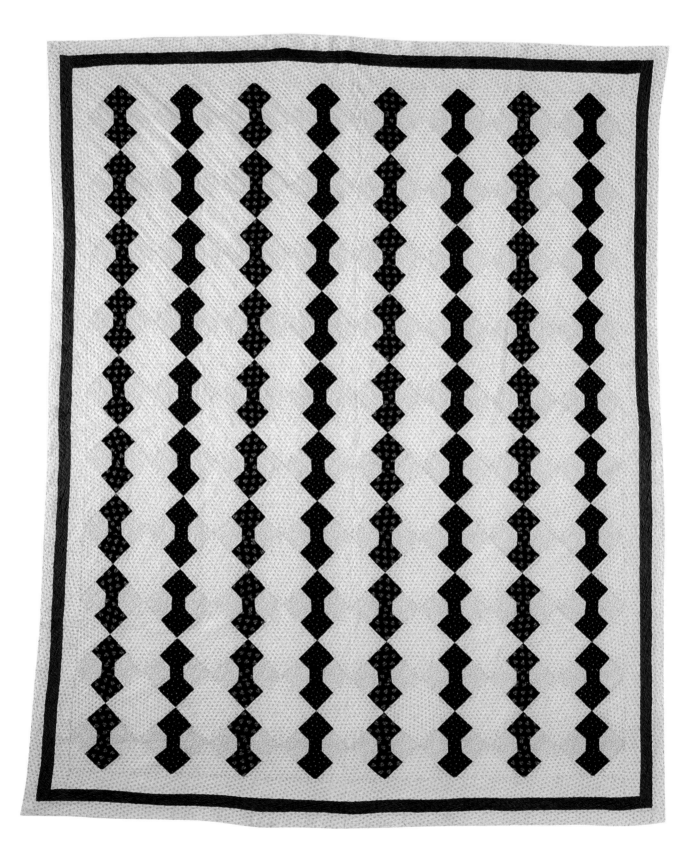

Although made as long as a hundred years ago, the crisp black-and-white color scheme of this antique Bow Tie quilt makes it look right at home in even the most modern of today's decorating schemes. The black print Bow Tie blocks are arranged to create rows of ties that run the length of the quilt. You can arrange your ties this way or run them in rows across the width of the quilt.

SKILL LEVEL: *Easy*

SIZE:

Finished quilt is approximately 78 × 95 inches
Finished block is 6 inches square (approximately
8½ inches on the diagonal)

NUMBER OF PIECED BLOCKS: 80

FABRICS AND SUPPLIES

- 4¾ yards of white print fabric (White Print 1) for setting pieces, borders, and binding
- 2 yards of a second white print fabric (White Print 2) for blocks
- 1¼ yards of black print fabric (Black Print 1) for half of the Bow Tie blocks
- 1¼ yards of a second black print fabric (Black Print 2) for half of the Bow Tie blocks
- ⅝ yard of black fabric with white pinstripes for middle borders
- 6 yards of fabric for the quilt back
- Batting, larger than 78 × 95 inches
- Template plastic (optional)
- Rotary cutter, ruler, and mat

A NOTE BEFORE YOU BEGIN

We've included two methods for cutting and piecing the Bow Tie blocks. The traditional method results in a block with set-in pieces, as shown in **Diagram 1.** For this method, you will need to make templates for pattern pieces A and B on page 209.

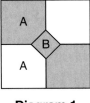

Diagram 1

The quick-piecing method makes a slightly different block, as shown in **Diagram 2.** For this method, all of the pieces can be cut with a rotary cutter and ruler. Read through all of the instructions before you begin the quilt to be sure you understand the instructions for the method you have chosen.

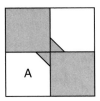

Diagram 2

CUTTING

First, cut the border and setting pieces. Then decide what method you will use and cut the block pieces. If you plan to piece the Bow Tie blocks traditionally with set-in pieces, follow the instructions in Cutting for Traditional Piecing. If you plan to quick-piece the blocks, follow the instructions in Cutting for Quick-Piecing.

Use a rotary cutter and ruler to cut the borders and setting pieces. Cut all strips across the width of the fabric. All measurements include ¼-inch seam allowances.

From White Print 1, cut:

- Nine 2½-inch-wide strips for the inner border
- Nine 2-inch-wide strips for the outer border
- 63 setting squares
  Quick-cut eleven 6½-inch-wide strips. Cut 6½-inch squares from the strips.
- 32 side setting triangles
  Quick-cut two 9¾-inch-wide strips. Cut eight 9¾-inch squares from the strips. Cut each square diagonally in both directions to make four triangles.
- 4 corner setting triangles
  Quick-cut two 5⅛-inch squares. Cut each square in half diagonally to make two triangles.
- Reserve the remaining fabric for binding

From the black pin-striped fabric, cut:

- Nine 2-inch-wide strips for the middle borders

Cutting for Traditional Piecing

Make plastic templates for patterns A and B on page 209. Using a large needle, such as a sewing machine needle, pierce holes through the templates at the dots marked at the corners of the patterns. As you trace around the templates on the fabrics, mark dots through the holes in the templates to use as matching points when pinning and stitching the pieces.

From White Print 2, cut:

- 160 A pieces

From Black Print 1, cut:

- 80 A pieces
- 40 B squares

From Black Print 2, cut:

- 80 A pieces
- 40 B squares

Cutting for Quick-Piecing

From White Print 2, cut:

- Fifteen 3½-inch-wide strips. Cut the strips into 3½-inch squares. You will need 160 squares.

From Black Print 1, cut:

- Eight 3½-inch-wide strips. Cut the strips into 3½-inch squares. You will need 80 squares.
- Three 1½-inch-wide strips. Cut the strips into 1½-inch squares. You will need 80 squares.

From Black Print 2, cut:

- Eight 3½-inch-wide strips. Cut the strips into 3½-inch squares. You will need 80 squares.
- Three 1½-inch-wide strips. Cut the strips into 1½-inch squares. You will need 80 squares.

MAKING THE BLOCKS

Follow the piecing method that corresponds to the cutting method you have used. Make 40 blocks using Black Print 1 and 40 blocks using Black Print 2.

Traditional Piecing Method

1. Referring to **Diagram 3**, lay out the following pieces for one block: two white print A pieces, and two A pieces and a B square from the same black print fabric.

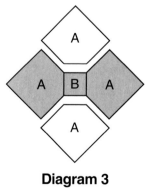

Diagram 3

2. Begin by making the black bow tie. Pin the matching points on one side of the B square to the matching points on the angled edge of one black A piece. Add additional pins as needed. Stitch the pieces together, sewing only between the matching

points. Leave the seam allowances free at the beginning and end of the seam so you can set in the white A pieces later. Backstitch to secure the beginning and end of your seams as you join pieces for the block.

3. In the same manner, stitch the angled side of the second black A piece to the opposite side of the B square.

4. To complete the block, set white A pieces into the openings. To set in the first A piece, begin by pinning and stitching the angled edge to one side of the B square. Next, pin and stitch the edges of the white A piece to the corresponding edges of the black A pieces. Repeat to set in the second white A piece. See page 6 in the "General Instructions" for details on setting-in.

Quick-Piecing Method

1. To make one block you will need two 3½-inch white print squares and two 3½-inch squares and two 1½-inch squares from the same black fabric. Press each small black square in half diagonally to create a stitching guideline.

2. With right sides facing and raw edges aligned, pin a small black square to one corner of a white square as shown in **Diagram 4.**

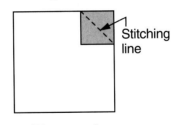

Diagram 4

3. Stitch diagonally from one corner of the black square to the opposite corner.

4. Trim off the excess corner as shown in **Diagram 5,** allowing a ¼-inch seam.

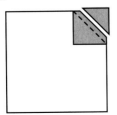

Diagram 5

5. Open out the black triangle so it completes the square, as shown in **Diagram 6.** Press the seam allowance toward the black triangle.

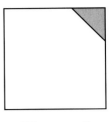

Diagram 6

6. Repeat Steps 2 through 5 to make a second **Diagram 6** unit for the block.

7. Referring to **Diagram 7,** join black squares and **Diagram 6** units to complete the block.

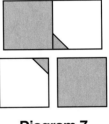

Diagram 7

ASSEMBLING THE QUILT TOP

1. Referring to the **Quilt Diagram,** lay out the Bow Tie blocks on point in eight vertical rows with ten blocks in each row. Use matching fabric bow ties for all ten blocks in each row; alternate types of rows.

2. Place white setting squares between the blocks, and fill in along the outside edges with the side setting triangles and corner setting triangles.

3. Join the pieces in diagonal rows, pressing the seams toward the setting squares and triangles. The heavy lines on the diagram define the rows. Then join the rows.

4. Make four inner borders by sewing eight 2½-inch-wide white strips together in pairs, joining the strips with diagonal seams. Instructions for joining strips with diagonal seams are on page 9 in the "General Instructions." Cut the remaining strip in half, and then sew one half to two of the long border strips.

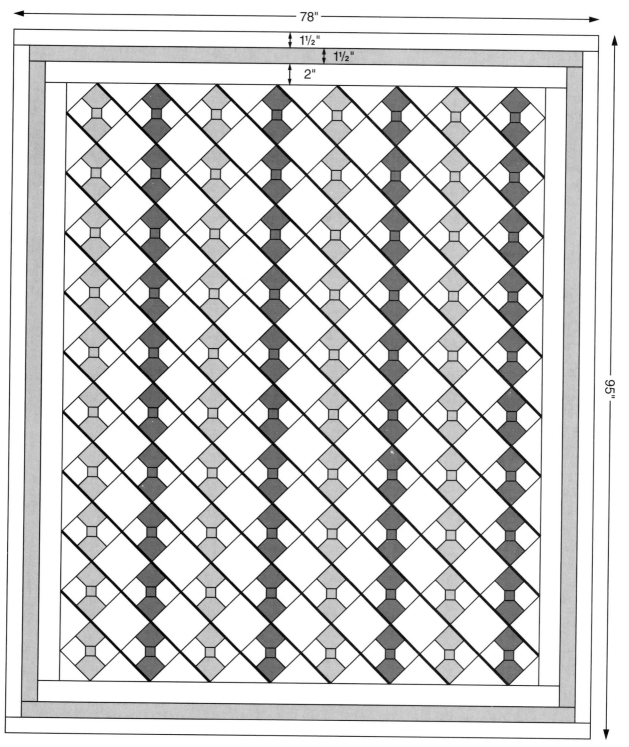

Quilt Diagram

5. Measure the length of your quilt top, measuring through the middle, and cut the two longer borders to this length (approximately 85½ inches). Sew the borders to the sides of the quilt top, pressing the seams toward the borders. Measure the width of the quilt top, again measuring through the middle, and cut the remaining two borders to this length (approximately 72½ inches). Sew the borders to the top and bottom edges; press the seams toward the borders.

6. In the same manner, add the black middle border, using the 2-inch-wide black pin-striped border strips, and the white outer border, using the 2-inch-wide white border strips.

QUILTING AND FINISHING

1. Mark quilting designs as desired on the completed quilt top. The quilt in the photograph was quilted with parallel diagonal lines.

2. To piece the quilt back, divide the backing fabric crosswise into two equal lengths. Cut one piece in half lengthwise. Stitch a half-panel to each side of the full-width panel. Press the seams away from the center panel.

3. Layer the quilt back, batting, and quilt top; baste. Quilt as desired.

4. From the remaining White Print 2 fabric, make approximately 10 yards (360 inches) of bias or straight-grain binding to finish the edges of your quilt. See page 13 in the "General Instructions" for details on making and attaching binding.

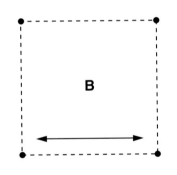

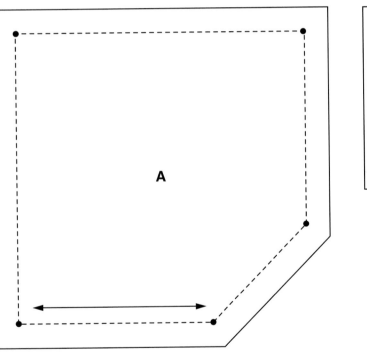

The dashed lines on the patterns indicate finished size. The solid lines include seam allowances.

All Flags Flying

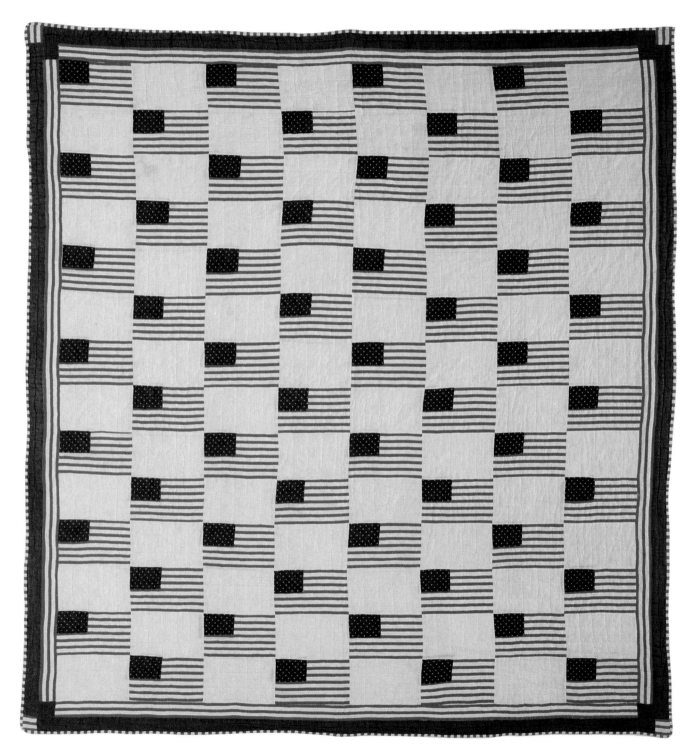

Flags fly high in this quick-and-easy quilt with an unabashedly patriotic theme. Fifty-six flags wave proudly, alternating with plain white rectangles. Simple striped borders and blue borders set off the central design with snappy red-and-white striped binding framing the outer edges. Patriotic fabrics, such as the blue print with white stars used in the flags, were produced in great quantities around the American centennial in 1876 and again during the bicentennial of 1976. During wars and other historic events that result in surges of patriotism, fabric manufacturers generally respond by bringing out commemorative fabric lines. During World War I, anti-German feelings ran strong throughout America. Iowa, with a large German immigrant population, was no exception: Even speaking German in public was outlawed. Perhaps as a reaction to such feelings, Anna and Ada Schnoor, two German-American sisters in Dallas County, Iowa, pieced this flag quilt in 1919 to proclaim their patriotism.

SKILL LEVEL: *Easy*

SIZE:

Finished quilt is approximately 76 × 81½ inches
Finished block is 5¼ × 8½ inches

NUMBER OF PIECED BLOCKS: 56

FABRICS AND SUPPLIES

- 4 yards of red-and-white striped fabric for flags, inner border, and binding
- 2½ yards of white fabric for setting rectangles
- ¾ yard of blue print fabric with white stars for flags
- ¾ yard of blue print fabric for outer border
- 5 yards of fabric for the quilt back
- Batting, larger than 76 × 81½ inches
- Rotary cutter, ruler, and mat

CUTTING

If you wish to cut the pieces using traditional methods, make templates for A and B. Pattern A appears full size on page 214; B is a 3 × 4-inch rectangle. If you prefer to quick-cut the pieces, follow the instructions below. Borders are cut longer than needed; trim them to the exact length when adding them to the quilt. All measurements include ¼-inch seam allowances. Cut all pieces across the fabric width unless instructed otherwise.

From the striped fabric, cut one 82-inch-long piece. From this piece, cut:
- Four 2½ × 82-inch inner borders
- 45 A rectangles with the stripes running lengthwise
  Quick-cut five 5¾ × 82-inch strips. From each strip, cut nine 5¾ × 9-inch rectangles for the flags.

From the remaining striped fabric, cut:

- 11 additional A rectangles
  Quick-cut two 9-inch-wide strips across the fabric width. From these strips, cut eleven 5¾ × 9-inch rectangles. You will have a total of 56 flag rectangles.
- Eight 2¼-inch-wide binding strips
- Four 2½-inch border corner squares

From the white fabric, cut:

- 56 A rectangles
  Quick-cut eight 9-inch-wide strips. Cut 5¾ × 9-inch rectangles from the strips.

From the blue fabric with white stars, cut:

- 56 B rectangles
  Quick-cut six 3-inch-wide strips across the fabric width. Cut 3 × 4-inch rectangles from the strips.

From the blue print border fabric, cut:

- Eight 2½-inch-wide outer border strips
- Four 2½-inch border corner squares

MAKING THE BLOCKS

1. To make one flag block, begin by pressing under the ¼-inch seam allowance on two adjacent sides of a blue B rectangle. See **Diagram 1.**

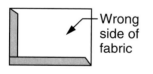

Wrong side of fabric

Diagram 1

2. Pin the prepared blue B rectangle to the upper left corner of a red-and-white striped A rectangle, aligning the raw edges at the corner. Appliqué the pressed-under edges of the blue rectangle to the striped rectangle. Baste the raw edges of the rectangles together at the corner, keeping the basting within the seam allowance so it will not show when the block is finished.

3. Repeat to make 56 flag blocks.

ASSEMBLING THE QUILT TOP

1. Referring to the **Quilt Diagram** on the opposite page, assemble the quilt top in 14 horizontal rows with four flag blocks and four white rectangles in each row. Make seven rows that begin with a flag and end with a white rectangle. Press the seams toward the flags. Make seven rows that begin with a white rectangle and end with a flag. Press the seams toward the flags.

2. Sew the rows together, alternating types of rows. The first row should begin with a flag block.

3. Measure the length of your quilt top, measuring through the middle rather than along the edges. Trim two striped borders for the sides of the quilt to this length (approximately 74 inches). Sew the borders to the sides of the quilt top. Press the seams toward the borders.

4. Measure the width of your quilt top, again measuring through the middle. Trim two striped borders for the top and bottom of the quilt to this length (approximately 68½ inches).

5. Sew a blue print border corner square to each end of the borders for the top and bottom of the quilt. Press the seams away from the corner squares. Sew the borders to the top and bottom of the quilt top.

6. Join pairs of blue print border strips to make four long borders. Sew them to the quilt top in a manner similar to that used for the striped borders, except use red-and-white striped corner squares.

QUILTING AND FINISHING

1. Mark quilting designs as desired. The quilt shown has very simple quilting, with a grid in the white rectangles and diagonal lines across the flags. If you prefer, add more interest to the setting rectangles with the star quilting design printed on the A rectangle pattern on page 214.

2. Divide the fabric for the quilt back crosswise into two equal lengths. Cut one piece in half lengthwise. Trim the selvages, and stitch a half panel to each side of the full-width panel. Press the seam allowances away from the center panel.

3. Layer the quilt back, batting, and quilt top; baste. Quilt as desired.

4. Join the red-and-white striped binding strips into one long piece, joining them with straight seams. Press the binding strip in half lengthwise. Sew the binding to the quilt. See page 13 in the "General Instructions" for details on making and attaching binding.

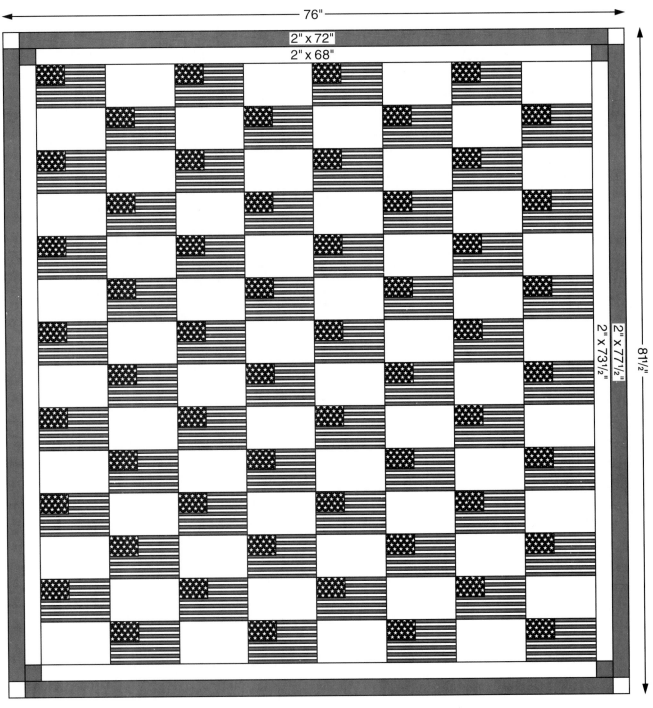

Quilt Diagram

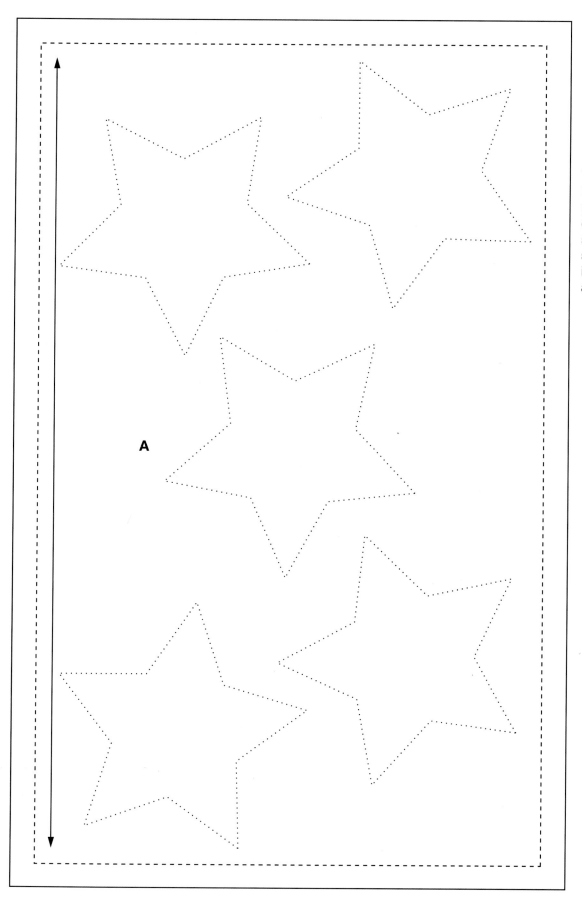

The dashed lines on the pattern indicate finished size. The solid lines include seam allowances.

A

· Grape Basket ·

Basket designs are perfect examples of quilt patterns inspired by everyday household objects. Famous quilt historian Carrie Hall wrote in 1935, "No quilt collection of our grandmother's day was complete without a basket quilt." Quilters of the 1990s are still in love with these charming patterns. Other popular basket designs include Cactus Basket, Cake Stand, and Flower Pot. One interesting feature of this particular basket quilt is the orientation of the baskets in the two outer rows. When the quilt is spread on the bed, those rows give you right-side-up baskets on both sides.

SKILL LEVEL: *Easy*

SIZE:

Finished quilt is approximately 70⅞ × 83¼ inches
Finished block is 8¾ inches square (approximately 12⅜ inches on the diagonal)

NUMBER OF PIECED BLOCKS: 30

FABRICS AND SUPPLIES

The antique quilt shown has 30 Grape Basket blocks. The dark triangles are brown print in 18 of the basket blocks, navy blue print in 8 blocks, and black print in 4 blocks. Various navy prints were used in the 8 blue blocks, but our supply list calls for the same blue print for the blocks, borders, and setting pieces. A pink checked fabric was used in the top portion of all the blocks. If you wish to make all the blocks identical, buy one more yard of navy fabric in addition to the amount listed below and omit the amounts listed for black and brown prints.

- 4¼ yards of navy blue print fabric for outer borders, setting pieces, and patchwork for eight blocks. (Purchase 5¼ yards if you wish to make all the blocks identical.)
- 2½ yards of white print fabric for block backgrounds
- 1½ yards of pink print fabric for inner borders and patchwork
- 1 yard of brown print fabric for patchwork
- ½ yard of black print fabric for patchwork
- 5 yards of fabric for the quilt back
- ¾ yard of fabric for binding
- Batting, larger than 70⅞ × 83¼ inches
- Template plastic (optional)
- Rotary cutter, ruler, and mat

CUTTING

If you wish to cut the pieces using traditional methods, make templates for pattern pieces A, B, C, D, and E on page 221. If you prefer to quick-cut all the pieces, follow the instructions here. All measurements include seam allowances. The measurements for the borders are longer than needed. Trim them to length when adding them to the quilt top. Cut all strips across the fabric width.

From the navy blue print, cut:
- Nine 3-inch-wide border strips
- Twenty 9¼-inch setting squares
  Quick-cut five 9¼-inch-wide strips. Cut the strips into 9¼-inch squares.
- 18 side setting triangles
  Quick-cut two 13⅝-inch-wide strips. From the strips, cut five 13⅝-inch squares. Cut each square in half diagonally both ways to make four triangles. You will have two extra triangles.
- 4 corner setting triangles
  Quick-cut two 7⅛-inch squares. Cut each square in half diagonally to make two triangles.
- 8 A triangles
  Quick-cut one 4⅜-inch-wide strip. Cut the strip into four 4⅜-inch squares. Cut each square in half diagonally to make two triangles.
- 64 B triangles
  Quick-cut three 2⅝-inch-wide strips. Cut the strips into 2⅝-inch squares. You will need 32 squares. Cut each square in half diagonally to make two triangles.

From the white print fabric, cut:
- 60 A triangles
  Quick-cut four 4⅜-inch-wide strips. Cut the strips into 4⅜-inch squares. You will need 30 squares. Cut each square in half diagonally to make two triangles.
- 120 B triangles
  Quick-cut four 2⅝-inch-wide strips. Cut the strips into 2⅝-inch squares. You will need 60 squares. Cut each square in half diagonally to make two triangles.
- 60 C triangles
  Quick-cut two 4¾-inch-wide strips. Cut the strips into 4¾-inch squares. You will need 15 squares. Cut each square diagonally both ways to make four triangles.
- 30 D squares
  Quick-cut two 2¼-inch-wide strips. Cut the strips into 2¼-inch squares.

- 60 E rectangles
  Quick-cut nine 2¼-inch-wide strips. Cut the strips into 2¼ × 5¾-inch rectangles.

From the pink print, cut:
- Eight 2½-inch-wide border strips
- 30 A triangles
  Quick-cut two 4⅜-inch-wide strips. Cut the strips into 4⅜-inch squares. You will need 15 squares. Cut each square in half diagonally to make two triangles.
- 120 B triangles
  Quick-cut four 2⅝-inch-wide strips. Cut the strips into 2⅝-inch squares. You will need 60 squares. Cut each square in half diagonally to make two triangles.

From the brown print fabric, cut:
- 18 A triangles
  Quick-cut one 4⅜-inch-wide strip. Cut the strip into nine 4⅜-inch squares. Cut each square in half to make two triangles.
- 144 B triangles
  Quick-cut five 2⅝-inch-wide strips. Cut the strips into 2⅝-inch squares. You will need 72 squares. Cut each square in half diagonally to make two triangles.

From the black print fabric, cut:
- 4 A triangles
  Quick-cut two 4⅜-inch squares. Cut each square in half diagonally to make two triangles.
- 32 B triangles
  Quick-cut two 2⅝-inch-wide strips. Cut the strips into 2⅝-inch-squares. You will need 16 squares. Cut the squares in half diagonally to make two triangles.

MAKING THE BLOCKS
When constructing the blocks, press the seams toward the darker fabric whenever possible. Follow the instructions to make one block. Make a total of 30 blocks.

1. Referring to the **Fabric Key** and the **Block Diagram,** lay out the following pieces for one block:

one pink A, one dark A, and two light A triangles; four pink B, eight dark B, and four light B triangles; two C triangles; one D square; and two E rectangles.

Fabric Key

- Dark fabric
- Light fabric
- Pink fabric

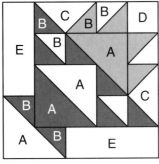

Block Diagram

2. Join one light A triangle and the dark A triangle to form a triangle-square, as shown in **Diagram 1.**

Diagram 1

3. Join a light B and a dark B triangle to form a triangle-square, as shown in **Diagram 2.** Add dark B triangles to two adjacent sides of the pieced square as shown to make a triangle unit. Make two of these units.

Diagram 2

4. Sew triangle units from Step 2 to two adjacent sides of the triangle-square from Step 1, as shown in **Diagram 3.**

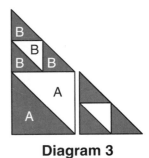

Diagram 3

5. Join pink B triangles to light B and light C triangles to form two strips as shown in **Diagram 4.** Be sure the B triangles are positioned correctly. Join a pink A triangle to one strip as shown. Add a D square to the end of the second strip; sew the strip to the side of the unit.

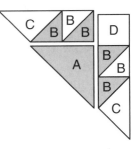

Diagram 4

6. Join a **Diagram 3** unit to a **Diagram 4** unit to form a square.

7. Sew dark B triangles to the ends of two E rectangles, as shown in **Diagram 5.** Sew these units to the sides of the block section.

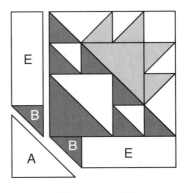

Diagram 5

8. Add a light A triangle to complete the block. Make 30 blocks.

ASSEMBLING THE QUILT TOP

1. Referring to the **Quilt Diagram** on page 220, lay out the blocks, setting squares, side setting triangles, and corner setting triangles in diagonal rows. Note that the blocks on the two outside rows on each side of the quilt point toward the center of the quilt. The baskets in the center row point toward the top of the quilt.

2. Join the blocks and setting pieces into diagonal rows as shown by the heavy lines in the diagram. Press the seams toward the setting squares. Join the rows.

3. To make the four pink borders, sew pairs of 2½-inch-wide pink border strips together with diagonal seams. See page 9 in the "General Instructions" for tips on piecing border strips.

4. Measure the width of the completed quilt top through the center of the quilt rather than along the sides, which may have stretched. Trim two of the pink borders to this length (approximately 62⅜ inches). Sew the borders to the top and bottom of the quilt. Press the seams toward the borders.

5. Measure the length of the quilt top, including the pink borders, measuring through the center of the quilt. Trim the two remaining pink border strips to this length (approximately 78¾ inches) and add them to the ends of the quilt top. Press the seams toward the borders.

6. Make four navy print border strips by sewing together pairs of 3-inch-wide strips with diagonal seams. Cut the remaining navy print border strip in half and add a half strip to each of the two side borders. Measure, trim, and sew the two shorter borders to the top and bottom of the quilt and the two longer borders to the sides of the quilt. Press the seams toward the border strips.

QUILTING AND FINISHING

1. Mark quilting designs as desired. The quilt shown has the all-over Baptist Fan quilting shown on page 31.

2. To piece the quilt back, divide the backing fabric crosswise into two equal lengths. Cut one of the pieces in half lengthwise. Sew a narrow panel to each side of the full-width panel. Press seams away from the center panel.

3. Layer the backing, batting, and quilt top; baste. Quilt as desired.

4. Make approximately 9 yards (324 inches) of straight-grain or bias binding to finish the edge of the quilt. See page 13 in the "General Instructions" for details on making and attaching binding.

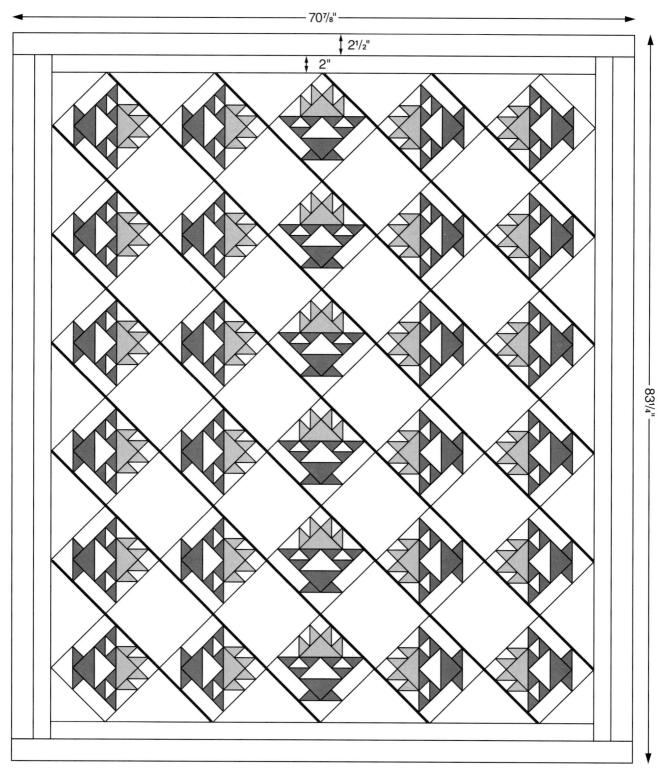

Quilt Diagram

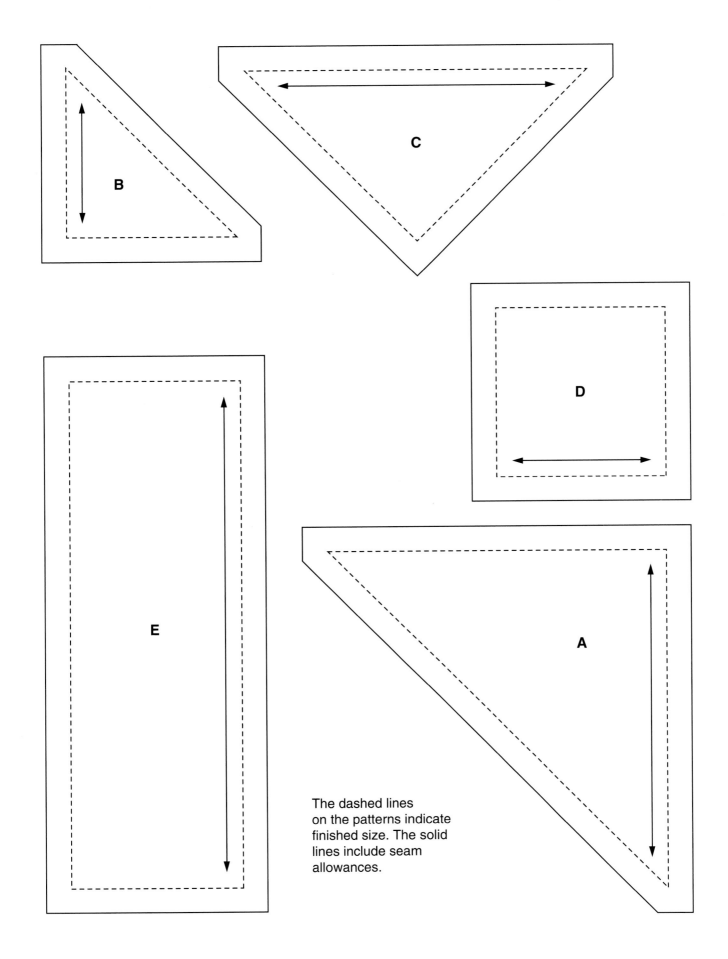

The dashed lines on the patterns indicate finished size. The solid lines include seam allowances.

· Country Schools ·

Two antique quilts, Chimneys and Cornerstones on page 236 and Little Red Schoolhouses and Birds on page 194, provided the inspiration for this quilt. The light and dark strips in the Chimneys and Cornerstones blocks frame the schoolhouses, and small red squares form chains across the quilt. We altered the top row of the schoolhouse block slightly to make the block square. Making the complex pieced zigzag borders will challenge your piecing skills.

SKILL LEVEL: *Challenging*

SIZE:

Finished quilt is approximately 73 × 93 inches
Finished block is 9 inches square

NUMBER OF PIECED BLOCKS:

18 Schoolhouse blocks
17 Chimneys and Cornerstones Log Cabin blocks

FABRICS AND SUPPLIES

- ¼ yard *each* of 18 or more different red print fabrics
- Scraps or ⅛ to ¼ yard *each* of 18 or more different light print fabrics (cream, beige, light gold, and white)
- Scraps or ⅛ to ¼ yard *each* of 18 or more different medium or dark print fabrics (blue, green, brown, black, and purple)
- 6 yards of fabric for the quilt back
- ¾ yard of fabric for binding
- Batting, larger than 73 × 93 inches
- Template plastic
- Rotary cutter, ruler, and mat

CUTTING

The cutting instructions are written so that you cut all the pieces for the Schoolhouse blocks first, then cut all the remaining pieces for the quilt.

Cutting the Pieces for the Schoolhouse Blocks

Cut the pieces for the Schoolhouse blocks from 18 different red print fabrics and assorted light print fabrics. Use either template-style cutting or quick-cut the pieces. For either method, refer to the **House Block Diagram** and the cutting chart to determine the numbers and types of pieces to cut.

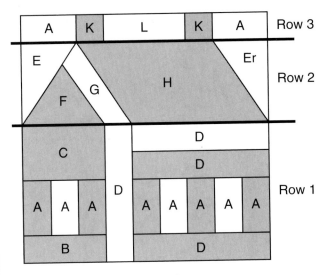

House Block Diagram

CUTTING CHART FOR SCHOOLHOUSE BLOCKS

Pattern Piece	Dimensions	Number to Cut per Block
A rectangle	1½ × 2½ inches	5 for house (red), 2 for windows (light), 1 for door (light), 2 for background (light)
B rectangle	1½ × 3½ inches	1 for house (red)
C rectangle	2½ × 3½ inches	1 for house (red)
D rectangle	1½ × 5½ inches	2 for house (red), 2 for background (light)
E and E reverse triangles	see pattern	1 each for background (light)
F triangle	see pattern	1 for house (red)
G piece	see pattern	1 for background (light)
H piece	see pattern	1 for roof (red)
K square	1½ × 1½ inches	2 for chimneys (red)
L rectangle	1½ × 3½ inches	1 for background (light)

If you plan to use template-style cutting, make templates for patterns A through H on pages 202–203. Since we altered the block slightly for this quilt, instead of using patterns I and J from the original block, you'll need to make templates for K and L on page 229.

If you plan to quick-cut the majority of the house pieces, you will still need to make templates for patterns E, F, G, and H. Refer to the cutting chart for the dimensions and quantities of pieces for quick-cutting. Measurements for quick-cut pieces include ¼-inch seam allowances.

Cutting the Remaining Pieces

Use a rotary cutter and ruler to quick-cut the pieces. Dimensions for pieces include ¼-inch seam allowances. Begin by cutting the number of 1½-inch-wide strips listed; if necessary, cut additional strips so you will have the needed number of each type of piece. Cut all strips across the fabric width.

From the red print fabrics left over from cutting the Schoolhouse blocks, cut 1½-inch-wide strips. Cut the following pieces from the strips:
■ 861 squares, each 1½ inches

From the light print fabrics left over from cutting the Schoolhouse blocks, cut 1½-inch-wide strips. Cut the following pieces from the strips:
■ Seventy 9½-inch-long rectangles
■ Seventy-eight 7½-inch-long rectangles
■ One hundred twenty-six 5½-inch-long rectangles
■ Four 4½-inch-long rectangles
■ Eighty-two 3½-inch-long rectangles
■ Four 2½-inch-long rectangles
■ Eighty-two 1½-inch squares

From the assorted medium and dark print fabrics, cut 1½-inch-wide strips across the full width of the fabrics. From these strips, cut:
■ Four 10½-inch-long rectangles
■ Eighty-two 9½-inch-long rectangles
■ Four 8½-inch-long rectangles
■ Eighty-two 7½-inch-long rectangles
■ Four 6½-inch-long rectangles
■ One hundred six 5½-inch-long rectangles
■ Eight 4½-inch-long rectangles
■ Eighty-six 3½-inch-long rectangles
■ Eight 2½-inch-long rectangles
■ Eighty-six 1½-inch squares

MAKING THE SCHOOLHOUSE BLOCKS

Follow the instructions below to make one block. As you assemble the pieces, press toward the red fabric whenever possible. Make a total of 18 blocks.

1. Referring to the **House Block Diagram** on page 223, lay out matching red print pieces and matching light print pieces for one block.

2. Make Row 1 in two units: a house front unit and a house side unit. For the house front, begin by joining two red A pieces and a light A door piece. Add a C rectangle to the top of the door unit and a B rectangle to the bottom.

3. For the house side unit, begin by joining three red A rectangles and two light A windows, as shown in the diagram. Sew a red D rectangle and a light D rectangle together along the long edges, and add them to the top of the window unit as shown. Sew a red D rectangle to the bottom of the window unit. To complete the house side unit, sew a light D rectangle to the left edge.

4. Join the house side unit and the house front unit to complete Row 1.

5. To make Row 2, begin by sewing a G piece to the right edge of the F triangle. Add an E triangle to the left edge of the FG unit. Sew the EFG house peak unit to the left edge of the H roof; add an E reverse triangle to the right edge.

6. To make Row 3, begin by sewing a red K chimney to each end of the L sky piece. Add an A sky piece to both ends of the KL unit.

7. Join the three rows. Press the seams in one direction. The block should measure 9½ inches square, including seam allowances.

MAKING THE CHIMNEYS AND CORNERSTONES BLOCKS

Small red squares divide the Chimneys and Cornerstones blocks diagonally both ways into four quarters. Two opposite quarters are light fabrics and two are medium and dark fabrics, as shown in the **Chimney Block Diagram.** The numbers on the diagram indicate the finished length of the pieces used; the

seam allowances have been deleted to simplify the drawing. For example, the number "3" indicates a piece that is cut 3½ inches long. Follow the instructions to make one block. Make 17 blocks.

1. Referring to the **Chimney Block Diagram,** lay out the following pieces for one block: 17 assorted red 1½-inch squares, 2 light and 2 dark 1½-inch squares, 2 light and 2 dark 3½-inch-long pieces, 2 light and 2 dark 5½-inch-long pieces, and 2 light and 2 dark 7½-inch-long pieces.

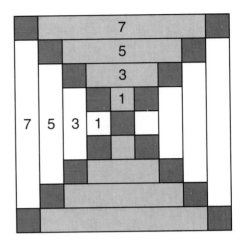

Chimney Block Diagram

2. Sew a red square to both ends of all the light pieces. You will have one extra red square to use as the block center. Press seams toward the light pieces.

3. Begin constructing the block by sewing a dark 1½-inch square to opposite sides of the red center square, as shown in **Diagram 1.** Press seams away from the center square.

Diagram 1

4. Referring to **Diagram 1,** sew the three rows of squares together to complete the center unit.

5. Add a 3½-inch-long dark piece to the opposite dark sides of the center unit, as shown in **Diagram 2.** Press the seams away from the center unit. Add the 3½-inch-long light strips with red squares attached to the other two sides. Press the seams away from the center.

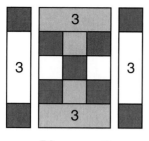

Diagram 2

6. Continue in this manner to add strips to opposite sides of the center. The completed block should measure 9½ inches square, including seam allowances.

ASSEMBLING THE INNER QUILT TOP

1. Referring to **Diagram 3,** lay out the Schoolhouse blocks, Chimneys and Cornerstones blocks, 9½-inch-long light and dark sashing strips, and red squares. Position the Chimneys and Cornerstones blocks so the dark sides are toward the dark sashing strips and the light sides are toward the light strips.

2. Make seven horizontal rows with five blocks and six sashing strips in each row. Press the seams toward the sashing strips.

3. Make eight horizontal rows with five sashing strips and six red squares in each row. Press the seams away from the red squares.

4. Join the rows in the order in which they're labeled on **Diagram 3.** Press the seams toward the sashing strip rows.

Schoolhouse	Chimneys and Cornerstones	Schoolhouse	Chimneys and Cornerstones	Schoolhouse
Chimneys and Cornerstones	Schoolhouse	Chimneys and Cornerstones	Schoolhouse	Chimneys and Cornerstones
Schoolhouse	Chimneys and Cornerstones	Schoolhouse	Chimneys and Cornerstones	Schoolhouse
Chimneys and Cornerstones	Schoolhouse	Chimneys and Cornerstones	Schoolhouse	Chimneys and Cornerstones
Schoolhouse	Chimneys and Cornerstones	Schoolhouse	Chimneys and Cornerstones	Schoolhouse
Chimneys and Cornerstones	Schoolhouse	Chimneys and Cornerstones	Schoolhouse	Chimneys and Cornerstones
Schoolhouse	Chimneys and Cornerstones	Schoolhouse	Chimneys and Cornerstones	Schoolhouse

Row 1 — Row 2 — Row 3 — Row 4 — Row 5 — Row 6 — Row 7 — Row 8 — Row 9 — Row 10 — Row 11 — Row 12 — Row 13 — Row 14 — Row 15 —

Diagram 3

MAKING AND ADDING THE PIECED BORDERS

The **Quilt Diagram** on page 228 shows the pieced borders for the quilt. The heavy lines at the corners define the division between the side and end borders.

A detail of the upper left quilt corner is shown in **Diagram 4.** The numbers on the diagram refer to the length of strips to use. As with the **Chimney Block Diagram,** the numbers have been abbreviated by omitting the seam allowance. For example, the number "3" indicates a piece cut 3½ inches long.

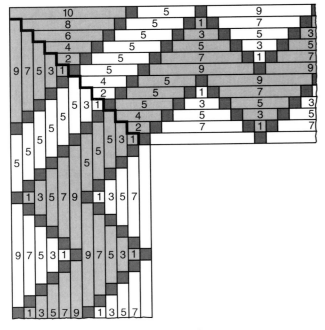

Diagram 4

1. Begin by making the border for the left side of the quilt. The border is made up of 11 long rows of 1½-inch-wide strips and squares. Refer to the **Quilt Diagram** and **Diagram 4** to determine the pieces to use for each row and the order in which to join them. Sew the pieces together to make the rows.

2. Sew the 11 rows together in order, starting with the innermost, shortest row. Leave approximately 3 inches of each border seam unsewn at the two ends of the strips. Leaving these seams unsewn will aid in attaching the borders to each other and to the quilt top once all the borders are ready.

3. In a similar manner, make the border for the right side of the quilt and the borders for the top and bottom. Pay careful attention to the diagrams as you assemble the borders, and use the partial seam method to join the individual border rows.

4. Join the left side border to the quilt top, sewing a complete seam from raw edge to raw edge. Repeat for the right side border.

5. Join Row 1 of the top border to the quilt top, stitching across the end of Row 1 of both side borders.

6. To finish the upper left border corner, complete the seam on the top end of Row 2 of the left side border, stitching across the end of the first row of the top border. Next, complete the seam on the left side of Row 2 of the top border, stitching across the end of Row 2 of the side border. Continue in this manner until the corner is complete.

7. Repeat to complete the upper right border corner.

8. Join the inner row of the bottom border to the quilt top, stitching across the end of the side borders.

9. Complete the lower left and the lower right border corners by completing the seams as described in Step 6.

QUILTING AND FINISHING

1. Mark quilting designs as desired. The Baptist Fan quilting design on page 31 was used on the quilt shown.

2. Divide the quilt back fabric crosswise into two equal lengths. Cut one piece in half lengthwise. Stitch a half panel to each long side of the full-width panel. Press the seams away from the center panel.

3. Layer the quilt back, batting, and quilt top; baste. Quilt as desired.

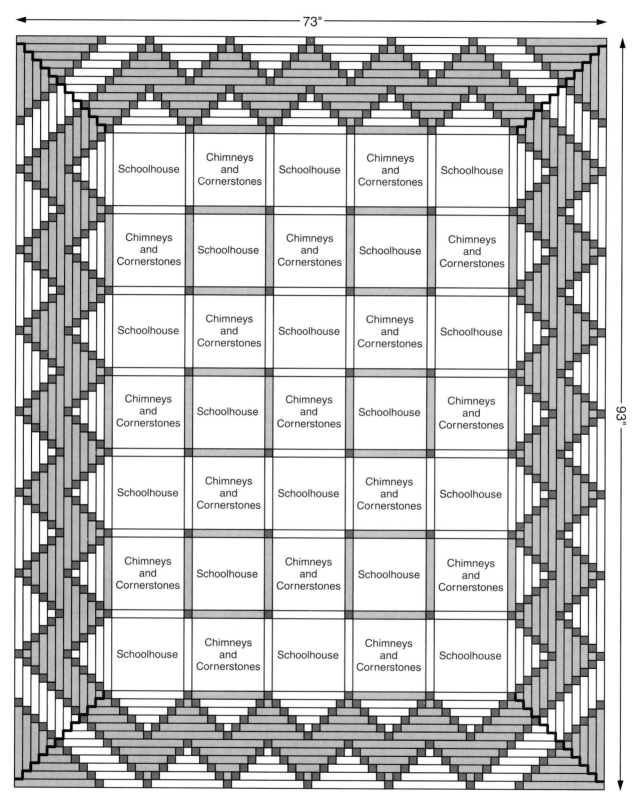

Quilt Diagram

4. From the binding fabric, make approximately 9¾ yards (350 inches) of straight-grain or bias binding. Sew the binding to the quilt. See page 13 in the "General Instructions" for details on making and attaching binding.

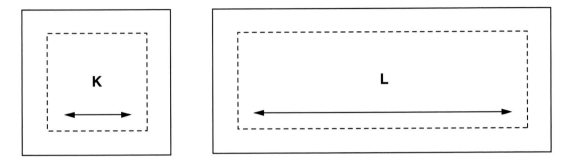

The dashed lines on the patterns indicate finished size.
The solid lines include seam allowances.

Strips
and
Strings

Long, narrow pieces, or fabric "strings," left over from other sewing found their way into patchwork that has become a genre all its own. Piecing strips to a paper or muslin foundation block was a quiltmaking fad that had its beginnings around 1860. Our instructions for two of the quilts in this chapter, the Midwest Windmill Blades and the Bull's Eye, involve using a fabric foundation block. Today's rotary cutter makes cutting strips in quantity a breeze.

Chinese Coins

Bar or strip quilts are much less common than the more typical block-format quilts. In this Victorian example, small logs of silk, taffeta, satin, wool, rayon, and cotton are joined into long strips. The pieced strips alternate with rust solid fabric strips. To make this otherwise plain quilt more elaborate and in keeping with Victorian taste, fancy embroidery was added along the seams that join the vertical pieces. Our instructions are for a quilt that finishes $61\frac{3}{4} \times 80$ inches, a comfortable size to use as a coverup while watching television. If you prefer a longer quilt, make longer pieced bars and purchase additional lengths of rust fabric and backing fabric.

SKILL LEVEL: *Easy*

SIZE:

Finished quilt is approximately $61\frac{3}{4} \times 80$ inches

FABRICS AND SUPPLIES

The antique quilt was pieced from a variety of "fancy" fabrics including silk, satin, wool, taffeta, and rayon. If you want your quilt to be washable, use fabrics such as cotton.

- Approximately $3\frac{3}{4}$ yards total of assorted fabrics for the small bar pieces. (For our quick-piecing method, you will need a total of 80 assorted strips, each $1\frac{1}{2}$ inches wide and approximately 40 inches long.)
- $2\frac{3}{8}$ yards of rust solid fabric for the separating strips
- 5 yards of fabric for the quilt back
- $\frac{3}{4}$ yard of fabric for binding (optional)
- Batting, larger than $61\frac{3}{4} \times 80$ inches
- Gold pearl cotton or embroidery floss and an embroidery needle for hand stitching OR machine embroidery thread for machine stitching (optional)

- Pearl cotton or embroidery floss in a color that coordinates with the quilt back and darning needle with large eye if you plan to tie the quilt (optional)
- Darning needle with large eye to tie the quilt (optional)
- Rotary cutter, ruler, and mat

CUTTING

Measurements for all pieces include $\frac{1}{4}$-inch seam allowances.

From the assorted fabrics for the pieced bars, cut:

- Eighty $1\frac{1}{2}$-inch-wide strips cut across the fabric width

From the rust solid fabric, cut:

- Seven $4\frac{1}{4}$-inch-wide strips cut the length of the fabric
- Two 3-inch-wide strips cut the length of the fabric

MAKING THE PIECED BARS

1. Divide the 80 assorted fabric strips into ten groups of eight strips each.

2. Stitch eight strips together into a strip set. Press all the seams in one direction. Make a total of ten strip sets.

3. Referring to **Diagram 1,** cut a total of eight 4¾-inch-wide segments from each strip set. You will have a total of 80 pieced segments.

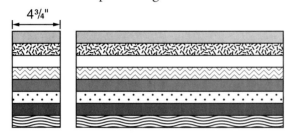

4¾"

Diagram 1

4. To make a pieced bar, choose ten assorted pieced segments. Join the segments into a long strip. Make eight long pieced bars.

5. Measure the length of a pieced bar (approximately 80½ inches). Trim all the rust strips to this length.

6. Referring to the **Quilt Diagram,** lay out pieced bars and rust strips. Be sure to place the 3-inch-wide rust strips on the outside edges. Sew the strips together, pressing the seam allowances toward the rust strips.

7. If desired, add decorative stitching along the vertical seams with embroidery thread. The antique quilt in the photo was embellished with the herringbone stitch, illustrated in **Diagram 2.** If your sewing machine will do decorative embroidery stitches, you may prefer to add decorative machine stitching along the seams using machine embroidery thread.

If you plan to hand or machine quilt your project rather than tie it, but prefer to do the embroidery work by hand, wait to do the embroidery until after you have completed the quilting.

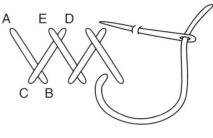

Diagram 2

FINISHING

1. To piece the quilt back, divide the backing fabric crosswise into two equal lengths. Cut one piece in half lengthwise. Stitch a half panel to each side of the full-width panel. Press the seams away from the center panel.

2. Layer the quilt back, batting, and quilt top; baste.

3. The antique quilt was tied, rather than quilted, with the ties on the quilt back. Use a square knot, as shown in **Diagram 3,** to secure the ties. Place ties along vertical seams, approximately every 4 inches. For a more durable cover, you may wish to quilt your throw. Hand or machine quilt in the ditch along the vertical seams. After quilting is complete, add decorative stitching along the seams if desired.

Diagram 3

4. The antique quilt was finished by bringing the back over to the front. To finish your quilt in the same way, begin by trimming the batting even with the quilt top. Trim the backing so it is 1 inch larger than the quilt top on all sides. Turn in ½ inch on the quilt back. Bring the folded edge to the front of the quilt and hand stitch in place.

If you prefer to finish your quilt with a separate binding, make approximately 9 yards (324 inches) of bias or straight-grain binding. See page 13 in the "General Instructions" for details on making and attaching binding.

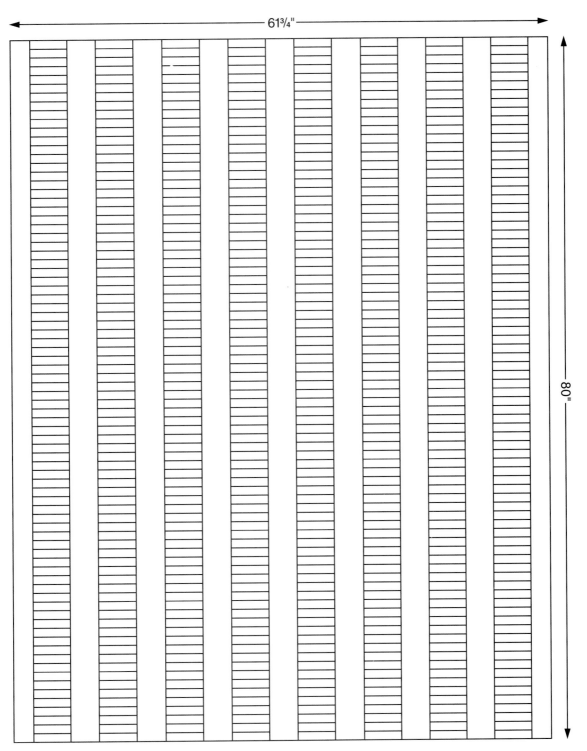

Quilt Diagram

Chimneys and Cornerstones

Log Cabin quilts, with their many variations, have long been a favorite with quilters. Examples of some types of Log Cabin quilts, such as Barn Raising and Straight Furrows, are very common in the Midwest and other regions of the country. The antique quilt in the photograph is a rare variation called Chimneys and Cornerstones. Small red squares, representing the chimneys and cornerstones of a log cabin, divide each block into four sections, two light and two dark, and create intersecting chains that run diagonally across the quilt in both directions. Here, we've written the directions so that you can make the quilt in either of two sizes. We were so intrigued with the design potential of this block that we couldn't resist experimenting with it. The Country Schools quilt, shown on page 222, evolved by alternating Chimneys and Cornerstones blocks with blocks similar to those used in the Little Red Schoolhouses and Birds antique quilt shown on page 194.

SKILL LEVEL: *Easy*

SIZE:

If you begin with strips cut 1½ inches wide,
  Finished quilt is 85 × 99 inches
  Finished block is 13 inches square
If you begin with strips cut 1¼ inches wide,
  Finished quilt is 63¾ × 74¼ inches
  Finished block is 9¾ inches square

NUMBER OF PIECED BLOCKS: 42

FABRICS AND SUPPLIES

The instructions for this quilt are organized to give you a choice of sizes. If you use strips cut 1½ inches wide, the finished quilt is ideal for a full- or queen-size bed. If you use strips cut 1¼ inches wide, the finished quilt makes a great coverup for watching television or reading. The fabric amounts and measurements for 1½-inch-wide strips are presented first, with the information for 1¼-inch-wide strips in parentheses. Be sure to refer to the same set of numbers throughout the directions.

- 6 (4½) yards total of assorted light print fabrics (white, tan, and yellow)
- 5 (4) yards total of assorted medium and dark print fabrics (blue, black, and gray)
- 2½ (2) yards total of red solid fabric
- 3 yards of 90-inch-wide (4½ yards of 44-inch-wide for the smaller quilt) fabric for the quilt back
- ¾ yard of fabric for binding (for both large and small versions)
- Rotary cutter, ruler, and mat

CUTTING

Measurements for all pieces include ¼-inch seam allowances. Begin by cutting the number of strips listed for each fabric; you may need to cut a few additional strips if your fabrics are narrower than 44 inches wide. Cut all strips across the fabric width. Label and set aside the strips for the strip sets.

From the assorted light fabrics, cut:
- Four 11½ (8¾)-inch-wide strips for the F strip sets
- Four 9½ (7¼)-inch-wide strips for the E strip sets
- Four 7½ (5¾)-inch-wide strips for the D strip sets
- Four 5½ (4¼)-inch-wide strips for the C strip sets
- Four 3½ (2¾)-inch-wide strips for the B strip sets
- Four 1½ (1¼)-inch-wide strips for the A strip sets
- Seventeen (thirteen) 1½ (1¼)-inch-wide strips. From the strips, cut forty-nine 13½ (10¼)-inch-long sashing strips.

From the assorted medium and dark fabrics, cut:
- Four 1½ (1¼)-inch-wide strips for the A strip sets
- Sixteen (twelve) 1½ (1¼)-inch-wide strips. From the strips, cut forty-eight 13½ (10¼)-inch-long sashing strips.
- Eighty-four 1½ (1¼)-inch-wide strips. From the strips, cut 84 each of pieces B, C, D, E, and F. Refer to the cutting chart below for the length to cut the pieces. You can speed the cutting process by stacking several strips and then cutting the pieces from the stacks.

From the red fabric, cut:
- Fifty-three (fifty-two) 1½ (1¼)-inch-wide strips. From three (two) of the strips, cut a total of fifty-six 1½ (1¼)-inch sashing squares. Reserve the remaining strips for the strip sets.

CUTTING CHART FOR CHIMNEYS AND CORNERSTONES BLOCK

Piece	Cut Length for 1½-inch strips	Cut Length for 1¼-inch strips
A	1½ inches	1¼ inches
B	3½ inches	2¾ inches
C	5½ inches	4¼ inches
D	7½ inches	5¾ inches
E	9½ inches	7¼ inches
F	11½ inches	8¾ inches

MAKING THE BLOCKS

Small red squares divide the Chimneys and Cornerstones blocks diagonally into four sections. Two opposite sections are light fabrics and two are medium and dark fabrics, as shown in the **Block Diagram.** Our quick-piecing instructions explain how to quick-piece the Nine-Patch block centers and the light fabric B, C, D, E, and F units with red squares attached. The medium and dark logs are added as individual pieces. Sashing strips with small red squares separate the individual blocks.

Block Diagram

Follow the instructions to make the 42 Chimneys and Cornerstones blocks for your quilt. As you make the strip sets, press the seam allowances away from the red fabric. As you add pieces around the block center, press the seam allowances away from the center of the block.

Piecing the Block Center Units

Use 1½ (1¼)-inch-wide strips for the A strip sets to make the block center units. You will need two types of strip sets: dark A strip sets and light A strip sets.

1. Referring to the **Fabric Key** and **Diagram 1,** make a dark A strip set by sewing together two medium or dark strips with a red strip between them. Make two dark A strip sets. Cut a total of 42 segments, each 1½ (1¼) inches wide, from the dark A strip sets.

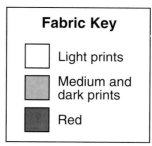

Fabric Key

Light prints

Medium and dark prints

Red

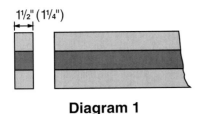

1½" (1¼")

Diagram 1

2. To make a light A strip set, sew together two red strips with a light strip between them, as shown in **Diagram 2**. Make four light A strip sets. Cut a total of 84 segments, each 1½ (1¼) inches wide, from the light A strip sets.

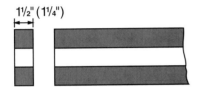

1½" (1¼")

Diagram 2

3. To make a block center, sew together two light A segments with a dark A segment between them, as shown in **Diagram 3**. Make 42 block center units.

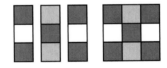

Diagram 3

Making and Adding the B Pieces

1. Make four B strip sets as shown in **Diagram 4** by sewing a red strip to both long sides of a 3½ (2¾)-inch-wide light strip. Cut a total of 84 segments, each 1½ (1¼) inches wide, from the strip sets.

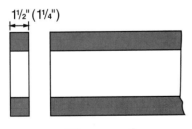

1½" (1¼")

Diagram 4

2. Referring to **Diagram 5,** sew a medium or dark B piece to the sides of the block center units that contain a dark A square. Then, sew segments from the B strip sets to the sides of the center units that contain a light A square.

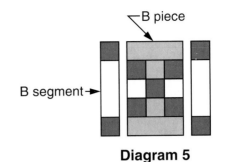

B piece

B segment→

Diagram 5

Making and Adding the C Pieces

1. Make four C strip sets as shown in **Diagram 6** by sewing a narrow red strip to both long sides of each 5½ (4¼)-inch-wide light strip. Cut a total of 84 segments, each 1½ (1¼) inches wide, from the strip sets.

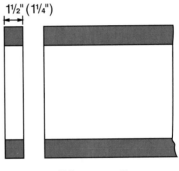

1½" (1¼")

Diagram 6

2. Referring to **Diagram 7,** sew a medium or dark C piece to the dark sides of the blocks. Then, sew segments from the C strip sets to the light sides of the blocks.

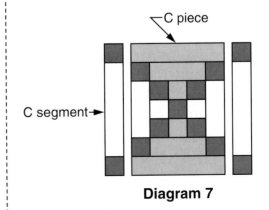

C piece

C segment→

Diagram 7

Making and Adding the D, E, and F Pieces

1. In the same manner, make four D, E, and F strip sets. Use 7½ (5¾)-inch-wide light strips for the

D sets, 9½ (7¼)-inch-wide light strips for the E sets, and 11½ (8¾)-inch-wide light strips for the F sets.

2. Cut 84 segments each from the D, E, and F strip sets, cutting each segment 1½ (1¼) inches wide.

3. Sew dark D pieces to the dark sides of the blocks; then, add light D segments to the light sides. Add E and F pieces in the same manner. The completed blocks should measure 13½ (10¼) inches square, including seam allowances.

Assembling the Quilt Top

1. Referring to **Diagram 8,** join six blocks into a row, placing light sashing strips between the blocks and at the beginning and end of the row. Make seven rows like the one shown in **Diagram 8.**

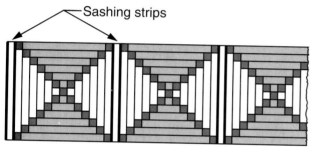

Diagram 8

2. Referring to **Diagram 9,** join six dark sashing strips into a row, placing red sashing squares between the strips and at the beginning and end of the row. Make eight rows like the one shown in **Diagram 9.**

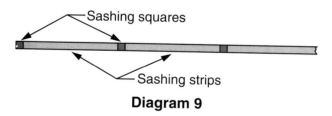

Diagram 9

3. Referring to the **Quilt Diagram,** sew the rows together, alternating sashing strip rows and block rows. The heavy lines on the diagram help define the horizontal rows.

Quilting and Finishing

1. If you are making the smaller quilt, piece the quilt back. Divide the backing fabric crosswise into two equal lengths. Cut one piece in half lengthwise. Trim the selvages, and stitch a half panel to each side of the full-width panel. Press the seams away from the center panel.

2. Layer the quilt back, batting, and quilt top; baste. Quilt as desired. The antique quilt in the photograph was quilted in the ditch around the patchwork pieces.

3. Make approximately 10½ (8) yards of bias or straight-grain binding to finish your quilt. See page 13 in the "General Instructions" for details on making and attaching binding.

Quilt Diagram

.Bull's Eye.

The Bull's Eyes in this quilt are formed where the red corners of four Roman Stripe blocks come together. While the quiltmaker left a whole row of incomplete Bull's Eyes, in our instructions we've added one more row of blocks to complete all of the four-block Bull's Eye sections. Like Log Cabin blocks, Roman Stripe blocks can be set different ways. We used Roman Stripe blocks for two contemporary quilts in this chapter, the Streak O' Lightning quilt and the Sunshine and Shadow wallhanging. Other setting variations are illustrated on page 256. To duplicate the antique quilt shown, we sewed strips on the diagonal to one-half of the foundation squares, leaving the other half of the squares unpieced. We used a different method, one that calls for strip combinations and quick-piecing, for our new projects that begin on page 254.

SKILL LEVEL: *Easy*

SIZE:

Finished quilt is approximately 85 inches square
Finished Roman Stripe block is 8½ inches square

NUMBER OF PIECED BLOCKS: 100

FABRICS AND SUPPLIES

The colors in parentheses are the predominant ones used in the antique quilt.

- ½ yard *each* of 13 dark print fabrics for foundation blocks and strips (indigo, navy, and medium blue prints and stripes; black prints and checks; and gray prints)
- ¼ yard *each* of four additional dark print fabrics for the strips (in the same colors described above)
- ½ yard *each* of 13 light print fabrics for foundation blocks and strips (various white-background prints with either small red or black motifs, narrow stripes, and small checks)
- ½ yard of red print fabric or the equivalent in scraps for strips

- ¼ yard of gold solid fabric for strips (optional)
- 8¼ yards of fabric for the quilt back
- Batting, larger than 85 inches square
- Rotary cutter, ruler, and mat

CUTTING

All the pieces for this quilt can be easily cut using a rotary cutter and ruler. The dimensions given include ¼-inch seam allowances. Cut all strips across the fabric width.

From *each* of the thirteen ½-yard pieces of dark fabric, cut:

- Four 9-inch squares
  Quick-cut one 9-inch-wide strip from each fabric. Cut the strips into 9-inch squares. You will need 50 squares.
- Five 1½-inch-wide strips

From *each* of the four ¼-yard pieces of dark fabric, cut:

- Four 1½-inch-wide strips

From *each* of the thirteen light fabrics, cut:

■ Four 9-inch squares
  Quick-cut one 9-inch-wide strip from each fabric.
  Cut the strips into 9-inch squares. You will need
  50 squares.
■ Four 1½-inch-wide strips

From the red print fabric, cut:

■ Nine 1½-inch-wide strips

From the optional gold fabric, cut:

■ Two 1½-inch-wide strips

MAKING THE BLOCKS

Follow the instructions to make one block. Use the
9-inch squares as foundation blocks for the strip
work. Select fabrics randomly to achieve the scrap
look of the original quilt. Make 50 dark blocks and
50 light blocks.

1. Fold a 9-inch square in half diagonally and
lightly press to form a crease line.

2. On the right side of the fabric, draw a placement line ¼ inch to one side of the crease line, as
shown in **Diagram 1.**

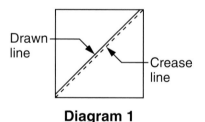

Diagram 1

3. Place a dark fabric strip *right* side together with
the foundation square, aligning the raw edge of the
strip with the drawn line, as shown in **Diagram 2.**
When working with a dark fabric foundation square,
be sure to begin with a strip that contrasts with the
foundation print. For example, use a black print for
the first strip on blue foundation squares. Use a blue
print for the first strip on a black print square.

4. Stitch the strip to the foundation square, using
a ¼-inch seam, as shown in **Diagram 2.**

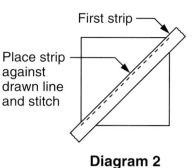

Diagram 2

5. Open the stitched strip so the right side is face
up, as shown in **Diagram 3,** and press flat. Trim off
excess strip to within ½ inch of the foundation
square, but wait to trim strips even with the foundation square until all strips are added.

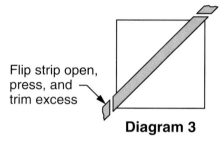

Diagram 3

6. Add the second strip by placing a light strip
right side together with the first strip, aligning the
raw edges. Stitch the light strip in place, sewing
through all three layers (two strips plus the foundation). Open the light strip so the right side is face
up and press. Trim off excess strip, as described
above. If desired, use a gold strip in this position on
approximately six blocks.

7. Referring to **Diagram 4,** continue to add strips,
adding a black print or a gray print strip next, then
a light strip, then a medium blue, and finally a red.
The numbers on the diagram show the order and
colors for strips.

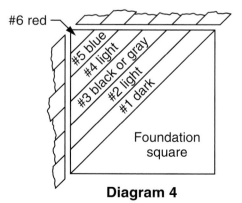

Diagram 4

8. Trim the excess strips even with the outside edges of the foundation square as shown in **Diagram 4.** The finished block should measure 9 inches square, including seam allowances.

ASSEMBLING AND FINISHING THE QUILT TOP

1. To make the Bull's Eye block units, sew two light blocks and two dark blocks together into a four-block unit, as shown in **Diagram 5.** Make 25 four-block units.

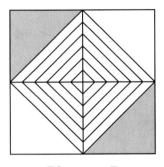

Diagram 5

2. Referring to the **Quilt Diagram,** lay out the four-block units in five rows with five units per row. Join the units in rows; join the rows. Note that, unlike the antique shown in the photo on page 242, the quilt in the diagram is made up of only complete four-block units.

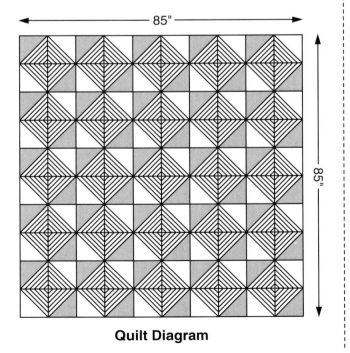

85"

85"

Quilt Diagram

3. To piece the quilt back, first divide the yardage into three 2¾-yard (99-inch) lengths. Trim the selvages and join two of the lengths. Measure the two-panel backing to see how wide it is. Cut a strip of fabric from the remaining panel wide enough to make the backing 99 inches wide. Sew the narrow panel to the two-panel quilt back. The remainder of the third panel can be used for a separate binding, if desired.

4. Layer the backing, batting, and quilt top; baste.

5. Quilt as desired. The quilt shown has straight-line quilting approximately ¼ inch away from the seams of the strips, as well as diagonal lines on the solid triangles, as shown in **Diagram 6.** If you plan to finish the edges of the quilt by turning them in, then stop quilting ½ inch away from the edge of the quilt top.

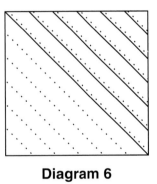

Diagram 6

6. The quilt shown was finished by turning in the front and back edges and hand stitching the folded edges together. To finish a quilt in this way, you must stop quilting ½ inch away from the edge of the quilt top. Trim backing and batting even with the edge of the quilt top. Separate the quilt top and backing from the batting, and trim off an additional ¼ inch of batting. Fold in ¼ inch along the raw edges of the quilt top and the backing. Slip stitch the folded edges together.

If you prefer to finish the quilt with a separate binding, use the leftover backing fabric to make approximately 10 yards (360 inches) of straight-grain or bias binding. See page 13 in the "General Instructions" for details on making and attaching binding.

Midwest
Windmill Blades

Not a true quilt, since it is tied rather than quilted, this stunning coverlet was made around 1893 by the grandmother of the Winterset, Iowa, gentleman who owns it. Creator Gertrude Buchner positioned the light and dark values of her fabrics with absolute mastery. The jagged edges of the patchwork, forming circle upon circle, are what give the quilt its illusion of movement, as though those blades are turning night and day on a windy midwest farm. The fabrics are lightweight wool, including twill, challis, and serge weaves, with velvet used for the checkerboard and plain borders. Strip and string quilts, such as Log Cabin, Pineapple, and Windmill variations like this one, were often constructed by stitching the narrow strips of fabric, possibly left over from other sewing, onto a foundation square. Our instructions call for a slightly updated version of that method—using a transfer pen to mark placement lines on the foundation fabric.

SKILL LEVEL: *Challenging*

SIZE:

Finished quilt is approximately 82½ × 94 inches
Finished block is 18½ inches square

NUMBER OF PIECED BLOCKS: 20

FABRICS AND SUPPLIES

- 5¾ yards of foundation fabric. (Choose the fabric type, cotton or cotton/polyester blend, recommended for use with the brand of transfer pen you will use.)
- 3 yards total of assorted deep red solid fabrics
- 2¾ yards of black solid fabric
- 2 yards of blue solid fabric. (Use blue fabric for the B, D, and F pieces for all blocks. Also, use blue solid for the U, W, and Y pieces for eight of the blocks.)
- 2 yards total of gold solid and light green tweed

fabrics for the O, Q, and S pieces
- 1¾ yards of black-and-gray checked fabric for U, W, and Y pieces for 12 of the blocks
- 1½ yards total of gray solid and light teal solid fabrics for the I, K, and M pieces
- 1½ yards of dark teal solid fabric for the N, P, and R pieces
- 1 yard of cream or off-white print fabric for the C, E, and G pieces
- 1 yard of brown velvet fabric for borders
- Approximately ½ yard total of assorted (gold, red, and tan) velvet fabrics for border squares
- 7¼ yards of fabric for the quilt back
- Fabric transfer pen
- 19-inch square of tracing paper
- Fine-tip permanent marking pen
- Pearl cotton or embroidery floss and needle to tie quilt
- Rotary cutter, ruler, and mat

CUTTING

When piecing a Windmill Blades block with the foundation square method, only the center A squares are cut to size. All other pieces are cut as strips, sewn to the foundation square (which has the sewing lines marked on it), and cut to size as the block is pieced. Use a rotary cutter and ruler to cut the fabric strips. Cut all strips across the fabric width. The number of strips to cut is approximate. You may need to cut additional strips depending on the width of your fabric. All measurements include ¼-inch seam allowances.

From the foundation fabric, cut:
■ Twenty 20-inch squares

From the assorted deep red solid fabrics, cut:
■ Six 1½-inch-wide strips for the AD position in the block corners
■ Sixty 1¼-inch-wide strips
■ Twenty 1¼-inch squares
  Quick-cut one 1¼-inch-wide strip. From the strip, cut 1¼-inch squares.

From the black solid fabric, cut:
■ Sixty 1¼-inch-wide strips

From the blue solid fabric, cut:
■ Thirty-seven 1¼-inch-wide strips

From the gold solid and light green tweed fabrics, cut:
■ A total of approximately forty 1¼-inch-wide strips

From the black-and-gray checked fabric, cut:
■ Thirty 1¼-inch-wide strips

From the gray solid and light teal solid fabrics, cut:
■ A total of approximately thirty 1¼-inch-wide strips

From the dark teal solid fabric, cut:
■ Thirty-five 1¼-inch-wide strips

From the cream or off-white print fabric, cut:
■ Twenty 1¼-inch-wide strips

From the brown velvet fabric, cut:
■ One hundred six 2¼-inch squares
  Quick-cut six 2¼-inch strips. From the strips, cut 2¼-inch squares.
■ Nine 1¾-inch-wide border strips

From the assorted velvet fabrics, cut:
■ One hundred six 2¼-inch squares

MAKING AND USING THE MASTER PATTERN

Patterns for the Windmill Blades block are on pages 251–253. Use them to create a full-size master pattern that indicates placement lines for the patchwork pieces. The master pattern is transferred onto each foundation square, and pieces are stitched and cut using the master pattern as a guide.

1. Fold a 19-inch square of tracing paper in half vertically, horizontally, and diagonally in both directions, and crease to create guidelines.

2. Refer to the **Block Diagram** as you make the master pattern. Place the center of the sheet of tracing paper over the center of the A piece on the pattern, and align the dashed lines on the pattern with the folds on the tracing paper. Trace the entire pattern onto the paper. Rotate the paper to repeat the pattern in the other sections of the paper. Trace patterns Q through Y on page 252 and patterns R through AD on page 253 onto the paper to complete

Block Diagram

the drawing. Label the paper pattern with the letters and suggested fabric colors.

3. Darken all lines with a permanent pen.

4. Following the manufacturer's instructions for your transfer pen, trace the master pattern. Use a hot iron to transfer the pattern onto each foundation square.

Piecing the Blocks

Follow the instructions to piece a block onto a foundation square. The pattern for the foundation square includes seam allowances, so the raw long sides of the opened-out fabric strips should line up with the lines on the foundation block. If the long sides of the strips extend beyond the foundation lines, trim excess fabric. If the long sides of the strips are a bit shy of meeting the foundation line, check to be sure the seam is pressed well, with no tucks or folds. If the piece still is a bit shy of the line, line up the new strip to be added with the foundation line rather than with the raw edge of the previous strip. The result will be that the underlying seam allowance on the previous strip will be slightly less than a perfect ¼ inch.

1. Working with the marked side of the foundation square facing you, pin a red 1¼-inch square onto the center of the foundation square within the master pattern guideline marked for the A piece.

2. From the blue solid fabric, cut four 1¼-inch-long B pieces.

3. With right sides facing and raw edges aligned, pin a blue B strip to one side of the A square. Taking a ¼-inch seam, stitch the B strip to the A square, as shown in **Diagram 1,** sewing through all layers.

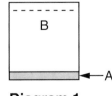

Diagram 1

4. Open out the B strip and finger press the seam, as shown in **Diagram 2.** Trim the excess B strip so its edges align with the foundation guidelines for the B piece.

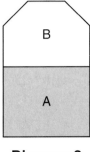

Diagram 2

5. In the same manner, position, sew, and trim a B strip to the opposite side of the A square. Sew a B strip to the remaining two sides of the square, as shown in **Diagram 3.**

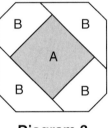

Diagram 3

6. With right sides facing and raw edges aligned, place the end of a white strip even with one edge of the center unit, as shown in **Diagram 4.** Place a pin at the other edge to indicate the end of the stitch line. Stitch the seam, stopping at the pin.

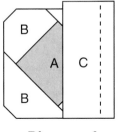

Diagram 4

7. Open out the C strip and finger press the seam, as shown in **Diagram 5.** Trim excess strip even with the lines on the foundation.

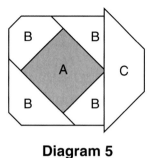

Diagram 5

8. Add a C strip to the opposite side of the center. Add a strip to the other two sides, as shown in **Diagram 6.** Trim the C pieces following the guidelines on the foundation square.

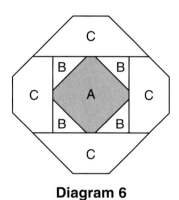

Diagram 6

9. Following the color suggestions on the patterns, continue to add strips around the center unit in alphabetical order until the block is complete. Use the 1½-inch-wide red strips for the AD pieces at the block corners.

10. When all pieces are added, baste within the seam allowance around the block. Trim the excess foundation square even with the edges of the strips.

ASSEMBLING THE QUILT TOP

1. Lay out the blocks in five horizontal rows with four blocks in each row.

2. Sew the blocks together in horizontal rows; press the seams in alternate directions from row to row.

3. Join the rows.

4. To make the velvet checkerboard borders, pair each brown square with a contrasting square. Sew pairs of squares together and press the seams toward the brown squares. Use a press cloth on top and a towel underneath the velvet to prevent damage to the velvet during pressing.

5. Alternating brown squares with colored squares, make two borders that are 53 squares long.

6. Measure the length of the quilt, measuring through the middle rather than along the sides (approximately 93 inches including seam allowances). Trim the checkerboard borders to this length.

7. Sew the velvet border strips into one long strip. From this strip, cut two borders the same length as the checkerboard borders.

8. Sew a brown velvet border to one side of each checkerboard border. Press the seams toward the brown borders. Sew the borders to the sides of the quilt, placing the brown velvet borders to the outer edges. Press the seams toward the borders.

9. Measure the width of the quilt, again measuring through the middle (approximately 83 inches including seam allowances). Cut two brown velvet borders to this length. Sew the borders to the top and bottom edges of the quilt top. Press the seams toward the borders.

FINISHING

1. Divide the backing fabric crosswise into three equal lengths. Trim the selvages and join the three panels, pressing the seams away from the center panel. The seams will run crosswise across the quilt.

2. With right sides facing, pin the pieced top to the backing. Sew the top and backing together, leaving an opening along one side for turning.

3. Trim the excess backing. Turn the quilt right side out through the opening. Stitch the opening closed.

4. To secure the layers, use embroidery floss to tie the top to the back at the centers, corners, and middle of each side of the blocks. A stitch diagram for making a square knot to tie a quilt is on page 234.

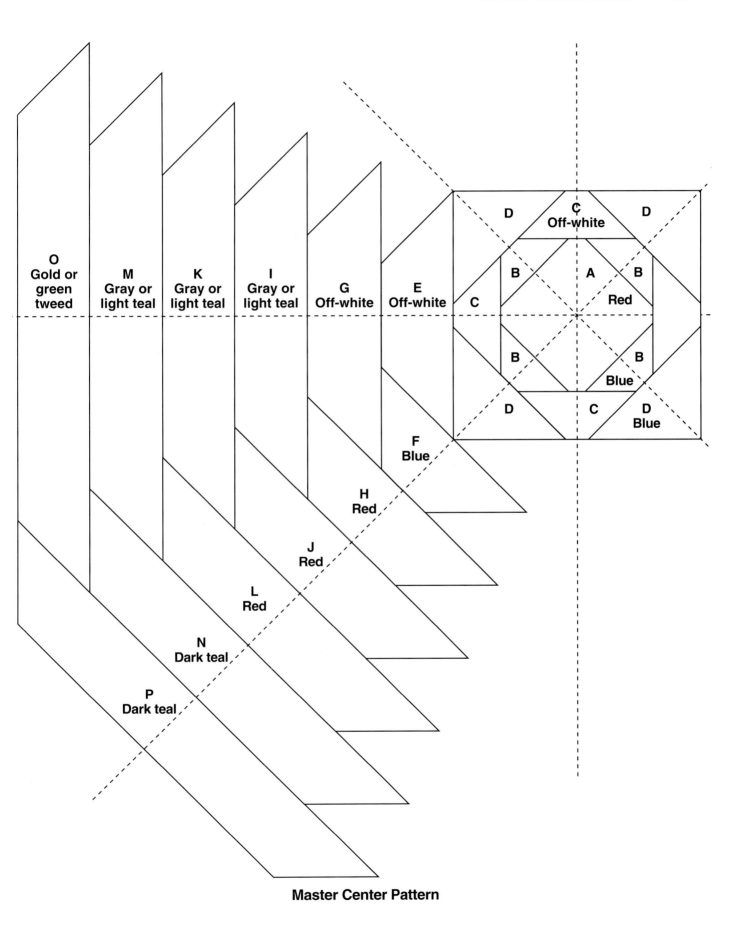

Master Center Pattern

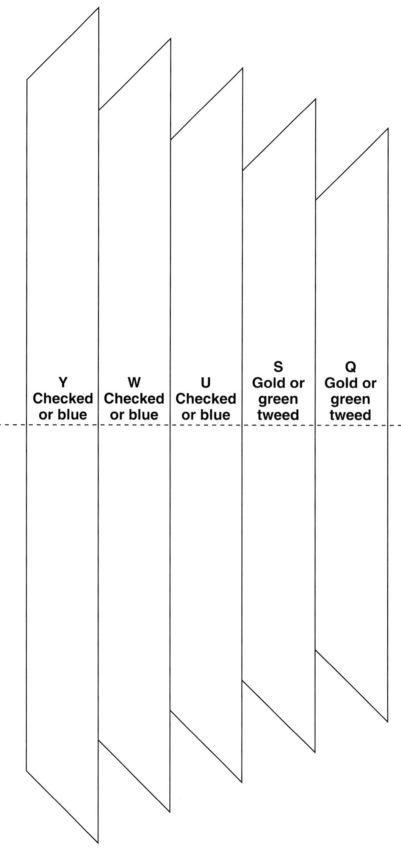

Master Pattern Q-Y

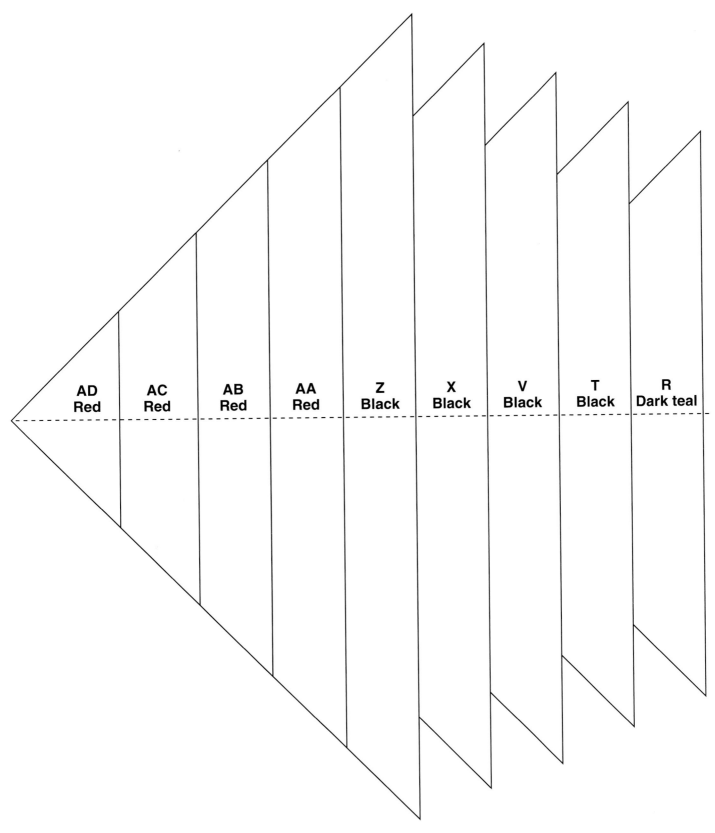

| AD | AC | AB | AA | Z | X | V | T | R |
| Red | Red | Red | Red | Black | Black | Black | Black | Dark teal |

Master Pattern R-AD

▪ Roman Stripe ▪ Variations

The simple Roman Stripe block is almost as versatile as that traditional favorite, the Log Cabin. Having both a pieced and a plain diagonal half, the blocks can be arranged so that the striped portion connects with others and forms a design, like the Streak O' Lightning shown in the photo at the bottom of the photo. Or the striped part can be isolated, as with the Sunshine and Shadow variation at the upper left. (Another setting for the Roman Stripe can be found in the Bull's Eye quilt on page 242.) Our instructions for these two quilts call for quick-cutting and strip piecing. Although not technically a Roman Stripe variation, the miniature Chinese Coins at the top right is related to the Sunshine and Shadow quilt; use your leftover strip-pieced fabric from the Sunshine and Shadow to create the pieced bars in the Chinese Coins.

Streak O' Lightning

SKILL LEVEL: *Easy*

SIZE:

Finished quilt is approximately 39½ × 49½ inches
Finished Roman Stripe block is 5 inches square

NUMBER OF PIECED BLOCKS: 48

FABRICS AND SUPPLIES

Use full-width (44- to 45-inch) pieces of fabric, rather than odd-sized scraps, to cut the solid-color strips for the strip sets. Using long strips will enable you to cut an adequate number of triangle units per strip set for the quilt. If you are buying fabric, purchase eighth yards if possible. If you cut strips from fabric on hand, you'll need only a strip or two of each fabric.

■ 1¼ yards of dark purple solid fabric for outer borders and setting pieces

■ ¾ yard of medium purple solid fabric for inner borders and binding
■ A total of thirty-five 1¼ × 44-inch strips of various solid-color fabrics for strip sets. (Colors used in the quilt shown include orchid, teal, light lavender, dark lavender, forest green, peach, medium gray, rust, light rust, light gold, medium blue, slate, light taupe, and medium taupe.)
■ 2½ yards of fabric for the quilt back
■ Batting, larger than 39½ × 49½ inches
■ Rotary cutter, ruler, and mat
■ Template plastic

CUTTING

The instructions for this quilt call for quick-cutting and quick-piecing. Use the pattern on page 261 to

Quilter's Schoolhouse

OTHER SETTINGS FOR ROMAN STRIPE BLOCKS

Like the Log Cabin block, the Roman Stripe has a dark and a light diagonal half. You can use these simple blocks in a variety of setting options. The diagrams below illustrate three of them.

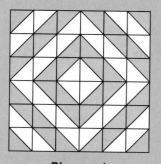

Diagram 1
Barn Raising

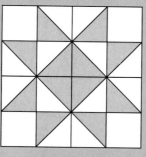

Diagram 2
Variable Star

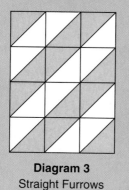

Diagram 3
Straight Furrows

make an X template to ensure super-accurate marking and cutting of the triangle units.

All measurements include ¼-inch seam allowances. Measurements for the border strips include extra length; trim them to the exact size when adding them to the quilt top. Cut all strips across the fabric width unless directed otherwise.

From the dark purple fabric, cut:
- Four 2½ × 45-inch *lengthwise* strips for the outer borders
- 48 setting triangles
  Quick-cut 5⅞-inch-wide strips. From the strips, cut 24 squares, each 5⅞ inches. Cut each square in half diagonally to make two triangles.

From the medium purple fabric, cut:
- Four 2½-inch-wide strips for the inner borders
- Four 3¼-inch corner squares
- Reserve the remaining fabric for binding

MAKING THE STRIP SETS AND ROMAN STRIPE BLOCKS

1. Sort the fabric strips into seven sets of five strips per set.

2. Referring to **Diagram 1,** join the strips into strip sets, offsetting the strips by 1¼ inches as shown. Press the seams to one side. Press on the right side, making sure all seams are flat. The strip set should measure 4¼ inches wide including seam allowances.

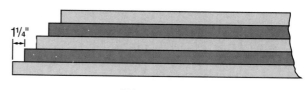

1¼"

Diagram 1

3. Position the strip set wrong side up, so that the seams are facing you. Use template X, as shown in **Diagram 2,** to mark six to seven units on each strip set. Cut on marked lines with scissors or a rotary cutter and ruler. Cut a total of 48 X triangles. Reserve the remaining portions of the strip sets to cut into straight segments for the pieced borders.

Diagram 2

4. Join X triangles and purple setting triangles, as shown in **Diagram 3,** to make a total of 48 Roman Stripe blocks. Press seams toward the purple triangles. While pressing, be careful not to stretch the bias edges of the strips.

Diagram 3

ASSEMBLING THE QUILT TOP

1. Referring to the **Streak O' Lightning Quilt Diagram,** lay out the completed Roman Stripe blocks in eight horizontal rows of six blocks per row.

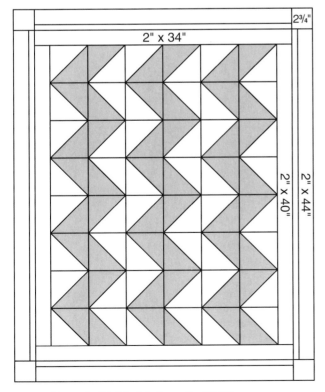

Streak O' Lightning Quilt Diagram

The shaded portion of the blocks in the diagram indicates the strip-pieced section of the block.

2. Join the blocks into rows, pressing the seams in opposite directions from row to row. Join the rows.

3. Measure the length of the quilt top, measuring through the middle rather than along the edges. Trim two of the medium purple borders to this length (approximately 40½ inches including seam allowances), and sew them to the sides of the quilt top. Press the seams toward the borders.

4. Measure the width of the quilt top, measuring through the center and including the side borders (which are approximately 34½ inches including seam allowances). Trim the two remaining medium purple borders to this length, and sew them to the top and bottom of the quilt. Press the seams toward the borders.

5. From the remaining scraps of the seven strip sets, cut 1¼-inch-wide segments as shown in **Diagram 4.** You will need approximately 42 segments, six to seven per strip set. If your fabric strips were less than 44 inches long, you may need to cut and piece a few additional 1¼-inch squares to have enough units for the pieced borders.

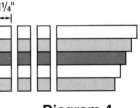

Diagram 4

6. Measure the length of the quilt top (approximately 44½ inches including seam allowances). Trim two of the dark purple borders to this length. Join enough of the **Diagram 4** segments to make two borders this length. If necessary, adjust the length by taking slightly deeper seams when joining the segments. Sew a pieced border to each purple border; sew the double borders to the sides of the quilt, positioning them so the purple borders are to the outside. Press the seams toward the outer borders.

7. Measure the width of your quilt, and trim the two remaining dark purple borders to length. Join **Diagram 4** segments as needed to make two borders this same length. Take deeper seams as needed to adjust the length. Join pieced borders and purple borders as before to make double borders.

8. Sew medium purple corner squares to the ends of the two double borders. Sew the borders to the top and bottom of the quilt. Press the seams toward the outer borders.

QUILTING AND FINISHING

1. Mark quilting designs as desired. The plume quilting design for the setting triangles is given full size on page 261.

2. The backing fabric should be at least 4 inches larger than the top on all four sides; piece the backing if necessary. Layer the quilt back, batting, and quilt top; baste the layers.

3. Quilt as desired. The quilt shown also has in-the-ditch quilting along the seams of the strip-pieced triangle areas and along the seams that join the blocks and borders.

4. From the remaining medium purple fabric, make approximately 5½ yards (198 inches) of straight-grain or bias binding. See page 13 in the "General Instructions" for details on making and attaching binding. See page 15 for instructions on making a hanging sleeve.

Sunshine and Shadow

SKILL LEVEL: *Easy*

SIZE:

Finished quilt is 26½ × 21½ inches
Finished Roman Stripe block is 5 inches square

NUMBER OF PIECED BLOCKS: 12

FABRICS AND SUPPLIES

Use full-width (44- to 45-inch) pieces of fabric, rather than odd-sized scraps, to cut the solid-color strips for the strip sets. Using long strips will enable you to cut an adequate number of triangle units per strip set for the quilt. If you are buying fabric, purchase eighth yards if possible. If you cut strips from fabric on hand, you'll need only a strip or two of each fabric.

- ¾ yard of medium lavender solid fabric for outer borders and quilt back
- ½ yard of light lavender solid fabric for setting triangles and binding
- Two 1¼ × 44-inch strips of medium blue solid fabric for inner borders
- A total of ten 1¼ × 44-inch strips of various solid-color fabrics. (Colors used in the quilt shown include light rust, beige, dark green, medium blue, taupe, dark gray, light maroon, medium gray, light blue, and peach.)
- Batting, larger than 26½ × 21½ inches
- Rotary cutter, ruler, and mat
- Template plastic

CUTTING

The instructions for this quilt call for quick-cutting and quick-piecing. Following the template pattern on page 261, make an X template to ensure super-accurate marking and cutting of the triangle units.

All measurements include ¼-inch seam allowances. Measurements for border strips include extra length; trim them to the exact size when adding them to the quilt top. Cut strips across the fabric width unless directed otherwise.

From the medium lavender fabric, cut:

- Four 3 × 27-inch *lengthwise* strips for the outer borders
- Reserve the remaining piece of fabric for the quilt backing

From the light lavender fabric, cut:

- 12 setting triangles
  Quick-cut one 5⅞-inch-wide strip. From the strip, cut six 5⅞-inch squares. Cut each square in half diagonally to make two triangles.
- Reserve the remaining fabric for binding

MAKING THE STRIP SETS AND ROMAN STRIPE BLOCKS

1. Sort fabric strips into two sets of five strips per set.

2. Referring to **Diagram 1** on page 256, join strips into strip sets, offsetting the strips by 1¼ inches as shown. Press the seams in one direction. Press on the right side, making sure all seams are pressed flat.

3. Position the strip set with the seams facing you. Using template X as shown in **Diagram 2** on page 257, mark six triangles on each strip set. Cut on the marked lines with scissors or a rotary cutter and ruler. Cut a total of 12 triangles. If you wish, reserve the remaining portions of the strip sets to make the Chinese Coins Miniature Quilt on page 260.

4. Join X triangles and light lavender setting triangles, as shown in **Diagram 3** on page 257, to make a total of 12 Roman Stripe blocks. Press the seams toward the light lavender triangles.

ASSEMBLING THE QUILT TOP

1. Referring to the **Sunshine and Shadow Quilt Diagram,** lay out the completed Roman Stripe blocks in three horizontal rows of four blocks per row. The shaded portion of the blocks in the diagram indicates the strip-pieced section of the block.

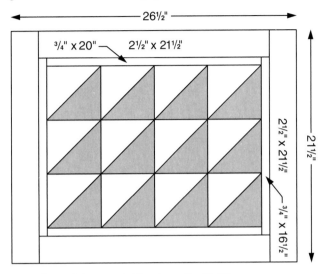

Sunshine and Shadow Quilt Diagram

2. Join the blocks into rows, pressing the seams in opposite directions from row to row. Join the rows.

3. Measure the width of the quilt top, measuring through the middle rather than along the edges. From the two 1¼-inch-wide medium blue border strips, cut two borders to this length (approximately 20½ inches including seam allowances). Sew the strips to the top and bottom of the quilt. Press the seams toward the blue borders.

4. Measure the length of the quilt top, again measuring through the middle (approximately 17 inches including seam allowances). Cut two blue border strips this length and sew them to the two sides of the quilt top. Press the seams toward the borders.

5. In the same manner, measure, trim, and sew the 3-inch-wide medium lavender borders to the quilt top. Press the seams toward the borders.

QUILTING AND FINISHING

1. Mark quilting designs as desired. The plume quilting design for the setting triangles is given on page 261 and the scroll quilting design for the borders is given on page 262.

2. Layer the quilt back, batting, and quilt top; baste the layers.

3. Quilt as desired. In addition to the plume and scroll designs, the quilt shown has in-the-ditch quilting along the seams of the strip-pieced triangle areas and along the seams that join the blocks and borders.

4. From the remaining light lavender fabric, make approximately 2¾ yards (99 inches) of straight-grain or bias binding. See page 13 in the "General Instructions" for details on making and attaching binding, and see page 15 for instructions on making a hanging sleeve.

Chinese Coins Miniature Quilt

SKILL LEVEL: *Easy*

SIZE:

Finished quilt is 11½ × 15½ inches

FABRICS AND SUPPLIES

- Leftover strip sets from Sunshine and Shadow
- ½ yard of medium purple solid fabric for sashing strips and quilt back
- ⅛ yard of medium blue solid fabric for binding
- Batting or flannel, larger than 11½ × 15½ inches

ASSEMBLING THE QUILT

1. From leftover strip sets, cut approximately nine 2½-inch-wide segments, as shown in **Diagram 4** on page 257.

2. Join the segments end to end to make three bands of bar patchwork with 16 bars in each band. Add additional single 1¼ × 2½-inch bars if you wish to make the bands longer. Press the seams in one direction.

3. From the medium purple fabric, cut two 1½-inch-wide sashing strips and four 2¼-inch-wide border strips. Cut the strips on the lengthwise grain so they are approximately 18 inches long.

4. Measure the length of a pieced band (approximately 12½ inches including seam allowances). Trim the sashing strips and two of the border strips to this length.

5. Join the three pieced bands and the two sashing strips, alternating strips as shown in the **Chinese Coins Quilt Diagram.** Press the seams toward the sashing strips. Sew a border strip to each side of the quilt. Press the seams toward the borders.

6. Measure the width of the quilt top (approximately 12 inches including seam allowances). Trim the remaining two border strips to this length. Sew the borders to the top and bottom of the quilt top. Press the seams toward the borders.

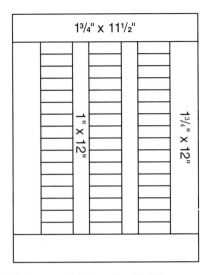

1¾" x 11½"

1" x 12"

1¾" x 12"

Chinese Coins Quilt Diagram

7. Mark quilting designs as desired. The miniature scroll pattern used for the quilt shown is on page 262.

8. Layer the quilt back, batting, and quilt top; baste the layers. Quilt as desired.

9. Make approximately 1¾ yards (63 inches) of straight-grain or bias binding. See page 13 in the "General Instructions" for details on making and attaching binding. For miniatures, we recommend single-fold binding.

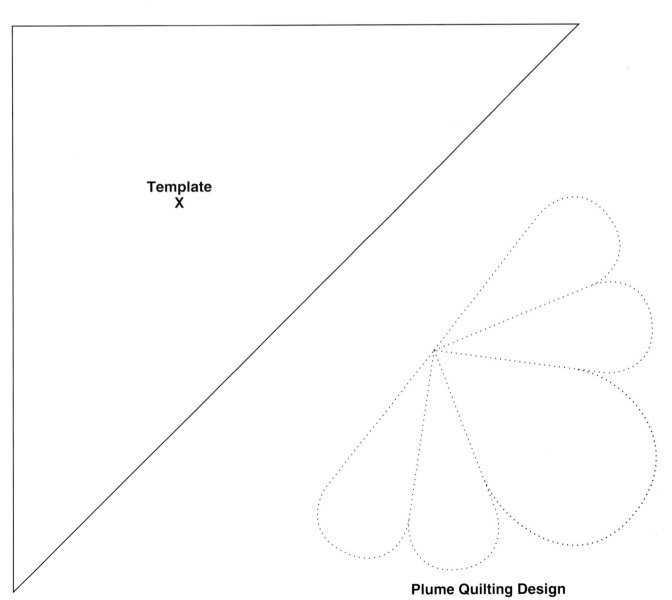

Template X

Plume Quilting Design

Scroll Quilting Design

Miniature Scroll Quilting Design